D1442481

FBI

100 YEARS

AN UNOFFICIAL HISTORY

HENRY M. HOLDEN

ZENITH PRESS

This book has neither been sponsored nor endorsed by the FBI and the author is solely responsible for the book's content. Reproduction of the Seal and FBI indicia on the front cover occurred with the special permission of the FBI and any unauthorized use, possession, or reproduction of the Seal and/or other FBI indicia is a violation of Federal law carrying a penalty of fines or imprisonment.

First published in 2008 by Zenith Press, an imprint of MBI Publishing Company, 400 First Avenue North, Suite 300, Minneapolis, MN 55401 USA.

© Henry M. Holden, 2008

All rights reserved. With the exception of quoting brief passages for the purposes of review, no part of this publication may be reproduced without prior written permission from the Publisher.

The information in this book is true and complete to the best of our knowledge. All recommendations are made without any guarantee on the part of the author or Publisher, who also disclaim any liability incurred in connection with the use of this data or specific details.

This publication has been prepared solely by MBI Publishing Company and is not approved or licensed by any other entity. We recognize that some words, model names, and designations mentioned herein are the property of the trademark holder. We use them for identification purposes only. This is not an official publication.

Zenith Press titles are also available at discounts in bulk quantity for industrial or sales-promotional use. For details write to Special Sales Manager at MBI Publishing Company, 400 First Avenue North, Suite 300, Minneapolis, MN 55401 USA.

To find out more about our books, join us online at www.zenithpress.com.

Front cover image:
Each symbol and color in the FBI seal has special significance. The dominant blue field of the seal and the scales on the shield represent justice. The endless circle of thirteen stars denotes unity of purpose, as exemplified by the original thirteen states. The laurel leaf symbolizes academic honors, distinction, and fame, as it has since early civilization. There are exactly forty-six leaves on the two branches, since there were forty-six states in the union when the FBI was founded in 1908. The significance of the red and white parallel stripes lies in their colors. Red traditionally stands for courage, valor, and strength, while white conveys cleanliness, light, truth, and peace. As in the American flag, the red bars exceed the white by one. The motto, "Fidelity, Bravery, Integrity," succinctly describes the motivating force behind the men and women of the FBI. The peaked beveled edge, which circumscribes the seal, symbolizes the severe challenges confronting the FBI and the ruggedness of the organization. The gold color in the seal conveys its overall value. FBI

Library of Congress Cataloging-in-Publication Data

Holden, Henry M.
  FBI 100 years : an unofficial history / by Henry M. Holden.
    p. cm.
  ISBN-13: 978-0-7603-3244-3 (hardbound w/ jacket)
  ISBN-10: 0-7603-3244-4 (hardbound w/ jacket) 1. United States. Federal Bureau of Investigation--History--20th century. 2. Subversive activities--United States--History--20th century. 3. Criminal investigation--United States--History--20th century. 4. Undercover operations--United States--History--20th century. I. Title.
HV8144.F43H647 2008
363.250973--dc22

                                        2007034689

Editor: Steve Gansen
Designer: Mandy Iverson

Printed in China

CONTENTS

FOREWORD

"Such is charged with the duty of investigating violations of the laws of the United States, collecting evidence in cases in which the United States is or may be a party in interest, and performing other duties imposed by law." What you have just read is inscribed on the credentials of every special agent who has served in the Federal Bureau of Investigation. It is a mere forty-word description of the vast responsibilities and duties assigned to the FBI since its formation in 1908.

With this charging statement as a basis, an array of images springs to mind when thinking about the FBI's history: the early rag-tag days when the original Bureau of Investigation was rife with corruption; Hoover and his reformed G-men fighting gangsters in the 1930s and enforcing civil rights laws while battling the Ku Klux Klan in the 1960s; the World War II Nazi saboteurs and spy investigations; Cold War Soviet spies such as the Rosenbergs, Alger Hiss, and Klaus Fuchs; to today's agents, providing vital investigative support for the 9/11 Commission and tracking al Qaeda terrorists.

Along the way there were the FBI investigations of dozens of political assassinations, including President John F. Kennedy, Dr. Martin Luther King Jr., and the attempted assassinations of such figures as Alabama governor George Wallace and Presidents Gerald Ford and Ronald Reagan. Throw into this mix the kidnappings, the church bombings, the airplane hijackings, the political corruption, the organized crime—from La Cosa Nostra to the new post-communist phenomenon of Russian and Asian organized crime, then add the FBI's leadership role in forensic science and law enforcement management and training, and one begins to develop a sense of the enormous task facing anyone who is interested in the one-hundred-year history of the FBI.

What does a writer include in such a story? What cases does the historian pursue? What investigations never make it into the word processor? Which of the millions of FBI cases and investigation are "essential" for a clear understanding of the FBI's role in our nation's history, and which ones are consigned to the "important" or just "interesting" categories? With these questions always at the forefront, Henry Holden, author of *FBI 100 Years: An Unofficial History*, has produced a comprehensive and readable account of the first hundred years of one of America's most important governmental institutions. It is a story that should be read by anyone who is interested in the history of the United States and is concerned, in any way, about the international challenges facing us in this new century.

—Raymond J. Batvinis, FBI special agent, 1972–1997,
including service in the FBI Intelligence Division Training Unit

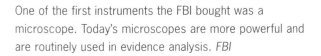

The FBI Medal of Valor is awarded to individuals for an exceptional act of heroism that occurs in the direct line of duty within the scope of FBI employment and in the face of a criminal adversary. Such an act must also involve the voluntary risk of personal safety and life, and it requires that the individual overcome obstacles to neutralize a significant life-threatening crisis. *FBI*

The FBI Shield of Bravery is awarded for brave and courageous acts occurring in the direct line of duty and/or within the scope of FBI employment. Such an act would include a voluntary risk in hazardous duty while extending major assistance in a grave situation or crisis confrontation associated with the highest priority cases of the FBI. An act deserving the Shield of Bravery would occur on duty and might include action in connection with a high-priority police cooperation matter or organized crime prevention. *FBI*

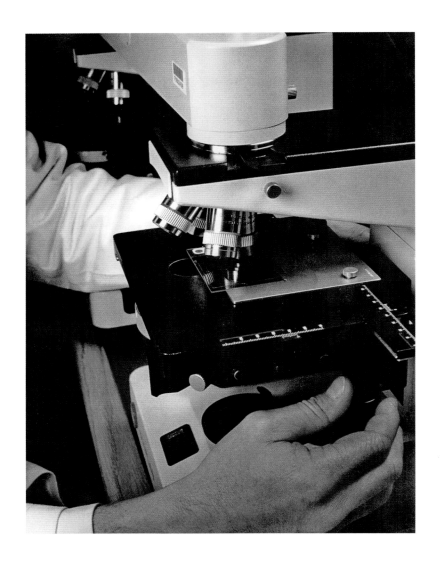

One of the first instruments the FBI bought was a microscope. Today's microscopes are more powerful and are routinely used in evidence analysis. *FBI*

FBI TEN MOST WANTED FUGITIVES

Michael Alfonso
UFAP - Murder,
Aggravated Stalking

Usama Bin Laden
Murder of U.S. Nationals
Outside the United States;
Conspiracy to Murder U.S.
Nationals Outside the
United States; Attack on
a Federal Facility Resulting in Death

James J. Bulger
RICO - Murder,
Conspiracy to Commit Murder;
Conspiracy to Commit Extortion,
Narcotics Distribution,
Conspiracy to Commit Money Laundering;
Extortion; Money Laundering

Genero Espinosa Dorantes
UFAP - Criminal Homicide

Robert William Fisher
UFAP - First Degree Murder,
Arson of an Occupied Structure

Victor Manuel Gerena
Bank Robbery;
UFAP - Armed Robbery;
Theft From Interstate
Shipment

Glen Stewart Godwin
UFAP - Murder, Escape

Richard Steve Goldberg
Sexual Exploitation of Children
(Production of Child Pornography);
UFAP - Lewd Acts Upon a Child,
Possession of Child Pornography

Diego Leon Montoya Sanchez
Conspiracy to Import and Possess
With Intent to Deliver Cocaine;
Possession With Intent to Deliver Cocaine;
Money Laundering; RICO - Drug Trafficking;
Conspiracy to Distribute or Manufacture
Cocaine Abroad With Knowledge or
Intent That it be Imported into the United States

Donald Eugene Webb
UFAP - Murder; Attempted Burglary

the FBI's **ten most** **wanted** *fugitives*

Donald Eugene Webb (lower right) is wanted for killing a police officer. He was added to the list in 1981 and has been on the list longer than anyone else. If still alive, he would be seventy-seven years old. Billie Austin Bryant spent the shortest amount of time on the list—two hours in 1969. *FBI*

By 1908, President Theodore Roosevelt had gone from a Rough Rider to a pale rider, seeing massive land frauds but doing little about them. Roosevelt is the source of the term "muckraker." During a speech in 1906, he likened investigative journalists to the man with the muckrake, a character in John Bunyan's Pilgrim's Progress (1678). Library of Congress

Chapter 1

THE "WILD WEST" YEARS

Teddy's Trust-busting Detective Force

The framers of the U.S. Constitution created a national government with limited authority and jurisdiction over matters that crossed state boundaries. The restrictions on interstate jurisdiction continued through the period of westward expansion in the nineteenth century, when the government was decidedly slow in creating a federal law enforcement system. It was not until June 22, 1870, that Congress created the Department of Justice, headed by the century-old attorney general's office. The job of attorney general became enforcement of the few existing federal laws. A year later, Congress appropriated $50,000 for the "detection and prosecution of crimes," and the attorney general appointed the first special investigator for this purpose. In 1908, Attorney General Charles J. Bonaparte put together a force of investigators, allowing the attorney general's office to grow into a viable law enforcement organization. This force would go on to become the Federal Bureau of Investigation—the FBI.

In 1905, Roosevelt appointed Charles J. Bonaparte as secretary of the navy. Both Harvard men, they had worked together previously. Later, as president, Roosevelt sought Bonaparte's services on the Board of Indian Commissions and then as special counsel to prosecute alleged frauds in the postal service. In December 1906, at the age of forty-five, Bonaparte became attorney general. He appeared before the Supreme Court personally in 560 cases and delivered 138 opinions, through the Department of Justice, to the president and heads of departments. He argued forty-nine cases orally before the Supreme Court and submitted seven on briefs. Twenty of these cases came under the antitrust laws, helping to dissolve the American Tobacco Company and earning Bonaparte another soubriquet—the "trust buster." *Library of Congress*

Prior to the creation of this federal force, Americans had looked to their local and state governments to fulfill law enforcement and other social responsibilities. The federal law enforcement's scope was limited to such crimes as antitrust, bad debts, neutrality, and bankruptcy fraud. Muckraking journalists in California, New Mexico, Oregon, Washington, Kansas, and Colorado wrote exposés of their states' social ills, including prostitution, child labor, land fraud, and other unchecked crimes spreading across the newly settled West.

By 1907, there was political pressure on President Theodore Roosevelt to do something about the rampant criminal activity. Roosevelt ordered Bonaparte to employ investigative personnel to conduct an official inquiry of Western land fraud and related crimes. Having to start nearly from scratch, Bonaparte borrowed Secret Service operatives from the Treasury Department to fill out his enforcement staff. Months later, his operatives presented their report. Roosevelt didn't see enough in the report's testimonies to mount an effective prosecution and ordered Bonaparte to try again.

Bonaparte commissioned new operatives to bring fresh blood to his second investigation, but the resulting report was largely a rehash of the first. Some newspapers suggested a cover-up by government officials. The land fraud issue was about to explode with serious consequences in Congress. It began to look as though successful prosecution of the crimes, although blatant and widespread, would be impossible. In 1907, Attorney General Bonaparte notified Congress that the Justice Department possessed neither the budget nor the law enforcement force capable of dealing with the massive caseload. Newspapers supported his claim that a weak system of federal enforcement was stretched to its limits and was only getting worse.

FBI: EVOLUTION OF THE NAME

July 26, 1908	No specific name has been assigned; referred to as the Special Agent Force
March 16, 1909	Bureau of Investigation
July 1, 1932	U.S. Bureau of Investigation
August 10, 1933	Division of Investigation (the division also included the Bureau of Prohibition)
July 1, 1935	Federal Bureau of Investigation

Congressional Hearings

Congressional hearings held in 1908 led the Justice Department to use Secret Service operatives to look into possible cover-ups and conflicts of interests. "We are obliged [. . .] to rely on the Secret Service of the Treasury Department for certain work," Bonaparte acknowledged in his hearing testimony on January 17. He suggested the best plan would be to have such a service under the control of the Department of Justice and available to assist other departments on occasion.

The hearings had unexpected consequences when it was revealed, among other things, that the Navy Department had used the Secret Service operatives to spy on a naval officer's illicit affairs. During the land fraud investigations, operatives assigned to the Justice Department had also spied on several congressional representatives. As a result, on May 27, 1908, Congress adopted an appropriations rider for the Department of the Treasury that restricted the Secret Service to the enforcement of counterfeiting laws and presidential protection, thus barring its use in conducting investigations beyond these statutory requirements. This rider formally ended the practice of loaning Secret Service agents to the Justice Department and, in turn, severely diminished Bonaparte's ability to conduct his investigations. Bonaparte had once considered the idea of an entirely new federal detective force. With his back against the wall and his job on the line, Bonaparte now pushed for its establishment.

Bureau of Investigation

As chief examiner of the Justice Department at the time, Stanley W. Finch had also advocated for an internal investigative squad. President Roosevelt seemed to agree, despite congressional opposition to so-called "secret services," "black cabinets," spies, and federal detectives. Some critics claimed such a bureau was illegal, but to no avail. Roosevelt went forward, directing Bonaparte to create a squad. On June 29, 1908, Bonaparte ordered the creation of a special agent force and gave Finch responsibility for oversight.

On July 26, 1908, ten Secret Service operatives of the Treasury Department were transferred and appointed permanent special agents of the Justice Department. These, together, with thirteen investigators who had been employed on peonage cases, and twelve examiners provided for by statute, constituted the founding members of the investigative force. Bonaparte declared that these investigators would handle all Department of Justice investigative matters. Bonaparte assumed personal responsibility over the Bureau's operations.

Congress had been wary of overreaching, so Bonaparte reassured them the new force would be confined to investigating federal antitrust violation, land fraud, copyright violations, and peonage, and would not be used to monitor personal and political activities or to otherwise subvert constitutional checks and balances. On March 16, 1909, Attorney General George W. Wickersham named this force the Bureau of Investigation (BOI).

FOUNDING ORDER

"All matters relating to investigations under the Department, except those to be made by bank examiners, and in connection with the naturalization service, will be referred to the Chief Examiner for a memorandum as to whether any member of the force of special agents under his direction is available for the work to be performed. No authorization of expenditure for special examinations shall be made by any officer of the Department, without first ascertaining whether one of the regular force is available for the service desired, and, in case the service cannot be performed by the regular force of special agents of the Department, the matter will be specially called to the attention of the Attorney General, or Acting Attorney General, together with a statement from the Chief Examiner as to the reasons why a regular employee cannot be assigned to the work, before authorization shall be made for any expenditure of any money for this purpose."

—Charles J. Bonaparte, attorney general, July 26, 1908

Men identified as aliens dig the New York City subway nearly a century ago. Aliens took whatever work they could, at almost any wage. Although they provided valuable services left vacant by men drafted, aliens still suffered the brunt of scorn, racism, and fear. Anti-immigrant feelings among the wider public would later give rise to the American Protective League. *Library of Congress*

FBI agents practice pistol shooting using a .38-caliber six-shot revolver. Congress did not authorize special agents to carry pistols until 1934. *FBI*

MISSION

The stated mission of today's FBI is to protect and defend the United States against terrorist and foreign intelligence threats, to uphold and enforce the criminal laws of the United States, and to provide leadership and criminal justice services to federal, state, municipal, and international agencies and partners.

By July 1909, there were thirty-five permanent agents and five temporary agents. Because the early Bureau provided no formal training, it looked for operatives with previous law enforcement experience or a background in the law. Much of the hiring would become tainted by accusations of political patronage and corruption which, by the advent of World War I, were virtually standard practice in law enforcement circles.

Initially, Finch and Bonaparte set rigid standards. Similar to present-day qualifications, the men were to be physically fit, well educated (preferably college graduates and/or members of the bar), ordinary in appearance to pass unnoticed in crowds, and knowledgeable in a foreign language, if possible. Agents brought over from the Secret Service trained the new agents in general police work.

Turf Battles

For the first decade, the Bureau's lack of powers of arrest made it too impotent to enforce high-level crimes of the politically powerful. During that time, the Secret Service saw the BOI as a fledgling interloper. By 1914, the two agencies were jockeying for intelligence-gathering responsibilities, a source of much friction.

Prior to World War I, no single federal agency had any substantial counterintelligence investigative capability, and the modern concept of a counterintelligence community did not exist. But on June 28, 1914, a Serbian dissident shot and killed the heir to the Austria–Hungary throne, Archduke Franz Ferdinand, and his wife. Within days, Europe was at war.

This poster, intended to draw aliens in to register, reads in six different languages: "If the war has affected your living or working conditions, if you want to learn the American language and become a citizen, if you wish employment, advice, or information without charge, apply to: Room 1820, Municipal Building, Mayor's Committee on National Defense, Committee on Aliens." *Library of Congress*

As the German war machine rumbled through Europe, anxiety in America escalated. Despite the likelihood of the United States entering the war, the Bureau was limited to gathering intelligence related to neutrality law violations. Attorney General Thomas Gregory argued against broadening the scope of the Bureau. Like Bonaparte, Gregory thought that the Justice Department's responsibility was to investigate violations of already-defined federal laws that, at the time, did not include espionage, sabotage, or enemy subversion.

Then, in late July 1915, the Secret Service scored a major counterintelligence victory. Agents had been tailing German diplomat Dr. Heinrich Albert. When Albert carelessly left a briefcase on a bus seat, a quick-thinking Secret Service agent who had been following him grabbed the case and ducked out the back door

New Jersey Governor Woodrow Wilson chats with Attorney General A. Mitchell Palmer, before either had gained national prominence. In May 1915, President Wilson ordered the Secret Service "to increase its surveillance of the German Embassy, its personnel, and other Germans." The words "other Germans" would soon bring havoc on law-abiding German-American citizens. Wilson made no effort to stop Palmer's raids or the illegal incarceration of hundreds of individuals. *Library of Congress*

of the bus. The briefcase contained a wealth of incriminating intelligence about German propaganda and sabotage efforts in the United States. Some of the contents were leaked to the press, resulting in a public relations coup for the Secret Service. In sharp contrast, the Bureau of Investigation was humiliated over its powerlessness to catch German agents.

Attorney General Gregory and Bureau Chief A. Bruce Bielaski condemned the press leak as counterproductive. The Justice Department would not be able to prosecute the foreign agent because of his diplomatic immunity, and this result would make it look as though the president was being soft on Germany. The controversy sparked a series of heated interagency battles. When the Bureau hired almost one hundred new agents in 1915 to handle Neutrality Act violations, the Treasury Department saw the increase as a potential threat to Secret Service

Emma Goldman emigrated from Russia in 1889 and spent almost thirty years in the United States as a radical feminist, anarchist, and birth control reformer. Goldman and fellow anarchist Alexander Berkman were arrested in June 1917 for violating the Selective Service Act. They had organized the No Conscription League in an attempt to assist those resisting registration for the draft. The courts found this organization constituted a conspiracy. Goldman received two years in prison and was fined $10,000. *Library of Congress*

activities. The Treasury Department attempted to recruit more investigators but was not as successful as the Bureau.

A rise in sabotage incidents in 1915 forced Gregory to address the wider war-related issues. The United States was facing a serious intelligence failure, and foreign agents had been acting with impunity across the country. Treasury Secretary William McAdoo prepared what appeared to be a reasonable proposal: centralize and coordinate all intelligence responsibility, especially counterintelligence, into a

A blindfolded official draws the first name from a lottery of draft-eligible men. The draft created angst, bitterness, and violence from the antiwar opposition. The draft also gave the BOI additional power to hunt down draft-dodgers. *Library of Congress*

so-called "Bureau of Intelligence" to be run by the Department of State or by his Treasury Department. Jealousy between McAdoo's department and the Justice Department was clear in the omission of the Justice Department from his proposal. McAdoo was optimistic, however, that the State Department would back the idea to decrease the duplication of work across agencies.

Interdepartmental jealousy and President Woodrow Wilson's opposition to such an agency doomed the proposal. Attorney General Gregory protested the very idea of a Bureau of Intelligence, arguing that his Bureau of Investigation and the U.S. Army were already coordinating their efforts under the State Department. "The only problem that Justice is encountering is the constant overreaching of authority by Secret Service and their presumption of responsibility in matters already delegated to Justice," he stated.

Anxious to preserve a major role for the Secret Service, McAdoo pointed out its experience in counterintelligence investigations dating back to the Civil War in addition to recent successes targeting German diplomats. The Bureau didn't have the same long history but had successfully enforced Neutrality Act cases dating back to the Mexican Revolution of 1910. In 1916 alone, the Bureau had gathered evidence leading to more than two hundred prosecutions for neutrality and antitrust violations. Neutrality Act provisions were even used with some success against saboteurs, but the attorney general said that additional legislation was needed to address the problem of Germany's domestic spying.

In June 1916, Assistant Attorney General Charles Warren counter-proposed "Spy Bill" legislation that would give the federal government the authority to arrest and prosecute dangerous plotters and alien enemies. At the time, the press damned the proposal as an unreasonable request for arbitrary and invasive power.

The State Department was the lead agency on domestic counterintelligence and broader intelligence matters, but it had little law enforcement power. By 1916, it had established an office of chief special agent, with offices in New York City and Washington, D.C., to oversee surveillance, just as the Secret Service had been doing. Also in 1916, Congress authorized the Bureau of Investigation to conduct domestic investigations on behalf of the secretary of state and, in doing so, balanced President Wilson's 1915 move that conferred similar authority on the Secret

MUST LIBERTY'S LIGHT GO OUT?

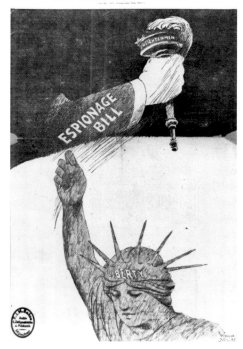

Espionage and alleged spying raised some serious angst in Congress and represented a throwback to the old despotic European kings. Representative Walter Smith (R-Iowa) declared in an article titled "Loan of Detectives" in the *Washington Evening Star* of April 21, 1908: "Nothing is more opposed to our race than a belief that a general system of espionage is being conducted by the general government." Representative John Fitzgerald (D-New York) warned against the dangers of a federal secret police. *Library of Congress*

These 815 men reported to Local Draft Board No. 17 on November 11, 1918—Armistice Day. They would be drafted, but they would not see battle. Despite the armistice, the BOI would continue to police "enemy aliens" and "pro-German organizations." No less than four hundred thousand pages of records related to German alien activities were accumulated by BOI investigators between 1908 and 1922. *Library of Congress*

NO WAR TALK!

Attorney General Gregory, says:

"OBEY THE LAW

Keep Your Mouth Shut!"

This poster illustrates the level of paranoia about foreign spies in America. Neighbors mistrusted each other, people acting suspiciously were reported, and there was a feeling that the Bureau was looking into the lives of every American. *Library of Congress*

MONTHLY REPORT

BABIES 164
CHILDREN .. 178
WOMEN 292
NON-COMBATANTS

MURDERED

A
Good
Month's
Business

BARRON COLLIER Patriotic Series No. 2

Every war brings out the worst in people—racism, bigotry, and hate. This poster clearly illustrates these phenomena during World War I. The war was especially hard on peaceful, law-abiding German-Americans in the United States. After the war, Americans' bias against immigrants shifted toward the growth of radical politics, resulting in the Bureau becoming a political police force. *Library of Congress*

Service. Because it did not have its own investigative force, the State Department was slow to take full control of domestic counterintelligence. It preferred to borrow agents from the Secret Service and Bureau of Investigation as needed. Given the anxiety between the Secret Service and the Bureau over these responsibilities, the State Department's arrangement proved unproductive.

The Secret Service took a broader view and assigned itself fewer self-imposed restrictions than the Bureau. Treasury Secretary McAdoo was one of "the most politically ambitious members of Wilson's cabinet," wrote one historian. McAdoo interpreted the service's authority to conduct investigations in the broadest sense, despite repeated congressional action to curtail such interpretations. He actively pursued intelligence matters, in contrast to Attorney General Gregory's reluctance to do so without specific legislation. As a result, the Secret Service felt free to probe (and did) the activities of German diplomats.

American Protective League

During a time when anti-German feelings were running high in America, three Chicago businessmen proposed to the Bureau the idea of an organization for patriotic citizens who either were too old for the draft or had medical deferments. The attorney general secretly approved its formation, and the

In the first seven months after America's entrance into this war for human freedom, enemy agitators in our midst caused 283,402 workers to lose 6,285,519 days of production. Our war industries were heavily handicapped by this unpatriotic strife.

LET US ALL PULL TOGETHER TO WIN THE WAR QUICKLY

This poster came out just seven months after America's entry into World War I. *Library of Congress*

Racy cartoons of the day suggested prostitution. The man is saying, "My sweet honey, I hope you are to be let with lodging." She replies, "No, sir, I am to be let *alone*." The Mann Act of 1910 expanded the BOI's jurisdiction to include prostitution, albeit on a limited basis. The act made it a crime to transport women over state lines for immoral purposes. It also provided a tool by which the federal government could investigate criminals who evaded state laws but had no other federal violations. *Library of Congress*

LODGINGS TO LET.

American Protective League (APL) was born March 22, 1917. The all-volunteer body of the APL consisted of every social and economic class of American. More than half the U.S. population lived in areas where the APL was active. Despite its patriotic front, egregious violations of the First and Fourth Amendments were committed in the process of seeking out "seditious and disloyal" conversations.

Secretary McAdoo sharply criticized the APL's activities. In a memorandum, he made clear how frustrated he was with the Department of Justice's "eyes and ears." He protested to Gregory that the APL was full of the "gravest danger of misunderstanding, confusion, and even fraud . . . [and] in the public interest, I am sending you my serious protest against the continuation under its present designation." He continued that "in arming a private organization with a power, the very existence

In September 1919, the Immigration Bureau issued arrest warrants for Goldman and Berkman for their anarchist beliefs, which made them subject to deportation under the 1918 Immigration Act. J. Edgar Hoover wrote the legal brief. Since Goldman claimed to be a U.S. citizen—through her father and husband—Hoover challenged the validity of her naturalization. In December 1919, the Immigration Bureau deported Goldman, Berkman, and 249 aliens to the Soviet Union on the "Soviet Ark." the USS *Buford.* Many of these people would disappear during the Stalin years. *Library of Congress*

In the early days of the twentieth century, police corruption was a crisis. To the general public, it seemed that there was corruption at every level in law enforcement, and in many instances, they were right. *Library of Congress*

A. Mitchell Palmer was the attorney general to whom J. Edgar Hoover reported. He was an anticommunist zealot cut from the same cloth as Hoover. *Library of Congress*

This FBI special agent is using an early portable telephone link—an ancient forerunner to today's palm-sized cellular phone. As communication improved over the decades, the Bureau's law enforcement techniques also improved. *FBI*

of which in private hands is detrimental to the public interest . . . the government cannot escape responsibility for their activities, whatever they may be." McAdoo was further troubled by the league's badges, which referred to the organization as a "secret service," even though it was not the official Secret Service under the Treasury Department.

On November 11, 1918, the Allies signed an armistice with Germany. However, most Americans still harbored deep-rooted bias against some foreigners immigrating to the United States. The focus of their hostility became less about racial prejudice and more about the growth of radical politics. This led to the first "Red scare" beginning in the latter years of World War I. America's business leaders accused Reds, anarchists, Bolsheviks, communists, and socialists of plotting to subvert what they saw as the American way of life. Foreigners, they said, were taking what few jobs were available, bringing with them both the evils associated with the Old World and the new evil of communism. Government leaders agreed that unless the communist revolution was stopped, it would destroy the country. Series of raids of enemy agents and homegrown and foreign radicals were staged throughout the war, climaxing with one last notable raid soon after the war ended.

On June 2, 1919, bombs exploded in eight American cities, including one in Washington, D.C., that damaged the home of Attorney General Alexander Mitchell Palmer. A search of the bomber's body turned up leaflets suggesting a Bolshevik conspiracy. In response, Palmer, with his assistant, J. Edgar Hoover, planned a series of retaliatory raids against radicals, Reds, and leftists, using BOI agents and citizen volunteers of the APL, with the Espionage and Sedition Acts as the basis of their actions.

Five months later, Palmer launched his raids. Raiders arrested thousands of people without cause, including many from the Union of Russian Workers. The media initially proclaimed Palmer a hero, but as the raids and ambushes continued, public opinion shifted. In the end, Palmer and the Bureau were rebuked.

Teapot Dome

The Teapot Dome scandal took its name from a rock formation in Wyoming that looked like a teapot and stood atop a large government naval oil reserve. As the most famous of several scandals that ruined the reputation of President Warren G. Harding and his administration, Teapot Dome became a symbol for the unseemly and often illegal relationship between big business and political influence.

In 1921, Harding had issued an executive order releasing control of naval oil reserves at Teapot Dome, Wyoming, and at Elk Hills, California, from the Navy Department to the Department of the Interior. President Wilson had set the oil reserves aside for the navy during World War I.

On April 15, 1922—the day after the *Wall Street Journal* reported that Albert Fall, a former senator from New Mexico, had secretly leased petroleum reserves to a private oil company without competitive bidding—Senator John Kendrick (D-Wyoming) introduced a resolution that would set in motion one of the most significant Bureau investigations of the era. When the Bureau looked into the matter, it found that Fall, as secretary of the interior and a friend of Harding's, had taken over $400,000 in bribes from oil executives. Oilman Harry Sinclair obtained an illegal no-bid lease to drill for oil at Teapot Dome, and Edward Doheny acquired a no-bid lease for reserves at Elk Hills. The Bureau's investigation led to criminal prosecutions, and Fall ended up as the first former cabinet officer to go to prison. He received a year in prison and was fined $100,000 after being convicted of accepting the bribes.

This sentence and a subsequent Senate inquiry triggered court cases testing the extent of the Senate's investigative powers. One of those cases resulted in the landmark 1927 Supreme Court decision, *McGrain v Daugherty*, which established Congress' right to compel witnesses to testify before its committees.

From Lawless to Lawful

More than simple corruption and a scandal-ridden Department of Justice confronted Attorney General Harlan Stone after his 1924 appointment by President Calvin Coolidge. The Bureau had become a political police force. As Stone recalled later, "The organization was lawless, maintaining many activities which were without any authority in federal statutes, and engaging in many practices which were brutal and tyrannical in the extreme."

Stone had a problem with the Bureau's domestic intelligence operation and had joined a committee of protest against Attorney General Palmer's roundup of radical aliens for deportation in World War I. Stone called for "a thorough [congressional] investigation of the conduct of the DOJ in connection with the deportation cases." He demanded the resignation of Bureau Director William J. Burns, who had achieved earlier fame as the founder of an international detective agency that bore his name. Stone was aware that Burns' assistant, J. Edgar Hoover, had also been involved in the raids. Stone, however, did not immediately remove Hoover because of his reputation within the department as an honest and efficient administrator. Instead, he asked Roger Baldwin, a lawyer with the American Civil Liberties Union (ACLU), to interview Hoover. During the interview, Hoover assured Baldwin that he had played an "unwilling part" in the activities of Palmer and Burns and, further, had not been in a position to stop them.

Hoover understood Baldwin's point of view and reason for questioning him, so he agreed that if he were retained at the Bureau he would shut down its so-called "radical division." Convinced of Hoover's sincerity, Baldwin wrote to Stone, "I think we were wrong in our estimate of his attitude." On behalf of the ACLU, Baldwin announced that the Justice Department's "Red-hunting" days were over. On the heels of the announcement, Attorney General Stone chose Hoover to be acting director, in charge of implementing the necessary reforms.

In a memo to J. Edgar Hoover dated May 13, 1924, Stone ordered that the activities of the Bureau "be limited strictly to investigations of violations of the law, under my direction or under the direction of an assistant attorney general regularly conducting the work of the Department of Justice." Stone also ordered a review of all the personnel in the Bureau and the removal of "those who are incompetent and unreliable." He wanted "men of known good character and ability, giving preference to men who have had some legal training."

Within a year, Hoover reported to his boss: "The work of the Bureau of Investigation at this time is [. . .] of an open character not in any manner subject to criticism, and the operations of the Bureau of Investigation may be given the closest scrutiny at all times."

Stone requested a review of the applicability of the federal criminal statutes to communist activities in the United States. Several patriotic organizations had been lobbying for communists to be prosecuted under the federal sedition conspiracy law, but the courts had ruled that this Civil War–era statute required proof of a definite plan to use force against the government.

The Justice Department lawyers rejected prosecution under the Logan Act, enacted in the 1790s, to punish hostile communications between American citizens and a foreign country. These conclusions reinforced the attorney general's decision to abolish the Bureau's domestic intelligence operations, although Stone told Baldwin that he had no authority to destroy the Bureau's massive domestic intelligence files, dated from 1916 to 1924, without an act of Congress. The Bureau thus retained its domestic intelligence files and a vague legal authority under the appropriations act to conduct investigations that went beyond the detection of federal crimes under the direction of future attorneys general.

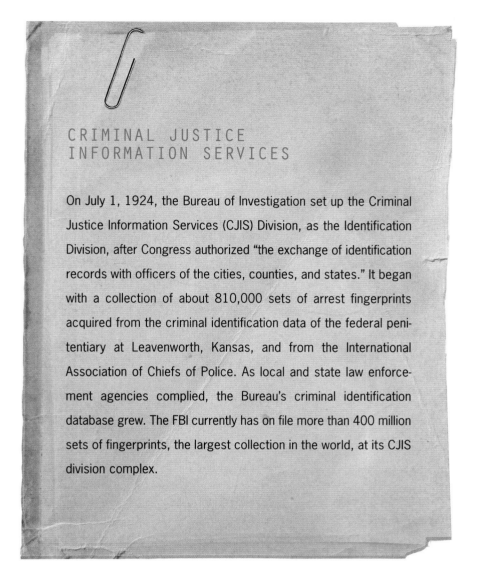

CRIMINAL JUSTICE INFORMATION SERVICES

On July 1, 1924, the Bureau of Investigation set up the Criminal Justice Information Services (CJIS) Division, as the Identification Division, after Congress authorized "the exchange of identification records with officers of the cities, counties, and states." It began with a collection of about 810,000 sets of arrest fingerprints acquired from the criminal identification data of the federal penitentiary at Leavenworth, Kansas, and from the International Association of Chiefs of Police. As local and state law enforcement agencies complied, the Bureau's criminal identification database grew. The FBI currently has on file more than 400 million sets of fingerprints, the largest collection in the world, at its CJIS division complex.

Stone asked Acting Director Hoover whether the Bureau would have the authority to investigate communist activities within the United States on behalf of the State Department in preparation for recognition of the new Soviet Union. Hoover replied that the appropriations rider of 1916 did allow such investigations upon formal request by the secretary of state and approval of the attorney general. In a memo to Attorney General Stone dated December 13, 1924, Hoover stressed that such investigations "should be conducted on an entirely different line than previously conducted by the Bureau of Investigation" and that there should be no publicity "because any publicity would materially hamper the obtaining of successful results."

Military intelligence had a duty, under an army emergency plan, to gather information "with reference to the economical, industrial, and radical conditions, to observe incidents and events that may develop into strikes, riots, or other disorders and to investigate, and report, upon the industrial and radical situation." Because the army

Department of Justice,
Bureau of Investigation,
Washington.

WJN:DJ

IDENTIFICATION
ORDER No. 1.

December 15, 1919.

TO ALL SPECIAL AGENTS, SPECIAL EMPLOYEES
AND LOCAL OFFICERS:

    William N. Bishop, a prisoner in the Camp Stockade at Camp
A. A. Humphreys, Virginia, escaped therefrom on Tuesday, December
2, 1919.

    At the time of his escape Bishop was wearing the uniform
of the United States Army. His description is as follows:

        Age 23 years,
        Height about 5' 7",
        Weight about 170 pounds,
        Short and heavyset in appearance,
        Gray eyes,
        Light brown hair,
        Massive lower jaw,
        Fair complexion,
        4 Vaccination scars 1" long on upper left arm,
        Smooth scar 3/4" long on left thumb,
        In back are pigmented mole near right armpit,
          smooth scars 3/4" long on left shoulder and
          2" long on left forefinger.

    It is thought probable that Bishop may communicate with #212 "C"
Street Southwest, Washington, D.C.; or Carlyle Davis, #44 Van Houton
Place, Belleville, New Jersey; or his sister Mrs. George Rich, #67 Grand
Avenue, Johnson City, New York.

    Attached hereto is photostat copy of a picture of subject which
was taken at Howard's studio, 706 Seventh Street, Washington, D. C.

    The Military Intelligence Division requests assistance of the
Bureau in locating and apprehending above subject. Make every effort
to locate and apprehend subject. Notify this Bureau, Military Intelligence Division, War Department, and Headquarters Military Police, Camp
A. A. Humphreys, Virginia.

                Very truly yours,

                FRANK BURKE,

                Assistant Director and Chief.

On December 15, 1919, the FBI issued its first wanted poster, called at the time, Identification Order (IO) No. 1. William N. Bishop, the subject of the notice, had escaped from the army's stockade at Camp A. A. Humphrys (today's Fort Belvoir) in northern Virginia. The army's Military Intelligence Division, established during World War I, requested the Bureau's assistance. The IO soon became a staple of crime fighting. It evolved into a standard eight-by-eight-inch size, and fingerprints, criminal records, and other background information were added. From 1919 through 2006, the FBI has issued more than 5,400 IOs. Bishop was apprehended less than five months later, on April 6, 1920. *FBI*

On November 24, 1932, the Bureau of Investigation established a technical laboratory in the Southern Railway Building on 13th Street and Pennsylvania Avenue NW in Washington, D.C. This small lab would one day grow into a world-class forensic laboratory. *FBI*

lacked the personnel for the job, the Bureau collected information about communist activities on the army's behalf but did not conduct official investigations since it did not appear that these activities violated any federal statutes.

Then, in the early 1930s, a special House of Representatives committee led by New York Congressman Hamilton Fish was authorized to investigate communism. A year later, the committee concluded that the federal intelligence community did not have the necessary authority to deal with the growing issue of communist activity. The committee proposed legislation in 1931 authorizing the Bureau to investigate "Communist and revolutionary activity." Covering his turf, Hoover opposed this and told Fish that rather than expanding the Bureau's power, it would be better to enact a criminal statute, especially since the Bureau had "never been established by legislation" and operated "solely on an appropriation bill."

The Immigration Bureau had jurisdiction to conduct these investigations and the obligation to deport communist aliens. If it did not do so, Hoover said, "It would be subject to criticism for its laxity along these lines." Hoover's position, expressed in a memo to the attorney general dated January 2, 1932, was not based on opposition to the idea of domestic intelligence but rather on his concern for the Bureau's authority if it resumed "undercover" activities that would be necessary "to secure a foothold in Communistic inner circles" and "to keep fully informed as to changing policies and secret propaganda on the part of Communists." ■

J. Edgar Hoover was the most powerful lawman in America for almost half of the twentieth century. It is possible that he exercised more power, longer, than any man in American history did. The fact that there is more remembered about Hoover than most presidents is revealing. Counting his time in the BOI, the predecessor organization of the FBI, his career spanned sixteen attorneys general and ten presidential administrations, from Woodrow Wilson to Richard Nixon. *Library of Congress*

Chapter 2

J. EDGAR HOOVER

The Man With the Secrets

Ralph Waldo Emerson said, "An institution is the lengthened shadow of one man." If this is true, then to understand the FBI, its actions, inactions, accomplishments, and transgressions, it is necessary to delve into the character of the man who cast his shadow over federal law enforcement for almost half a century.

J. Edgar Hoover died at the age of seventy-seven on May 2, 1972, at his home on Thirtieth Place NW in Washington, D.C. His body was already in rigor mortis when his housecleaner discovered it at 8:30 a.m. There was no autopsy performed, and, according to the coroner, Hoover had suffered from hypertensive cardiovascular disease—a heart attack caused by high blood pressure.

STANLEY W. FINCH,
DIRECTOR
JULY 26, 1908–APRIL 30, 1912

As chief examiner, Mr. Finch advocated the creation of an investigative squad within the Justice Department, eventually becoming its first leader. Attorney General Bonaparte created a special agent force in the Department of Justice. Oversight of that newly organized force, later named the Bureau of Investigation (BOI), was assigned to Mr. Finch. Stanley W. Finch, the first chief of the Bureau, faced criminal and political issues no one before him had faced. *Library of Congress photo*

Hoover's personal physician issued a statement that Hoover had lived with a mild case of hypertension, or slightly elevated blood pressure, for more than twenty years, but had shown no signs of heart disease. The fact that Hoover was not being treated for high blood pressure, or taking medication for high blood pressure, was left out of the findings. Despite no evidence of foul play, this conspicuous omission provided ammunition for conspiracy theorists.

The acting attorney general, Richard Kleindienst, delayed the announcement of Hoover's death for several hours. The lack of a family member's request or official suspicion of foul play meant no autopsy could be ordered, despite the seemingly insufficient conclusion that Hoover died of natural causes. This determination only added fuel to the conspiracy theories. (In Washington, D.C., and in most states, autopsies are only performed at the request of a family member if the cause of death is unknown or if there is a suspicion that death was caused by something other than natural causes.)

With the announcement of the Watergate break-in shortly after Hoover's death, more fuel was added to the conspiracy fire. Arthur Egan, a reporter for the *Manchester Union Leader*, off-handedly referred to "the murder of J. Edgar Hoover" in his testimony to the Ervin Committee (the Senate Select Committee to Investigate Campaign Practices). He said later, "Somebody in the Watergate thing murdered Hoover." The reporter eventually admitted that he had only a feeling and no proof.

Congress authorized Hoover's body to lie in state in the Capitol Rotunda. Only twenty-one others—American presidents, war heroes, and political leaders—had received this honor, and never before had an individual viewed by some as little more than a cop who had grown increasingly despotic with age. To protect his remains from persons seeking to deface it, Hoover's remains were placed in a lead-lined coffin that weighed over one thousand pounds. Hoover was buried in the Congressional Cemetery, just a dozen blocks from where he had been born seventy-seven years earlier.

During his lifetime, few dared challenge his actions; his power and influence were unmatched. After his death, Hoover became a lightning rod for anyone displeased with what they saw as the intrusive tactics of the FBI or with personal misconduct of individual agents. Documents later revealed Hoover was a willing accomplice to more than one president in circumventing the law. In spite of controversies, including rumors of extra-legal misconduct and a homosexual relationship, one thing is clear: Hoover completely reshaped federal law enforcement. He extended the purview of the Bureau and transformed its special agents into a cadre of elite and credible crime fighters.

Early Life and Career

John Edgar Hoover was born on January 1, 1895, on Seward Square in Washington, D.C. His father was of English and German descent, and his mother came from a Swiss background. Hoover was the youngest of four children, born to Dickerson Naylor Hoover and Annie Marie Scheitlin, two years after the death of their third

A. BRUCE BIELASKI,
DIRECTOR

APRIL 30, 1912-FEBRUARY 10, 1919

Mr. Bielaski entered the Bureau of Investigation and rose to become Mr. Finch's assistant. In that position, he was in charge of administrative matters for the Bureau. At the end of April 1912, Attorney General Wickersham appointed Mr. Bielaski to replace the retiring Finch. As chief, Mr. Bielaski oversaw a steady increase in the resources and responsibilities assigned to the Bureau. *Library of Congress photo*

child. His brother, Dickerson Jr., was fifteen years his senior, and his sister, Lillian, was older by thirteen years.

Hoover was shorter than other boys his age (although he topped off at five feet ten inches in adulthood) and suffered from the neglect of an alcoholic father. Dickerson Hoover worked for the U.S. Coast and Geodetic Survey office as head of the printing division. He suffered from depression, was in and out of hospitals, and spent his last eight years in an asylum. Hoover's mother was demanding but loving.

The young Hoover had a stuttering problem, which he self-corrected in his pre-teen years. He developed a rapid staccato speech, joined a debate team in high school, and turned himself into a persuasive public speaker. He taught Sunday school and became a role model for the young people in his Presbyterian church. It is said he even considered the ministry as a career. Some of his critics speculate that he played up this part of his story as a ploy to represent his personal conduct as above reproach.

Hoover's mother was his best friend, confidante, and the overpowering influence in his life. She knew his idiosyncrasies, approved his friends, and helped him budget his money. She raised him to be obsessive, persistent, and precise. These traits were obvious throughout Hoover's life. He was precise to the point of issuing the instruction that all outgoing correspondence from the Bureau must be proofread four times. He became outraged if even one typo made it into a report. He insisted that all incoming correspondence be answered within forty-eight hours and all FBI employees answer the telephone by the fourth ring. Offenders were subject to disciplinary action. One agent, working in the public relations section, gave a correspondent the wrong ingredient measurements for Hoover's personal popover recipe, relying on memory rather than hard files. For this infraction, Hoover placed an official letter of reprimand in the agent's file.

Annie Hoover instilled in her son a sense of responsibility, albeit one woven around guilt from a constant litany of the sacrifices and suffering she had made for their family. For Hoover, marriage, dating, or continuing his education beyond his law degree were out of the question. Hoover lived with his mother for forty-three years, only moving out upon her death in 1938.

WILLIAM J. FLYNN,
DIRECTOR

JULY 1, 1919-AUGUST 21, 1921

In 1919, Mr. Flynn was named director of the Bureau of Investigation. Attorney General Palmer praised his new appointee as "the leading, organizing detective of America . . . Flynn is an anarchist chaser . . . the greatest anarchist expert in the United States." On September 27, 1921, Mr. Flynn resigned saying he had a "private business matter to accept." Attorney General Harry Daugherty accepted the resignation immediately and appointed William J. Burns to the position. *Library of Congress photo*

President Woodrow Wilson heads to his second inauguration. Wilson would give the Bureau a new role as the keeper of domestic intelligence when the country approached World War I. When Congress authorized President Wilson to go to war, the Bureau's responsibilities expanded to enforcing the Espionage, Sedition, Selective Service, and Sabotage Acts. *Library of Congress*

After completing high school, Hoover began working as a clerk at the Library of Congress and attended night classes at George Washington University Law School. In 1916, he earned his bachelor's degree and the following year his master's degree. Along with completing his master's degree and passing the bar exam, Hoover registered for the draft, a requirement for all men between the ages of twenty-one and thirty-one. He was at that time the sole financial support for his parents, so he did not enlist, nor was he drafted.

Hoover joined the Department of Justice on July 26, 1917, as a clerk and rose quickly through the ranks. In *Hoover's FBI*, Cartha DeLoach said, "[Hoover] got his first taste of authority under circumstances in which he could disregard the normal constitutional restraints on the power of the state." In November 1918, Hoover was named assistant to the attorney general. He soon headed the Enemy Alien Registration Section, a.k.a. the Enemy Alien Bureau (EAB).

The fact that many other young employees of the Justice Department had enlisted gave Hoover the opportunity for a rapid ascent through the ranks. A *New Yorker* profile said, "He dressed better than most . . . he had an exceptional capacity for detail work, and he handled small chores with enthusiasm and thoroughness. He constantly sought new responsibilities to shoulder and welcomed chances to work overtime."

In 1921, Director William J. Burns appointed twenty-six-year-old J. Edgar Hoover as his assistant director. On May 10, 1924, Attorney General Harlan Fiske Stone appointed Hoover as acting director of the Bureau of Investigation. Later that year, President Coolidge approved Hoover as director of the Bureau. Hoover would soon develop a reputation as a true gangbuster but one who was more respectful of the Bill of Rights than his predecessors.

Hoover's appointment as director went largely unnoticed by the press. The BOI was perceived as just another mismanaged and corrupt organization in a burgeoning federal bureaucracy. The *Washington Evening Star* ran the Hoover announcement on the obituary page. It said, "The old-time detective, the man of 'shadows' and 'frame-ups' and 'get the goods any way you can' is a thing of the past."

Hoover was by choice almost friendless within the Department of Justice, and he rarely associated with his coworkers outside the office setting. Typically, when the other employees arrived at work, Hoover was already at his desk, reviewing evidence of newly uncovered subversives; he was still there when they left in the evening. The conjecture was that Hoover was a dedicated employee with no romantic attachments to complicate his life. Hoover was, however, devoted to his Masonic brothers. On November 20, 1920, he was raised to a Master Mason in Federal Lodge No. 1, Washington, D.C., just two months before his twenty-sixth birthday. He later became a Royal Arch and would go on to receive the highest title of Scotch Rite, 33rd Degree Inspector General.

Not long after Hoover took over the Bureau, he obtained a charter for the Bureau's own Masonic Lodge, the Fidelity Chapter. Attendance at the weekly meeting was voluntary, but astute agents soon caught on that if they wanted advancement, seeing the director in this semi-social environment was practically mandatory. For many years, this clique of Masons meant few Catholics ever rose to top positions in the FBI, and, with the notable exception of Hoover's eventual second in command, Harold "Pop" Nathan, Jewish agents were also rare in the higher ranks.

After becoming Director, Hoover eliminated the "Buzzard's Roost," a room where agents would congregate, swap stories, and drink alcohol. He fired the political appointees and those he considered unqualified, including an agent who was in jail for grand larceny but was listed as temporarily suspended. At the time, less than 17 percent of the investigative personnel possessed legal training and less than 14 percent had any accounting background. Within six months, Hoover had fired almost forty special agents, and the support staff fell from 216 to about 100 employees. *Library of Congress*

Reforms

In the early 1920s, the Bureau had approximately 650 employees, including 441 special agents. Many of its agents were unqualified, including numerous political appointees, accountants without accounting degrees or qualifications, criminals, and others who had no prior law enforcement experience. Such appointments grew in prevalence during World War I. After Burns became director on August 22, 1921, that practice quickly reached epidemic proportions. The principal qualification of an applicant was previous employment as a private detective or by a detective agency. In many instances, the prior employment had been with the William J. Burns International Detective Agency. Many were appointed as political or personal favors, and there were no age limits or educational requirements. Many appointees did not have so much as a high school education, and some were past sixty years of age when they joined the Bureau.

Hoover took over a BOI that was a cesspool of corruption. Newspapers were influencing public perception of the Bureau as a national disgrace. Nonetheless, Hoover proceeded to build an organization of professional law enforcement officers.

This 1917 cartoon by J. H. Cassel shows an enemy alien being stripped of the flag he is hiding behind. Hoover, who early in his career headed the Enemy Alien Registration Section, a.k.a. the Enemy Alien Bureau (EAB), shared a belief held by many other Americans that enemy aliens will hide behind the U.S. flag and exploit the Constitution's free speech protections. *Library of Congress*

Assistant Secretary of the Treasury Lincoln C. Andrews, right, and the commissioner of prohibition, Roy C. Haynes, meet outside of the House of Representatives. Prohibition was the cornerstone for organized crime. It created a lawlessness that touched every aspect of American life. Before prohibition, the country had about fifteen thousand legal bars. Prohibition spawned more than thirty-two thousand speakeasies in New York City and another twenty thousand in Chicago, where alcohol was served illegally. *Library of Congress*

The first female hired as an agent, Alaska P. Davidson was hired as a special investigator under Director William J. Burns, beginning her duty on October 11, 1922. She was fifty-four years old at the time and reportedly had only three years of public schooling. She stayed only a few years, as did two other women who followed her. Despite these early advances, Hoover would see to it that the agent population was kept exclusively male until his death in 1972. *FBI*

One story about Hoover's appointment harkened with the headline, "Days of 'old sleuth' are ended," which turned out to be accurate.

Unfortunately, Hoover's idea of building a professional law enforcement organization meant removing the only three female special agents in the Bureau. Hoover's antipathy to female agents was hardly a secret. He viewed women through the eyes of his Victorian upbringing, where there were only two kinds of women: good and bad. Good women were decorous creatures, and bad women were predators. Neither, in Hoover's judgment, would make good agents. Hoover said that women "could never gunfight, and all our agents must know how to do that." He feared women's cleverness and intuition. "Machine Gun" Kelly's wife was a typical example of Hoover's idea of a bad woman. "When a woman turns professional criminal," he said, "she is a hundred times more vicious and dangerous than a man." He made this statement after allegedly suppressing evidence that sent her to prison for twenty-six years—evidence that some claimed would have exonerated her.

It wasn't until 1971—the year prior to his death—that Hoover rescinded his order for female employees to wear dresses or skirts to work, even on snowy, winter days. Men could smoke at their desks, but women could not. In his last year, two women who were denied entry to the FBI Academy sued Hoover, and he fired two female clerks who attended peace protests.

In Anthony Summers' 1993 book, *Official and Confidential: The Secret Life of J. Edgar Hoover*, a former male special agent recalled that women were tolerated "only to perform the boring clerical functions required to keep the Bureau paper flowing. The prevailing attitudes seemed to be that it was perfectly all right to bullshit 'em and ball 'em; just don't tell 'em any secrets." (Sources in the FBI disagree that this was ever the attitude.)

Hoover set up what he saw as a standard of excellence for all employees. He abolished the seniority rule for promotions and introduced

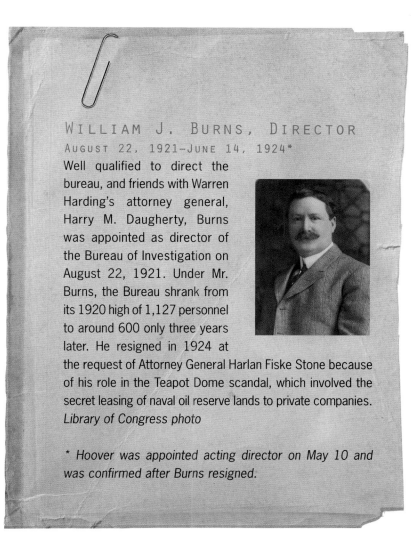

WILLIAM J. BURNS, DIRECTOR
AUGUST 22, 1921–JUNE 14, 1924*

Well qualified to direct the bureau, and friends with Warren Harding's attorney general, Harry M. Daugherty, Burns was appointed as director of the Bureau of Investigation on August 22, 1921. Under Mr. Burns, the Bureau shrank from its 1920 high of 1,127 personnel to around 600 only three years later. He resigned in 1924 at the request of Attorney General Harlan Fiske Stone because of his role in the Teapot Dome scandal, which involved the secret leasing of naval oil reserve lands to private companies. *Library of Congress photo*

* *Hoover was appointed acting director on May 10 and was confirmed after Burns resigned.*

Louis "Lepke" Buchalter, center, is handcuffed to J. Edgar Hoover, on the left. Buchalter controlled the New York garment workers' unions and the bakery delivery-drivers union, collecting a penny a loaf tax on all bread delivered. The FBI had him in its sights for restraint of trade and for drug smuggling. Meyer Lansky decided Buchalter should turn himself in to take the heat off the mob, and a friend arranged for it on the condition he would only be charged with drug smuggling and be out in five years. While in prison, a gangland snitch implicated Buchalter in murder, and he was sentenced to death. *Library of Congress*

uniform performance appraisals. In January 1928, he established a formal training course for new agents, including the requirement that new agents had to be between twenty-five and thirty-five years old to apply. He also returned to the earlier requirement that special agents possess either law or accounting degrees.

Hoover's agents had to excel in all areas, meeting higher standards than any other federal, state, and local law enforcement officers. He ordered background checks, interviews, and physical testing for new agent applicants. By the end of the decade, he had created approximately thirty field offices staffed by a new breed of special agents.

Hoover's goal was to fashion the Bureau into a model of public service, ethics, action, and appearance—an organization that would both intimidate criminals and win the admiration of law-abiding citizens. The results of Hoover's public relations campaign made children want to become "junior G-men" and persuaded tens of

Buchalter stands in court during his sentencing on December 2, 1941. Despite attempts to cut a deal, Buchalter went to the electric chair on March 4, 1944, making him the only major mob boss ever executed by state or federal authorities for his crimes. *Library of Congress*

The early days of the Bureau saw science take a prominent role in solving crime. The chemistry lab seen here would be the start of a world-class forensics laboratory. One of the first cases the laboratory solved was a murder by poisoning at a veteran's hospital. *FBI*

Clyde Tolson (left) was Hoover's second in command and constant companion for more than forty years. The pair often vacationed together, and one acquaintance described their relationship as "spousal"; others imagined a romantic relationship existed. Sherman Billingsley, a friend of Hoover and owner of the Stork Club in New York City, referred to the pair as "Mr. and Mrs. Hoover." However, nothing in their public behavior suggested anything more than a best-friends relationship. Both were lifelong bachelors. *Library of Congress*

thousands of qualified young men to join the Bureau during his tenure, despite the modest pay, long hours, and family disruptions that came with the job. These efforts developed universal respect for the Bureau (which after being endowed by Congress with greater powers became the Federal Bureau of Investigation in 1935), making it easier for agents to obtain the cooperation of citizens and other law enforcement officers. Hoover rewarded extraordinary loyalty in his agents but also took acute action against agents who displeased him. He commonly transferred agents to far-reaching and career-killing field offices, although some would get back on Hoover's good side and in some cases were even promoted. One (possibly apocryphal) story has Hoover firing agents who had "pointy heads," looked too much "like bus drivers or milkmen," or who otherwise "didn't look right."

In 1971, an agent attending a course at John Jay College of Criminal Justice in New York City remarked to his instructor in writing that he had problems with Bureau personnel policies. The agent made the mistake of having the letter typed in the FBI typing pool, and a copy went to Hoover. Hoover ordered all the agents enrolled in the course to drop out, and he transferred the complaining agent to the FBI field office in Butte, Montana.

Hoover would prove to be astute in controlling his sometime collaborator, sometime nemesis—the press. He used the media to create the persona of his agents as the invincible slayers of America's antiheroes, killers such as John Dillinger, Nazi spies, communists, and violent criminals. Noting the press' widespread interest in the war against crime, Hoover realized that he could use the media to carry the

JOHN EDGAR HOOVER,
DIRECTOR
MAY 10, 1924–MAY 2, 1972

message of the Bureau's work to the people. In 1932, Hoover published the first issue of the *Fugitives Wanted by Police*. It would later become *The FBI Law Enforcement Bulletin*.

On August 10, 1933, the Bureau of Investigation became the Division of Investigation (the Division also included the Bureau of Prohibition). Prior to 1933, Bureau agents were perceived by the public as interchangeable with other federal law enforcement officers. In a matter of a few years, Hoover's influence on the media made identification with the FBI a source of pride among its employees, and instant recognition and respect from the public.

Hoover took the art of media management to a new level. He generally had the cooperation of Congress, but in lieu of that, he used scare tactics, including Nazi or communist threats, to squeeze more funding from Congress. In his book, *Masters of Deceit* (ghostwritten by Courtney Riley Cooper), Hoover says, "They (Communist) try to paint our agents as brutal thugs in the hope of driving a wedge between them and their members and the government."

In general, the press was sympathetic during Hoover's early tenure, and he used that sympathy to project his FBI as an incorruptible institution and a model of science and technology. After his death, it would be difficult to maintain that stellar reputation of incorruptibility.

Hoover's Secret Life

Although Hoover was notorious in the gay community for his persecution of lesbian, gay, and bisexual individuals, speculation about his own sexuality followed him his entire adult life. Since at least the early 1940s, rumors circulated that Hoover was himself a homosexual, but no concrete evidence to support those claims has ever materialized. An FBI memorandum dated June 11, 1943, reports a woman spreading gossip of Hoover being "queer" and keeping "a large group of young boys around him." The memo reports the woman allegedly overheard the conversation at a

The J. Edgar Hoover reading room in the main library at the FBI Academy in Quantico contains memorabilia of the longest tenured director. Over the years, Hoover doggedly defended "his" bureau. When a governor criticized a local FBI field office, Hoover struck back like the bulldog he resembled. (Removal of a boil from his nose in childhood left him with a pushed-in nose and bulldog look.) "Let me reiterate my oft-stated position that as long as I am director of this Bureau, any attack on an FBI employee who is conscientiously carrying out his official duties will be considered an attack on me personally." *Henry M. Holden*

LOUIS PATRICK GRAY III, ACTING DIRECTOR
MAY 3, 1972–APRIL 27, 1973

In 1970, President Nixon appointed Mr. Gray as assistant attorney general for the Civil Division in the Department of Justice. In 1972, Mr. Gray was appointed deputy attorney general, but before he could be confirmed by the full Senate, his nomination was withdrawn. Instead, President Nixon designated him as acting director of the FBI. Gray served in the position for less than a year.

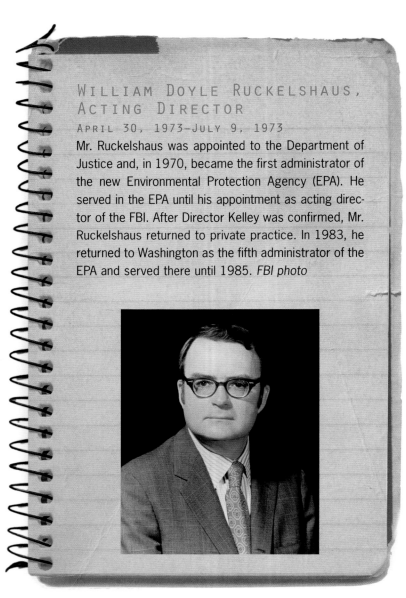

WILLIAM DOYLE RUCKELSHAUS, ACTING DIRECTOR
APRIL 30, 1973–JULY 9, 1973

Mr. Ruckelshaus was appointed to the Department of Justice and, in 1970, became the first administrator of the new Environmental Protection Agency (EPA). He served in the EPA until his appointment as acting director of the FBI. After Director Kelley was confirmed, Mr. Ruckelshaus returned to private practice. In 1983, he returned to Washington as the fifth administrator of the EPA and served there until 1985. *FBI photo*

restaurant in Baltimore, Maryland, in 1941. In retaliation, Hoover reportedly "opened files" on some of his accusers.

No one really knows whether the rumors of homosexuality were true or not, but he was said to have decorated his garden with classical statues of nude men, and his fashion sense as a bit of a "dandy" fit a certain stereotype. There is no available evidence of Hoover having romantic attachments with women and not so much as one eyewitness account of a female date known to be on record.

In the 1950s, the FBI began discreetly following both Hoover and Associate Director Clyde Tolson as a security precaution. While both men knew agents kept an eye on them, they usually did not see them lurking in the shadows. When Hoover died, Tolson inherited his estate of approximately $551,000 and moved into his home. Tolson also accepted the flag that draped Hoover's casket. Tolson, who died three years later, is buried a few yards away from Hoover in the Congressional Cemetery.

Despite the continued speculation, many agents categorically refute the idea that Hoover was homosexual. According to W. Mark Felt, who was an associate director under Hoover, "I never . . . saw any indication of homosexual tendencies in Hoover. To my knowledge, neither did any of my colleagues in the FBI. Hoover was married to his job."

The allegation that Hoover was also a cross-dresser is considered by most people to be an urban legend, fueled by the 1977 movie, *The Private Files of J. Edgar Hoover.* The cross-dressing rumors were further energized by Anthony Summers' *Official and Confidential: The Secret Life of J. Edgar Hoover.* Summers writes that an individual named Susan L. Rosenstiel reportedly "saw Hoover in the Plaza Hotel on two occasions, once dressed in a fluffy black dress and a second time in a red dress wearing lace stockings and high heels, and he had makeup on and false eyelashes."

Rosenstiel's character later came into question when it was revealed that Summers had paid her for the interview, and she had earlier perjured herself and served time in a New York City jail. There is speculation that she wanted to get even with Hoover, who she felt had stacked the deck against her in her divorce suit. Another get-even factor could have been that Rosenstiel's ex-husband, Lewis, funded the J. Edgar Hoover Foundation.

There were also rumors that the Chicago mafia and mob boss Meyer Lansky had blackmailed Hoover with photos of him in drag and performing homosexual acts. These rumors are used by some to explain why he never seriously went after organized crime. Mafia sources deny the existence of such photos, and if such photos ever did exist, most likely they would have found their way to the public by now. In addition, with the FBI constantly wiretapping the mob, any discussions of Hoover's cross-dressing by the mobsters would have made it to the FBI grapevine in a matter of hours; none ever surfaced.

There are allegations that the FBI purposely did not pursue the mob. Despite federal laws barring the shipment of stolen goods across state lines, the Mann Act, and the Dyer Act, Hoover denied the existence of the mafia. He knew those cases would consume his time and manpower, and he feared the unlimited money the mob had at its disposal might even corrupt his agents. He knew there was more publicity mileage to be had with quick arrests and convictions. In fact, a number of attorneys general did not make the mafia a priority, perhaps because they were afraid of what Hoover might have on them. It wasn't until Attorney General Robert F. Kennedy took over and ordered Hoover to take down the mob that the FBI set about doing so with the help of new congressional antiracketeering legislation.

Hoover's personal history was also clouded by anomalies in the personal records of his family history and genealogy. Journalist Edward Spannaus discovered that Hoover's siblings had birth certificates filed within days of their births, but Hoover's was not filed until he was forty-three years old and only after his mother's death. African-American author Millie McGhee claimed to be related to Hoover, that Hoover's father was Ivy Hoover in Mississippi, and that he was taken at a young age to Washington, D.C., to live with the Hoovers of Washington. George Ott, a professor of genealogy, found Mississippi census records that confirmed McGhee's personal history, passed down from her grandparents and including some suspicious alterations to records pertaining to the Hoovers of Washington. However, there does not seem to be unequivocal proof of that particular Ivy Hoover being J. Edgar's father. According to Spannaus, "Many former FBI agents recall that rumors about Hoover's ancestry were prevalent within the Bureau."

The Secret Files

Many individuals' fear of Hoover originated in the files he began to compile soon after he became director. Rumors persisted about these secret files for most of Hoover's tenure. The most volatile were filed under "Personal and Confidential," while less damaging information was kept under "Official and Confidential."

Hoover recognized early in his career the value of having secret files apart from the FBI's central records system. If sensitive documents were easily accessed, they would be vulnerable to congressional subpoena, review of senior Justice Department officials, or the White House. If there was no record made in the central records system, then nothing officially existed, and the secret file could be destroyed, leaving no paper trail.

In an October 1941 memo from Hoover, he reported that his files contained "various and sundry items believed inadvisable to be included in the general files of the Bureau." After Hoover's death, Acting Associate Director Felt incorporated most of the Official and Confidential files into the FBI's central records.

CLARENCE M. KELLEY, DIRECTOR
JULY 9, 1973–FEBRUARY 15, 1978

Clarence Kelley joined the FBI as a special agent on October 7, 1940. He was on military leave from the FBI while serving in the United States Navy from July 22, 1944, to April 9, 1946. Kelley's first assignment after returning from military service was in the Kansas City office. He was transferred to the Houston office and later Seattle, where he served as assistant special agent in charge. He served as special agent in charge of the Memphis office until his retirement in October 1961. Kelley was nominated for director by President Nixon on June 7, 1973, and was sworn in on July 9, 1973.

As a result of the increasing volume of these files over Hoover's tenure, there was an alleged document called the "D (destruct) list" that, in case of Hoover's death, or any calamitous event, specified the immediate destruction of certain files, films, and audiotapes, and of the list itself. Immediately following Hoover's death, Helen Gandy began destroying the files on the so-called D-list. There were several hundred folders containing close to twenty thousand pages of material, spanning almost fifty years in the Personal and Confidential files.

Before President Richard Nixon announced Hoover's death to the public, he ordered Chief of Staff H. R. Haldeman to secure Hoover's files (among them was a file on Nixon from his initial application to become an FBI agent). Haldeman in turn passed the order to Acting Attorney General Richard Kleindienst, who passed the word to John Mohr, an assistant to the director.

By 11:40 a.m. on the morning of Hoover's death, the files were secure and, according to Mohr, "The contents of the office are exactly as they would have been had Mr. Hoover reported to the office this morning." In a memo to Kleindienst, Mohr reported, "After having the lock changed, I have in my possession the only key to the office."

Temporary operational command of the Bureau passed to Associate Director W. Mark Felt, who was Hoover's second in command at the time. The following day, Nixon appointed L. Patrick Gray III, a Justice Department official with no FBI experience, as acting director, with Felt remaining as associate director.

That afternoon, Gray headed to the director's office on the fifth floor of the Justice Department building. He wanted access to the secret files. Mohr would later testify

JAMES B. ADAMS, ACTING DIRECTOR
FEBRUARY 15, 1978–FEBRUARY 23, 1978

James Blackburn Adams was appointed acting director of the FBI, serving from February 15, 1978, until February 23, 1978. Adams entered on duty with the Bureau on July 9, 1951. As a special agent, Mr. Adams served in the Seattle Division, San Francisco Division, and Administrative Services Division. In 1959, he was appointed assistant special agent in charge of Minneapolis. He subsequently served in several leadership positions before being appointed special agent in charge of San Antonio in 1972. The next year, he was appointed assistant director of the Office of Planning and Evaluation. He was appointed assistant to the director/deputy associate director for investigations in 1974, served as acting director in early 1978, and was appointed associate director on April 6, 1978, the number two position in the Bureau. He retired from the Bureau on May 11, 1979, and returned to Texas, where he served in various law enforcement–related positions until 1987. *FBI photo*

before a special House Subcommittee that he told Gray there were no secret files in Hoover's private office. He was right. The FBI's Personal and Confidential files were under the ever-watchful eye of Hoover's personal secretary, Helen Gandy, in her outer office. Most likely, Gandy had already shredded the most damaging files. The *New York Times* quoted an anonymous FBI source in the spring of 1975 as saying, "Gandy had begun almost a year before Mr. Hoover's death and was instructed to purge the files that were then in his office."

On May 4, 1972, Gandy handed over 164 folders containing approximately 17,700 pages of Official and Confidential files to Mark Felt. Among the 164 folders, which now reside in the National Archives, were eight folders that had been originally marked Personal and Confidential files but were transferred to Official and Confidential by Hoover in November 1971. One folder contains a description of the director's "Do Not File" procedures to preclude the discovery of illegal activities. A second folder records efforts to get the assistance of Supreme Court Justice Abe Fortes in a case before the Court.

The real Personal and Confidential files were never turned over to Felt. Gandy worked for a week in her office going through those files. She then transferred at least three dozen file drawers of papers to Hoover's basement recreation room at his residence, where she continued working on those files until mid-July. Exactly how many existed, and what the files contained, will never be known.

In 1975, during Congress' investigation of FBI harassment of Martin Luther King Jr., Gandy testified that Hoover had left instructions to destroy his personal papers upon his death. According to Clyde Tolson and L. Patrick Gray, Gandy reportedly said, "I can give you my word, I know what there was—letters to and from friends, personal friends, and a lot of letters. [After reviewing them] I tore them up, put them in boxes, and they were taken away to be shredded." Although many on the subcommittee said they did not believe her, no one who was called before Congress disputed her testimony. The only other person who could have known what was in the Personal and Confidential files was dead.

According to Laurence Silberman, appointed deputy attorney general in early 1974, Director Clarence M. Kelley thought such files either did not exist or had been destroyed. After the *Washington Post* broke a story on the files in January 1975, Kelley searched and found some files in his outer office. None were the kind alleged to have existed.

The contents of the infamous files allegedly included blackmail material on an influential politician, his sons, their wives, and other women. There were also allegations of two homosexual arrests, which Hoover leaked to help defeat a Democratic presidential candidate; the surveillance on one of America's best-known first ladies and her alleged lovers, both male and female, white and black; child molestation documentation Hoover used to control and manipulate a Red-baiting politician; a list of the Bureau's spies in the White House during eight administrations; evidence that an attorney general had received payoffs from the Chicago syndicate; and all the distasteful gossip Hoover could amass on some of Hollywood's biggest names, such as Charlie Chaplin

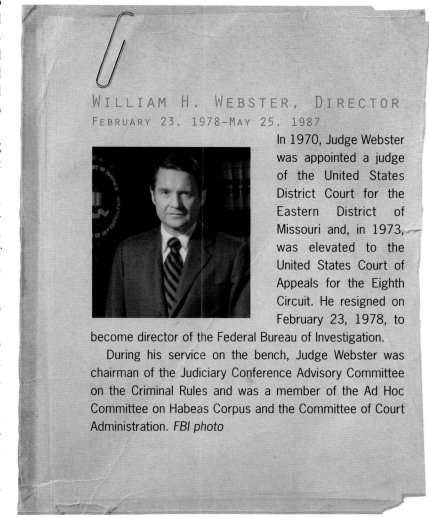

WILLIAM H. WEBSTER, DIRECTOR
FEBRUARY 23, 1978–MAY 25, 1987

In 1970, Judge Webster was appointed a judge of the United States District Court for the Eastern District of Missouri and, in 1973, was elevated to the United States Court of Appeals for the Eighth Circuit. He resigned on February 23, 1978, to become director of the Federal Bureau of Investigation.

During his service on the bench, Judge Webster was chairman of the Judiciary Conference Advisory Committee on the Criminal Rules and was a member of the Ad Hoc Committee on Habeas Corpus and the Committee of Court Administration. *FBI photo*

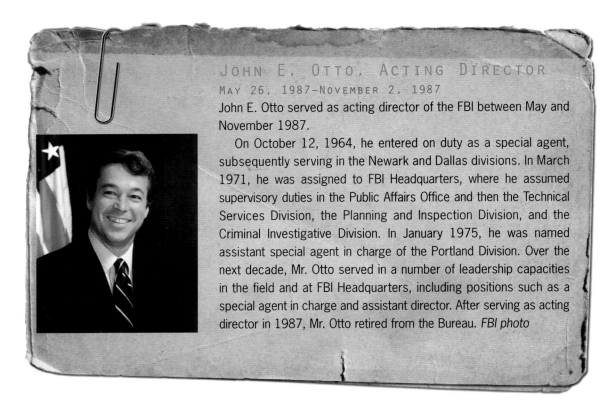

JOHN E. OTTO, ACTING DIRECTOR
MAY 26, 1987–NOVEMBER 2, 1987

John E. Otto served as acting director of the FBI between May and November 1987.

On October 12, 1964, he entered on duty as a special agent, subsequently serving in the Newark and Dallas divisions. In March 1971, he was assigned to FBI Headquarters, where he assumed supervisory duties in the Public Affairs Office and then the Technical Services Division, the Planning and Inspection Division, and the Criminal Investigative Division. In January 1975, he was named assistant special agent in charge of the Portland Division. Over the next decade, Mr. Otto served in a number of leadership capacities in the field and at FBI Headquarters, including positions such as a special agent in charge and assistant director. After serving as acting director in 1987, Mr. Otto retired from the Bureau. *FBI photo*

and Rock Hudson, writers such as John Steinbeck and Ernest Hemingway, politicians such as Adlai Stevenson, and activists such as Gloria Steinem.

While most of these files were destroyed after his death, not all of the secrets went with him to the grave. For instance, Hoover investigated Eleanor Roosevelt after she made statements he thought were contrary to most Americans' political beliefs. The FBI also opened a file on Marilyn Monroe when she became associated with (and eventually married) playwright Arthur Miller, an alleged member of the Communist Party. The FBI also tracked her as one of John F. Kennedy's suspected lovers. The files contained other sensitive documents discussing Hoover's authorizations of black bag jobs, wiretaps, and other illegal or politically motivated investigatory activities.

Associate Director Felt said that while the Official and Confidential files did exist, the information in them was not as explosive as some believed. Included in the files was personal correspondence between Hoover and public figures such as RCA founder David Sarnoff, New York archbishop Francis Cardinal Spellman (whose home had been bombed), television personality Bishop Fulton Sheen (a frequent speaker at Bureau functions), and movie mogul Jack Warner, for whose studio Hoover was an unpaid consultant on the 1959 film *The FBI Story* and again in 1965 for the TV series *The FBI.* According to Felt, the files were available on a need-to-know basis, with top-secret clearances necessary. The catch was that these clearances would have had to come with Hoover's approval, which he rarely granted.

After Hoover's death, the "intimidation factor" of the FBI in the public perception diminished despite the continued existence of the files. The news of his death allowed some people to speak out for the first time without fear of reprisal. For instance, Hoover had maintained surveillance on Martin Luther King Jr. and questioned the motives of some of his associates. King's widow, Coretta Scott King, made no attempt to hide her acrimony against the man she felt tried to destroy her husband. She told the

Washington Post, "We are left with a deplorable and dangerous circumstance. The files of the FBI gathered under Mr. Hoover's supervision are replete with lies and are reported to contain sordid material on some of the highest people in government, including presidents of the United States. Such explosive material has to be dealt with in a responsible way. Black people and the black freedom movement have been particular targets of this dishonorable kind of activity."

Another longtime adversary of Hoover was Gus Hall, the general secretary of the Communist Party USA (CPUSA). As reported in the *New York Times* on May 3, 1972, he called the late FBI director "a servant of racism, reaction, and repression," and a "political pervert whose masochistic passion drove him to savage assaults upon the principles of the Bill of Rights."

The FBI cannot divulge the exact number of files it maintains today, but one recent estimate was more than six million. At one point, the Associated Press used the Freedom of Information Act to request every "High Visibility Memorandum" filed between 1974 and 2005. The AP's request produced more than five hundred memos totaling nearly 1,500 pages. The agency has long maintained that its era of surveillance for political purposes is over, reflecting changes that followed FBI Director J. Edgar Hoover's death in 1972. But there no doubt remains plenty of nuggets of past behavior tucked away on FBI letterhead.

Two days after Hoover's death, and while the new FBI building was under construction, President Nixon named the building the J. Edgar Hoover Building. President Gerald Ford dedicated the building on September 30, 1975. By 1987, a debate was on whether or not the building should be renamed. Director William Sessions said, "Mr. Hoover built the FBI. It was his genius; it was his inspiration . . . . The fact that there are circumstances that suggest that there were problems in his administration, I think is unfortunate." In July 2002, a bill was introduced in Congress to rename it the "Federal Bureau of Investigation Building." As of 2007, the bill was still in a subcommittee. *FBI*

WILLIAM S. SESSIONS, DIRECTOR
NOVEMBER 2, 1987–JULY 19, 1993

Judge Sessions was a private practitioner of law in Waco, Texas, from 1958 until 1969, when he left his firm to join the Department of Justice in Washington, D.C., as chief of the Government Operations Section, Criminal Division. In 1971, he was appointed U.S. attorney for the Western District of Texas. In 1974, Judge Sessions was appointed United States district judge for the Western District of Texas and, in 1980, became chief judge of that court. He has served on the board of the Federal Judicial Center in Washington, D.C., and on commit-tees of both the State Bar of Texas and the Judicial Conference of the United States.

On November 1, 1987, Judge Sessions resigned his position as United States dis-trict judge to become director of the Federal Bureau of Investigation and was sworn in on November 2, 1987. *FBI photo*

In June 1941, Roosevelt named William J. Donovan to the Office of the Coordinator of Information (COI) and the first overall chief of the United States intelligence community. At the insistence of Hoover, the FBI retained its independence and control of domestic intelligence. In 1942, the COI became the Office of Strategic Services (OSS). The OSS was responsible for espionage and sabotage in Europe and in parts of Asia. The OSS was kept out of South America by Hoover's hostility to Donovan and out of the Philippines by General Douglas MacArthur. According to the 9/11 Commission Report, the OSS was disbanded because of "lobbying by the FBI, combined with fears of creating a U.S. Gestapo led the FBI's being assigned responsibility for internal security functions and counterespionage." *Library of Congress*

President Roosevelt's funeral was held April 14, 1945. By the time President Franklin Roosevelt took office, the Bureau, while in reality a part of the Justice Department, appeared more like an independent agency. At the time of FDR's death, Hoover had amassed power and influence and ran the FBI as a quasi-autonomous organization. *Library of Congress*

Taken at the Yalta Conference in February 1945, this photo shows Prime Minister Winston Churchill, a weak and ailing President Roosevelt, and Premier Joseph Stalin of the Soviet Union. Hoover had studied Lenin, Trotsky, and other communist writings, and he discovered "a conspiracy so vast, so daring, that few people at first could even grasp the sweep of Communist vision . . . ." Hoover decided communism was "the most evil, monstrous conspiracy against man since time began." Roosevelt would die within weeks of the conference, and his vice president, Harry Truman, would face a despotic-like Hoover and a real threat from Stalin. *Library of Congress*

Hoover and the Presidents

Hoover's relationships with the eight presidents he served ranged from friendly to fiery. Some of Hoover's more contentious relationships were with John F. Kennedy, Lyndon Johnson, and Attorney General Robert F. Kennedy. Presidents Truman, Kennedy, Johnson, and Nixon each considered removing Hoover but concluded that the political cost of doing so would be too great. Johnson tried to retire Hoover by offering him an ambassadorship. The old dog, however, did not bite.

Hoover also used two future presidents as secret informants. Gerald Ford kept Hoover informed on the Warren Commission hearings, and Ronald Reagan reported on the activities of Screen Actors Guild members during his tenure as SAG president.

During Hoover's term, presidents regularly requested that the Bureau collect information on their political opponents and critics. Hoover complied with these requests and, either directly or through surrogates, told each president about the questionable personal conduct of not only the president's political opponents but of those within the administration. When it benefited him, Hoover would tell those on whom he held a file that it would be held in the strictest confidence. By doing so, he built reluctant lifetime enablers. These were allegedly some of the Personal and Confidential files destroyed by Helen Gandy.

Hoover and President Truman are all smiles for the camera. Away from the camera, Hoover had little respect for Truman. He considered him "a pig farmer from Missouri," who needed to learn how Washington worked, even though Truman had been in the Senate for almost ten years before ascending to the presidency. *FBI*

A MATTER OF ETHICS

On July 19, 1983, following a Justice Department inspector general investigation of ethics violations committed by Director William Sessions, President Bill Clinton removed him from office and appointed Deputy Director Floyd I. Clarke as acting director.

Franklin D. Roosevelt

In August 1936, President Roosevelt called a meeting with Hoover to discuss "subversive activities, particularly fascism and communism." FDR wanted Hoover to discreetly provide him with a broad picture of both movements. With war looking inevitable, Hoover took the opportunity to resume his domestic surveillance activities.

By late fall of 1939, Hoover had resurrected the structure of the old General Intelligence Division of World War I and set up a custodial detention plan for those who should be rounded up in case of war. The FBI expanded in authority, jurisdiction, and size during FDR's administrations.

Harry S. Truman

As early as 1945, Harry S. Truman complained that Hoover and his agents were "dabbling in sex life scandals and plain blackmail when they should be catching criminals."

Their relationship did not begin well. Hoover sent an agent from Truman's Missouri hometown to the White House to convey Hoover's welcome. After some small talk with the agent about home, Truman asked why the agent was there. The agent replied, "Mr. Hoover wants you to know that he and the FBI are at your personal disposal and will help you in anyway you ask."

Truman saw through the message and replied, "Any time I need the services of the FBI, I will ask for it through my attorney general," effectively dismissing the agent and Hoover in one sentence. According to William Sullivan, who would be promoted to assistant director of domestic intelligence in 1961, "From that time on, Hoover's hatred of Truman knew no bounds."

John F. Kennedy

Hoover knew Kennedy's secrets, and Kennedy knew Hoover had files on him. Hoover had moral and security concerns about President Kennedy. His files revealed that Kennedy had an affair with Judith Campbell Exner, who was simultaneously having an affair with Sam Giancana, the boss of the Chicago mafia, while Giancana was conspiring with the CIA to assassinate Fidel Castro.

In the summer of 1963, FBI Director J. Edgar Hoover went to Robert Kennedy and said, "We have information that not only your brother, the president, but others in Washington have been involved with a woman whom we suspect as a Soviet intelligence agent, someone who is linked to East German intelligence."

Ellen Rometsch was born in Kleinitz, Germany, in 1936. After World War II, Kleinitz became part of East Germany. In 1955, Rometsch immigrated to West Germany. Her second husband was Rolf Rometsch. As a West German military aide assigned to Washington, D.C., Mrs. Rometsch arrived in the United States on April 6, 1961.

Copies of some of Hoover's files on Rometsch were moved to Robert F. Kennedy's personal files. A memo shows that while discussing the Rometsch issue with Attorney General Robert Kennedy, Hoover broached the subject of the possibility that President John Kennedy might replace him as FBI director.

In a declassified FBI memo dated October 28, 1963, Hoover briefed Senate leaders Everett Dirksen (R-Illinois) and Mike Mansfield (D-Montana) and asked them to keep to themselves whatever knowledge they had of the situation. At the bottom of the memo, Hoover indicated that he had accepted an invitation to lunch with the president on October 31, 1963. Had Hoover warned the president or blackmailed him?

A July 1963 FBI memo called for an end to the investigation of the Rometsch case. Memos show that after taking office following President Kennedy's assassination, President Johnson encouraged further investigation into the Rometsch case. Files show that the FBI at least initially did not make files concerning Rometsch available to Robert Kennedy's replacement as attorney general, Nicholas Katzenbach. Another memo summarizes a 1965 FBI interview with Robert Kennedy concerning Ellen Rometsch, John F. Kennedy, and former publisher of the *Washington Post*, Philip Graham. Files show that the FBI failed to develop any information connecting Rometsch with intelligence activities in the United States. Specific results of the FBI investigation were unpublished. The memos, however, show the dissemination of that information and the interest of others to see it. Yet another memo indicates that some FBI files on Rometsch had been intentionally destroyed by the FBI.

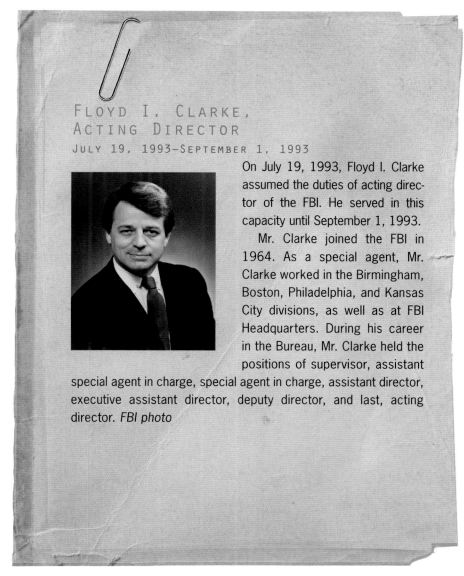

FLOYD I. CLARKE, ACTING DIRECTOR
JULY 19, 1993–SEPTEMBER 1, 1993

On July 19, 1993, Floyd I. Clarke assumed the duties of acting director of the FBI. He served in this capacity until September 1, 1993.

Mr. Clarke joined the FBI in 1964. As a special agent, Mr. Clarke worked in the Birmingham, Boston, Philadelphia, and Kansas City divisions, as well as at FBI Headquarters. During his career in the Bureau, Mr. Clarke held the positions of supervisor, assistant special agent in charge, special agent in charge, assistant director, executive assistant director, deputy director, and last, acting director. *FBI photo*

President Lyndon Johnson both feared and loathed Hoover. Johnson made one weak effort to remove Hoover from office. In 1967, he told Secret Service Agent Rufus Youngblood to go to FBI Headquarters and "take over." Youngblood hung out in the Bureau for several days; Hoover ignored him, and L.B.J. changed his mind. *FBI*

Lyndon B. Johnson

Lyndon Johnson was fearful of the Kennedy family and ordered FBI checks on high officials in the Democratic National Committee. When the *Washington Star* attacked him editorially, Johnson asked Hoover to find out if there was any Kennedy money behind the paper.

When Johnson's aide, Walter Jenkins, was involved in a homosexual episode in 1964, L.B.J. suspected that a Barry Goldwater supporter might have set up the arrest. He angrily ordered Hoover to seek derogatory material on Goldwater's Senate staff to be held for use if the senator made an issue of the Jenkins matter in the presidential campaign. Goldwater never did so.

Richard M. Nixon

Hoover had a close relationship with Dwight D. Eisenhower's vice president, Richard Nixon, which dated back to the 1940's Alger Hiss case. Alger Hiss was a U.S. State Department official and a Soviet spy. In 1948, Whittaker Chambers accused Hiss of being a communist, which he denied. Publicity surrounding the case fed the political career of Nixon, helping him move from the House of Representatives to the United States Senate in 1950, to the U.S. vice presidency in 1952, and ultimately to the presidency in 1969.

President Nixon, in office at the time of Hoover's death, had been at odds with Hoover over the director's refusal to break the law for some "black bag" jobs.

President Nixon, who was in office at the time of Hoover's death, in his eulogy called Hoover a "giant (whose) long life brimmed over with magnificent achievements and dedicated service to the country he loved . . . He became a living legend while still a young man, and he lived up to his legend as the decades passed. He personified integrity, he personified honor, he personified principle, he personified courage, he personified loyalty and patriotism." Nixon later wrote: "He died at the right time: fortunately, he died in office. It would have killed him had he been forced out of office or had resigned even voluntarily . . . . I am particularly glad that I did not force him out at the end of last year."
Library of Congress

Louis J. Freeh, Director
September 1, 1993–June 25, 2001

Director Freeh served as an FBI special agent from 1975 to 1981 in the New York City field office and at FBI Headquarters in Washington, D.C. In 1981, he joined the U.S. Attorney's Office for the Southern District of New York as an assistant U.S. attorney. Subsequently, he held positions there as chief of the Organized Crime Unit, deputy U.S. attorney, and associate U.S. attorney.

During that time, Director Freeh was the lead prosecutor in the Pizza Connection case, the largest and most complex investigation ever undertaken at the time by the U.S. government.

Following the investigation, in July 1991, President George Bush appointed Freeh as U.S. District Court judge for

the Southern District of New York. While serving in that position, he was nominated to be the director of the FBI by President Clinton on July 20, 1993. He was confirmed by the Senate on August 6, 1993, and sworn in as director on September 1, 1993.
FBI photo

Named for the satchels that carried the break-in tools, black bag jobs were illegal break-ins, usually to plant bugs, photographs, or steal materials, a practice that at one time had been frequently ordered by Hoover. These jobs included breaking into embassies, homes of antiwar radicals, members of the Ku Klux Klan, and the Rev. Dr. Martin Luther King Jr. In 1966, Hoover felt political pressure developing to expose these illegal activities; he forbid them in July 1966 and reiterated his mandate in 1967. Hoover's adamant position caused Nixon to form his own Special Investigations Unit, a.k.a. the "White House Plumbers."

Top: The FBI conducts physical and defensive training on the rooftop of the Department of Justice in this 1940s-era photo. When Hoover took over the Bureau, there was no formal physical training. Hoover quickly realized that his agents must maintain good physical conditioning, and he began a formal program. Bottom: The modern FBI trains its agents at Quantico, Virginia. Once applicants have successfully completed the rigorous selection process and background check, they will join a class with other new agent trainees for seventeen weeks of intensive training. *Both images: FBI*

THOMAS J. PICKARD, ACTING
DIRECTOR
JUNE 25, 2001–SEPTEMBER 4, 2001

Mr. Pickard began his career as a special agent of the FBI on January 13, 1975. On September 10, 1996, FBI Director Louis Freeh named Mr. Pickard to the position of assistant director in charge of the Washington field office (WFO). During his tenure at WFO, Mr. Pickard supervised such matters as the investigation and arrest of FBI Special Agent Earl Pitts for espionage and the capture of convicted CIA killer Mir Aimal Kasi. On November 1, 1999, Mr. Pickard was appointed deputy director, the number two position at the FBI. On June 25, 2001, Mr. Pickard was appointed acting director of the FBI by Attorney General John Ashcroft. *FBI photo*

Although Hoover had secretly helped Nixon become president, Nixon twice unsuccessfully tried to remove Hoover (July and October 1971) from the FBI. Both times, he changed his mind after meeting with Hoover. Nixon allegedly said on one of those occasions, "I want to discuss the issue of retirement." Hoover allegedly replied, "Mr. President, you are too young to retire." Nixon dropped the matter.

J. Edgar Hoover had a problem coming up with a new name for the Bureau, so he ordered his senior agents to submit ideas on changing the name. Edward Tamm, an assistant director and close friend of Hoover, came up with "Federal Bureau of Investigation." Hoover was only convinced when another agent suggested the letters "FBI" could also stand for Fidelity, Bravery, and Integrity, all characteristics Hoover wanted in his agents. The motto has been memorialized on this courtyard sculpture at the J. Edgar Hoover building. *FBI*

A Faltering Reputation

The death of Hoover, the Watergate scandal, and the Vietnam War left the FBI vulnerable to congressional scrutiny. Critics contended that the FBI's campaign against subversion had also targeted peaceful, legitimate antiwar and civil rights protests. Also embarrassing to the Bureau were revelations that Hoover had compiled dossiers on prominent Americans that contained compromising information that Hoover could use to embarrass his opponents and bolster his own power.

After Hoover's death, public confidence in the FBI eroded dramatically. According to the 9/11 Commission Report, a 1966 Gallup poll revealed that 84 percent of the public gave the Bureau a "Highly Favorable" rating. By 1970, that rating had fallen to 71 percent. By 1973, approval of the FBI had fallen to 52 percent, and dropped further to 37 percent in 1975 and lower still in 1979. As a result, the FBI dissolved its Domestic Intelligence Division. Operating under stringent guidelines, the FBI sought to restore public trust in the Bureau. The FBI reduced its domestic security investigations and foreign counterintelligence. Organized crime and white-collar crime became the Bureau's principal concerns during the late 1970s.

While Hoover fired agents who committed crimes, he sometimes put himself above the law. In January 1978, a Justice Department report on "The Relationship between U.S. Recording Co. and the FBI" revealed that Hoover engaged in behavior that he would have considered unacceptable for his agents. Hoover had FBI employees build a front portico on his house in Washington, dig a fishpond with lights and a water pump, maintain his yard, paint the house yearly, and even prepare his income tax returns, all on government time. There were (and still are) federal statutes that bar conversion of federal property to personal use and the misuse of federal property.

Hoover's death signaled an end of an era. He had built an empire on information. And yet, he led a double life. He was a gangbuster and a blackmailer, and a hero and a hypocrite. He was more famous than the movie stars and perhaps more powerful than the presidents he served. Despite the negative perceptions of him that persist to this day, the fact remains that he almost single-handedly took a corrupt and dismal organization and built it into an impressive law enforcement agency. That part of the Hoover legacy remains intact. ∎

ROBERT S. MUELLER III, DIRECTOR
SEPTEMBER 4, 2001–PRESENT

Robert Mueller became the sixth director of the FBI on September 4, 2001. Mr. Mueller graduated from Princeton University in 1966 and earned a master's degree at New York University in 1967. He joined the United States Marine Corps and served as an infantry officer for three years in Vietnam. Following his military service, Mr. Mueller earned a law degree from the University of Virginia Law School in 1973. In 1993, he became a partner at Boston's Hale and Dorr, specializing in complex white-collar crime litigation. He returned to public service in 1995 as senior litigator in the Homicide Section of the District of Columbia United States Attorney's Office. In 1998, Mr. Mueller was named U.S. attorney in San Francisco and held that position until 2001. He served as acting deputy attorney general of the Department of Justice before becoming FBI director. *FBI photo*

Louis Buchalter, facing front, sits with Emanuel "Mendy" Weiss and Philip "Little Farvel" Kovolick, who shield their faces, and Louis Capone, in a courtroom during jury selection. Kovolick was a member of Murder Inc. and was eventually convicted on narcotics charges in late 1941. The New York Times reported that Kovolick was found sealed in a steel drum at the bottom of a rock pit in Hallandale, Florida, after disappearing on April 7, 1971. Library of Congress

Chapter 3

GANGBUSTERS

The FBI came of age in the Great Depression. During that time of turmoil in America, the organized-crime syndicate was in its embryonic stage. Two events in those years forced the expansion of the Bureau's jurisdiction. The first was the rise of colorful but ruthless gangsters, such as Al Capone, who conducted their murderous crime sprees with virtual impunity. The second watershed event was the Lindbergh baby kidnapping, which revealed the nation's uneasy relationship with its immigrant population and took the love-hate feelings between the legal system and the media to new heights.

The expression "bootleg" came from this unique way of hiding a pint flask of whiskey. *Library of Congress*

There weren't exactly high-speed chases in the 1930s, but the wrecked automobile had been eluding Bureau agents. The paddy wagon on the left awaits the passengers of the wrecked vehicle. Advocates of expanded federal law enforcement argued that prohibition had created gangs that operated between states, and the automobile and airplane quickly put criminals beyond the reach of local law enforcement. Defenders of traditional state and local law enforcement argued that expanding federal crime control would undercut local efforts and be counterproductive. FBI

Police raid a gambling den in Washington, D.C. Prohibition brought organized crime into illegal trafficking of alcohol, drugs, prostitution, and gambling. *Library of Congress*

Al "Scarface" Capone

In 1925, Alfonso (Al) "Scarface" Capone rose to power as a mob boss. Capone in many ways created the mold for organized crime. He built a fearsome reputation, and he ruled most of Chicago's rackets. His crime syndicate terrorized Chicago for a decade, referred to by many as the "gangster years." His organization committed assaults, murders, and controlled gambling, prostitution, and illegal alcohol sales. The Internal Revenue Service estimated Capone's illegal businesses took in $105 million in 1927 alone, and he had not paid any tax on the money.

However, the Supreme Court decision *United States v Sullivan* (1927) ruled that unlawful income was subject to federal income tax. On March 29, 1929, the Bureau of Investigation arrested Capone after he failed to respond to a subpoena to appear as a witness in a prohibition case.

The attorney general had ordered the Bureau to review an affidavit that requested a postponement of Capone's court appearance. Capone's lawyers submitted a physician's statement asserting that Capone was in Miami, suffering from

Al Capone and his organization went largely untouched by local law enforcement because Chicago politics and organized crime were usually intertwined. Federal agents of the Prohibition Bureau were never able to gather enough evidence to indict Capone on bootlegging. As fast as the booze came into the city, the feds would dump it into the city's sewers. Demand continually outstripped supply, and bootleggers made fortunes. *Library of Congress*

bronchial pneumonia. The Bureau, however, obtained statements that Capone, at that time, had attended racetracks in the Miami area, and that he had made a plane trip to the island of Bimini.

Capone had appeared before the grand jury on March 20, 1929, and completed his testimony on March 27. As he left the courtroom, Bureau agents arrested him for contempt of court, an offense that threatened a year of incarceration and a $1,000 fine. Capone posted $5,000 bond and was released. On February 28, 1930, the jury

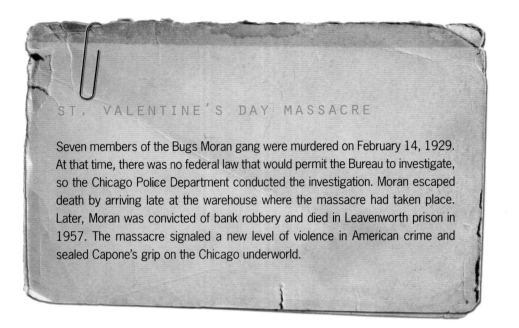

ST. VALENTINE'S DAY MASSACRE

Seven members of the Bugs Moran gang were murdered on February 14, 1929. At that time, there was no federal law that would permit the Bureau to investigate, so the Chicago Police Department conducted the investigation. Moran escaped death by arriving late at the warehouse where the massacre had taken place. Later, Moran was convicted of bank robbery and died in Leavenworth prison in 1957. The massacre signaled a new level of violence in American crime and sealed Capone's grip on the Chicago underworld.

found Capone guilty of the contempt charge. The judge sentenced him to six months in Cook County Jail.

Meanwhile, the Treasury Department had obtained an indictment against Capone for income tax fraud, and on October 17, 1931, he was convicted on five counts of tax evasion. Capone was released from a federal prison in November 1939 after serving over seven years and paying all fines and back taxes. He died at his home in 1947 of syphilis, which he contracted in his youth.

Critics have said the tax evasion and contempt charges were trivial when compared to the more serious crimes for which Capone had never been charged: extortion, racketeering, prostitution, gambling, and murder. Capone's first killing was in 1924, after another mobster had called Capone's Jewish friend, Jack Guzik, an anti-Semitic name. Capone shot the mobster six times in front of witnesses. An assistant state attorney interrogated Capone but released him for lack of evidence. All the witnesses had suddenly suffered memory loss. The inability of the government to prosecute Capone on witness tampering was a function of the Bureau's limited jurisdiction, as the more serious charges fell under local law enforcement jurisdiction.

Special agents check for fingerprints and other clues, circa 1933. Fingerprints were the only way to make an accurate identification until DNA typing came along decades later. *Library of Congress*

Charles Lindbergh was at the height of his fame for his pioneering transatlantic flight years earlier when his infant son was kidnapped and murdered. Called the "Crime of the Century," it shocked a world that was already mired in the Great Depression, and had an enormous impact on both the legal system and the relationship between celebrity and media. *Library of Congress*

THE MAFIA NETWORK

The 1930s structure of the mafia took on the look of corporate America. There was a national commission composed of three Jewish and three Italian delegates. Its job was to sanction murders and mediate disputes between rival mafia groups. There was a New York commission, which ruled on serious issues and controlled the five New York families. The Eastern states controlled by the mafia at the time were Florida, Michigan, Ohio, New York, New Jersey, Pennsylvania, and Louisiana. There was a separate Chicago mafia, also under the national commission, as were the Western states of California, Kansas, and Illinois. Nevada would enter the mafia ranks when Las Vegas became a hot spot for gambling in the 1950s.

Lindbergh Baby Kidnapping

The 1929 stock market crash and the Great Depression brought hard times to America. Gangsters ruled many of the large cities, and the public disregard and violation of the prohibition law sent strong messages to the federal government.

Prior to the 1930s, the Bureau's mandate was limited. On the run up to and during World War I, there had been some expansion of its role. After the war, because of its abuse of power, Congress had purposely limited the Bureau's role and budgets. Most law enforcement continued to be the responsibility of state and local authorities.

In an example of early crime scene photography methods, this FBI agent takes a picture of a heel print left at the scene. Still in its infancy, crime scene photography was of little help in solving the Lindbergh case. *FBI*

This 1930s-era photo shows agents in the old photographic unit processing photographic prints. Today, digital cameras and computers have made the chemical baths obsolete. *FBI*

The BOI's first technical laboratory was initially equipped with only a microscope (which cost $590), ultraviolet light equipment, a helixometer (a device to measure the bore or interior of a gun barrel), and a drawing board. Note the air conditioning on the far right wall. *FBI*

The Lindberghs received thirteen ransom notes; the tenth upped the ransom to $70,000. The other notes were about delivering the money and the return of the child. Dr. John F. Condon met with "John" to reduce the demand to $50,000. Condon handed the stranger the money in exchange for a receipt and the thirteenth note, saying that the kidnapped child was on a boat called Nellie near Martha's Vineyard, Massachusetts. In response to the Lindbergh kidnapping case, Congress passed the Federal Kidnapping Act on June 22, 1932. The act gave the Bureau authority to investigate kidnappings where the victims were taken across state borders (*New York Times* front page: March 2, 1932).

This separation between local and federal crime control began to narrow with President Roosevelt's New Deal administration of 1933, which signaled a major shift in the government's involvement in economic issues caused by the Depression. Until then, private enterprise and local charities were responsible for most economic recovery and relief. This shift in policy also extended to law enforcement after the Lindbergh baby kidnapping.

The debate about law enforcement jurisdiction effectively ended when the infant son of Charles and Anne Morrow Lindbergh was kidnapped. On March 1, 1932, at about 9 p.m., the child was discovered missing from his nursery on the second floor of the Lindbergh home near Hopewell, New Jersey. A ransom note demanding $50,000 was found on the nursery windowsill. The New Jersey State Police took over the investigation. At the time, the Bureau had no jurisdiction to investigate the kidnapping.

The police questioned the household employees and groundskeepers, and Lindbergh asked friends to communicate with the kidnappers. They made widespread appeals for the kidnappers to start negotiations. The Bureau followed thousands of leads throughout the United States, but to no avail.

On March 2, Attorney General Homer Cummings and J. Edgar Hoover informed the New Jersey State Police that the Department of Justice would assist and cooperate in the investigation. Hoover advised the police that they could call upon the Bureau for any facilities or resources needed.

Shortly after Hauptmann's apprehension, specimens of his handwriting were sent to the Bureau's Document Section laboratory in Washington, D.C. A comparison of the writing on the Lindbergh baby ransom notes with that of the exemplars disclosed remarkable similarities in inconspicuous personal writing habits, which resulted in a positive identification by the handwriting experts of the FBI Laboratory. *FBI*

At one point, Dr. John F. Condon, a retired school principal, published an offer in the *Bronx Home News* to act as a go-between. Eventually, Condon met with an individual named "John," an alleged go-between for the kidnappers.

On May 12, investigators found the infant's body partly buried and badly decomposed, just five miles from the Lindbergh home. The coroner's examination showed that the child had been dead for about two months, killed by a blow to the head.

On May 13, President Roosevelt instructed all government investigative agencies to place themselves at the disposal of the New Jersey State Police to catch the criminals. The Bureau, he said, would serve as a clearinghouse and coordinating agency for all investigations related to the case that were conducted by other federal agencies.

Forty-thousand dollars of the ransom money had been paid in gold certificates and, at the time, a large portion of this money had not been returned. The attorney general asked the commissioner of the Internal Revenue Service for a detailed report of all work performed by the IRS Intelligence Unit. On January 17, 1933, the New York BOI office issued a letter to all banks in New York City requesting a watch for the gold and silver notes used to pay the ransom.

On May 2, 1933, the Federal Reserve Bank in New York discovered 296 $10 gold certificates and one $20 gold certificate with serial numbers that matched the ransom money. The Federal Reserve traced the bills back to one deposit slip bearing the name and address of J. J. Faulkner, 537 West 149th Street. Despite an intensive investigation, the Bureau never located the depositor.

In late August and into September, sixteen more gold certificates showed up in New York City. As each bill was recovered, a colored pin marking the location of the recovered bill was inserted in a large map at the BOI office. These pins created a

The Lindbergh baby kidnapping posed new technological challenges for the fledgling crime lab. There was no definitive evidence at the scene. Traces of mud were found on the floor of the nursery. There were some smudged footprints under the nursery window, but there were no bloodstains or fingerprints anywhere. Here, Lab technicians analyze mud from shoes in a thermal analyzer to identify the clay content. *FBI*

The case against Hauptmann was based on circumstantial evidence. Tool marks on the ladder matched tools owned by Hauptmann. Wood in the ladder was similar to wood used as flooring in his attic. The FBI Lab examined the ladder and determined that, although it was crudely built, the builder was familiar with woodworking. A wood expert with the U.S. Forest Service disassembled the ladder and identified the types of wood used. He concluded it was likely that some wood had been used before in indoor construction. He summarized his findings in a report, which played a critical role in the trial of the kidnapper. *FBI*.

The Supreme Court of New Jersey upheld the lower court's verdict on Hauptmann. The U.S. Supreme Court denied Hauptmann's appeal on December 9, 1935, and he was scheduled to die on January 17, 1936. However, the governor of New Jersey granted a thirty-day stay, pending the review of court documents. Hauptmann was resentenced to death during the week of March 30, 1936. The Pardon Court denied Hauptmann's petition for clemency, and on April 3, 1936, Hauptmann was executed (*New York Times* front page: April 4, 1936).

pattern illustrating that the ransom money was coming from the Yorkville area. The Bureau also had a description of the individual passing these bills. It fit the description of "John" given by Dr. Condon.

In September 1933, Roosevelt stated in a meeting with Hoover that all work on the case would be centralized in the Department of Justice. Soon after FDR had taken office, he had issued a declaration requiring the return to the Treasury of all gold certificates.

For several months, New York City banks and their branches kept a close watch for the ransom certificates. In February 1934, all Bureau offices were supplied with copies of a pamphlet containing the serial numbers of ransom bills. Copies also went out to bank employees, clearinghouses, grocery stores, insurance companies, gasoline filling stations, airports, department stores, post offices, and telegraph companies.

Finally, on September 18, 1934, the manager of a bank at 125th Street in New York City telephoned the New York Bureau office and reported a teller had discovered a $10 gold certificate a few minutes earlier. They traced the bill back to a gasoline station located two blocks away.

The gasoline attendant had received a $10 bill in payment for five gallons of gasoline from a man whose description fit "John." The attendant was suspicious of the

The Bureau discovered that Bruno Hauptmann, thirty-five years old, was a native of Saxony, Germany. He had a criminal record, and had spent time in prison. After two failed attempts at entering the United States, Hauptmann succeeded in November 1923. On October 10, 1925, Hauptmann married Anna Schoeffler, a New York City waitress. Anna bore a son in 1933. Until the spring of 1932, Hauptmann worked as a carpenter. However, shortly after March 1, 1932, the date of the kidnapping, Hauptmann began to trade in stocks and never worked again. *FBI*

$10 gold certificate and recorded the license plate number of the automobile. The car belonged to Bruno Richard Hauptmann of East 222nd Street, Bronx, New York. Federal and local authorities put Hauptmann's house under surveillance. On September 19, 1934, Hauptmann left his house. Bureau agents and local police took him into custody.

Hauptmann was identified as a German carpenter who had been in the United States for approximately eleven years. A $20 gold certificate from the ransom was found in his pocket, and his description fitted perfectly that of "John." In his house, police found a pair of shoes that had been purchased with a $20 ransom bill recovered on September 8. The following day, ransom money in excess of $13,000 was found in Hauptmann's garage. Dr. Condon identified Hauptmann as the "John" to whom he had paid the ransom.

On October 8, 1934, Hauptmann was indicted for murder. The trial began on January 3, 1935, and lasted five weeks. On February 13, 1935, the jury found Hauptmann guilty of first-degree murder and sentenced him to death. The defense appealed but lost. Bruno Richard Hauptmann was executed on April 3, 1936.

George "Machine Gun" Kelly

George "Machine Gun" Kelly was one of the most infamous criminals of the gangster era. He was born George Kelly Barnes on July 18, 1895, to a wealthy family in Memphis, Tennessee. At the age of nineteen, Kelly married Geneva Ramsey and quit school. He fathered two children with Geneva and took a job as a cab driver. Working long hours for low wages, the couple struggled financially. Distraught and broke, Kelly quit his job, became a bootlegger, and began making money.

After being arrested several times for bootlegging, Kelly left town with a new girlfriend. He changed his name to George R. Kelly to preserve the respect and name of Geneva Barnes and his law-abiding family back home.

By 1927, Kelly had earned a reputation. He had been arrested several times and served time in jail. In 1928, he was caught smuggling liquor onto an Indian reservation and went to Leavenworth Penitentiary for three years.

Eventually, Kelly moved to Oklahoma City, where he met a minor bootlegger named Steve Anderson. Kelly fell for Anderson's mistress, Kathryn Thorne, a criminal herself. One day, Thorne's husband turned up dead. The official cause of death was suicide, but the investigators suspected that Kathryn was involved. Just days before, she had made comments that she was going to "kill that god-damned Charlie Thorne." Kelly and Kathryn married in September 1930.

Historians believe that Kathryn Thorne Kelly was the creator of the "Machine Gun" Kelly image and the mastermind behind several bank robberies. In July 1933, Kathryn and Kelly schemed to kidnap wealthy oil tycoon Charles Urschel. Kelly, carrying his trademark Tommy gun, and two other men carrying pistols entered the

Urschel's home in Oklahoma City. The Urschels were playing cards with friends when Kelly stormed in and threatened to "blast everybody away." Urschel was taken to a ranch in Texas, and Kelly demanded a $200,000 ransom. A family friend delivered the money and ended the eight-day nightmare for an unharmed Urschel.

In August 1933, the Bureau published wanted posters describing Kelly as an expert machine gunner. George and Kathryn both dyed their hair to conceal their identities and enjoyed a lavish lifestyle. After several weeks in hiding, the couple made their way back to Memphis to stay with longtime friend, John Tichenor. On the morning of September 26, 1933, Memphis police, along with Bureau agents, surrounded Tichenor's house and made a forced entry. Witnesses say it was then that Kelly coined a new term when he shouted out, "G-men, don't shoot," but this is considered apocryphal by FBI historians. Nevertheless, "G-man," short for "government man," became synonymous with the Bureau's special agents in the public's imagination.

The couple stood trial, and both received life sentences. Eventually, the kidnapping accomplices were arrested, and all received life sentences. George "Machine Gun" Kelly went back to Leavenworth in 1951 and died of a heart attack on July 18, 1954. Kathryn Thorne Kelly was released from prison in 1958 and took a job at an Oklahoma hospital as a bookkeeper.

Kansas City Massacre

On the morning of June 17, 1933, multiple murders took place in front of Union Railway Station in Kansas City, Missouri. The killings took the lives of three police officers, one federal agent, and their prisoner. In the wake of the Kansas City Massacre, Congress passed a number of federal crime laws that significantly enhanced the Bureau's jurisdiction.

The May/June Crime Bills of 1934 made it a federal crime to kill or assault a federal officer. Congress also created the Fugitive Felon Act and gave the Bureau full powers of arrest in crimes under its jurisdiction. Prior to this legislation, Bureau agents could only make a citizen's arrest and call a U.S. Marshal or local police officer to make the official arrest. In granting arrest powers, Congress required the Bureau to obtain a warrant from a federal judge prior to the arrest. To obtain the warrant, the Bureau had to show probable cause that the suspect had committed or was about to commit a federal felony, and the judge had to agree.

The law also made robbing a member bank of the Federal Reserve System a federal crime. Transportation of stolen property across state lines and fleeing across state lines to avoid prosecution or to avoid giving testimony all fell into the Bureau's lap.

"Baby Face" Nelson

Unlike many of the murderous gangsters of the 1930s, Lester M. Gillis, a.k.a. "Baby Face" Nelson, went out of his way to kill. Richard Lindberg, author of *Return to the Scene of the Crime*, said, "Standing only five feet four inches, Gillis compensated for his physical limitations with a murderous temper and a willingness to employ a switchblade or a gun without hesitation or remorse for the intended victim."

In 1928, Nelson met a sales clerk named Helen Wawzynak, whom he would later marry. His wife retained the surname Gillis throughout their marriage.

In Sausalito, California, Nelson met John Paul Chase, and the two became fast friends. In April 1934, Nelson, Helen, and Chase went to Chicago and joined the

"Baby Face" Nelson, so named for his juvenile appearance, was born Lester M. Gillis in 1908 in Chicago, Illinois. Nelson's early criminal career included stealing tires, operating stills, bootlegging, and armed robbery. By the age of fourteen, he was an accomplished car thief. In 1922, Nelson was convicted of auto theft and was remanded to a boys' home. In 1924, he was released on parole but returned to the home five months later on a similar charge. In January 1931, Nelson robbed a bank in Chicago and received a sentence of one year to life. A year later, Nelson was tried on another bank robbery charge in Wheaton, Illinois. On February 17, 1932, he escaped while being returned to Joliet Prison. *FBI*

Dillinger gang. Chase remained in Chicago, while Nelson and his wife joined the Dillinger gang on vacation at the Little Bohemia Lodge in northern Wisconsin.

The Bureau learned of the gang's location on April 22, 1934, and special agents were dispatched to the lodge. Dogs alerted the gangsters, who escaped in the dark, leaving the women behind. Nelson fled to a nearby home, forced his way in, and took two hostages. Later, Special Agents J. C. Newman and W. Carter Baum arrived at the scene with the local sheriff. When their car stopped, Nelson rushed to the car and ordered the occupants to get out. Before they could comply, he shot all three men, killing Special Agent Baum.

On June 23, 1934, Attorney General Cummings offered a reward for Nelson's capture or information leading to his arrest. A week later, Nelson robbed the Merchants National Bank in South Bend, Indiana, killing a police officer during the crime. Nelson, John Dillinger, and Homer Van Meter participated in the robbery. Afterward, the three men fled to Chicago. Two police officers were later shot outside Chicago, as they approached the gang's meeting place.

Inspector Samuel P. Cowley of the Bureau's Washington, D.C., headquarters had been assigned to search for Nelson. On November 27, 1934, Cowley received word that Nelson had been seen driving a stolen car. Two agents spotted Nelson's vehicle near Barrington, Illinois. Nelson brought the car around behind the agents, and John Paul Chase fired five rounds into the agents' car. One of the agents returned fire, and one shot pierced the radiator of Nelson's car, partially disabling it.

In another car, Cowley and Special Agent Herman Edward Hollis pursued Nelson and Chase. Suddenly, Nelson veered off the highway and stopped. Before Cowley and Hollis could get out of their car, Nelson and Chase began firing machine guns at them. Special Agent Hollis died during the gun battle, which lasted about five minutes. Inspector Cowley died the next morning.

Baby Face Nelson died of his gunshot wounds about 8 p.m. that evening. An anonymous caller told Bureau agents they could find his body, ironically, in a cemetery. More than ten thousand "mourners" attended his funeral.

On December 31, 1934, John Paul Chase became the first person to be tried under the law that made it a federal crime to murder a special agent of the Bureau in the performance of his duty. Chase's trial began on March 18, 1935. One week later, the jury found him guilty of murdering Inspector Samuel P. Cowley. He was sent to Alcatraz Island, California, on March 31, 1935. Paroled from Leavenworth on October 31, 1966, Chase worked in California as a custodian for seven years. He died of cancer in Palo Alto, California, on October 5, 1973.

Bonnie and Clyde

Bonnie and Clyde were the bad seeds of the Depression. Clyde Barrow was an angry young man. He had been born dirt-poor, the fifth of seven children, and it got worse during the Great Depression. He killed in cold blood and always tried to justify the murders as if he had a right to pull that trigger. His weapon of choice was a Browning automatic rifle (BAR), and he used it to be feared and envied. His legend outsized his five-foot seven-inch frame.

By the time Bonnie and Clyde had become known, many ordinary folks believed they were striking back at big business and government. They were anti-heroes, in the same mold as John Dillinger and Baby Face Nelson.

The two knew they could not last long in the bank robbery business. The evidence lay all around them—criminals shot dead by law enforcement. They decided to celebrate until the bullets cut them down. Bonnie Parker's last request to her mother was, "Don't bring me to a funeral parlor. Bring me home."

Their murderous crime spree involved state and local violations over a span of less than two years. The Bureau became interested in Clyde in late December 1932 through a mistake on his part. An automobile that Clyde had stolen in Pawhuska, Oklahoma, turned up abandoned near Jackson, Michigan, three months later.

A year after that, the Bureau caught up with the two in Louisiana. After one of the most stunning manhunts the nation had seen up to that time, Clyde Barrow and Bonnie Parker attempted to run a roadblock. On May 23, 1934, they were cut down in a hail of bullets. Each had been shot over fifty times, according to some reports.

Clyde Chestnut Barrow, twenty-one, stood five feet seven inches, weighed 130 pounds, and had slicked-back, thick brown hair in the style of the day. His eye color matched his hair. Women found him attractive. Bonnie Parker, nineteen, stood four feet eleven inches, weighed 90 pounds, and had Shirley Temple–colored strawberry-blond ringlets. She was freckle-faced and, according to those who knew her, she was very pretty. At the time of their death, Barrow had been wanted for twelve murders in the preceding two years, and Parker was wanted as his accomplice. *FBI*

Dillinger's crime spree, from September 1933 to July 1934, was not well timed. The Crime Bills were passing through Congress in early 1934 and were about to be signed by President Roosevelt. J. Edgar Hoover wanted to make Dillinger an example of why crime didn't pay. Dillinger wore a twelve-pound bulletproof vest (pictured) on many of his bank robberies but left it at home the night he went to the Biograph Theater. *FBI*

As evidence of the legendary status the criminals had reached, thirty thousand mourners attended Clyde's funeral.

By 1934 criminal enterprises were running amuck, contributing to a period of unrest in America. J. Edgar Hoover authorized the "flying squads"—special agent groups tasked with capturing the most notorious gangsters, including John Dillinger, who flagrantly violated federal law during the commission of his crimes.

John Dillinger

In the 1930s, many Americans saw the bank as their enemy. Banks had failed, wiping out the life savings of millions of Americans. As the Depression deepened, the banks that survived foreclosed on homes, farms, and businesses. Americans did not view bank robbers as terrible criminals. To them, John Dillinger was like Robin Hood, stealing from the rich banks and, as an ancillary benefit, sometimes destroying the mortgage records at the banks he hit. The daring robberies and skilled getaways were fantasies for Americans who had lost everything.

For some time, Dillinger eluded the traps set for him. In April 1934, the gang needed a place to hide. One of them suggested a summer resort in northern Wisconsin called Little Bohemia. Emil Wanatka, an emigrant of Bohemia, had built the lodge a few years earlier. Wanatka and his wife were frightened to death of the gang's reputation. Wanatka wrote a letter to someone he knew in the U.S. attorney's office and had his wife pass it on to her brother, who mailed it. She also mentioned the note to another family member who was staying at her husband's lodge. That family member quietly contacted the Bureau in Chicago.

Melvin Purvis was the special agent-in-charge of the Chicago office. Purvis, unlike his fellow agents, loved the public spotlight. This vice would be his ultimate downfall. As soon as he got the news about Dillinger, Purvis called Hoover, who promised to fly in reinforcements from the St. Paul, Minnesota, office.

Along with the reinforcements came Assistant Bureau Director Hugh Clegg. The agents from Chicago and St. Paul met at the airport in Rhinelander, Wisconsin. Just as the Bureau forces were preparing for the attack, Dillinger and his mob were getting ready to move. It was past 6 p.m. when the Bureau agents landed at Rhinelander. They had planned to conduct the raid at 4 a.m. the next morning but changed their plan when they learned that Dillinger was about to flee.

Clegg and Purvis formulated a plan: three agents wearing bulletproof vests would storm the lodge. Ten others would flank the lodge and intercept anyone who tried to escape. The gang would be trapped on three sides. The fourth side, the lake, was impassable.

It was a good plan, but three key terrain factors were missing from the Bureau's maps: a ditch on the left of the lodge, a barbed-wire fence on the right, and the steep bank near the lake, which could cover an escape along the shore, and no one knew about the two watchdogs on the premises.

As the agents quietly approached the brightly lit lodge, the watchdogs barked angrily. The agents took cover, believing that the element of surprise was gone. The dogs, however, had barked so frequently that the gang members initially ignored the noise. The agents did not realize that Dillinger had left the lodge hours earlier. The ensuing gun fight mortally wounded several gang members, but Dillinger and most of his gang had escaped and scattered.

One person played a major role in ending Dillinger's crime spree: Anna Sage, a Romanian-born madam who had run three houses of prostitution, one in Chicago, one in East Chicago, and one in Gary, Indiana. She would come to be known as the "lady in red."

Sage claimed Purvis made a deal with her. She was under a court deportation order, and Purvis knew that Dillinger frequented her establishment. He would get the order rescinded if she cooperated, or so she claimed.

For five hectic months, the Bureau chased the elusive Dillinger back and forth across the Midwest. Then, on Sunday, July 22, 1934, at 5 p.m., Purvis's phone rang. It was Anna Sage. In a whispered voice, she said, "He's here. We are leaving in five minutes for either the Biograph or the Marbro Theater." With that, she hung up.

Purvis dispatched several agents to the Marbro Theater but decided to stake out the Biograph Theater himself with more men.

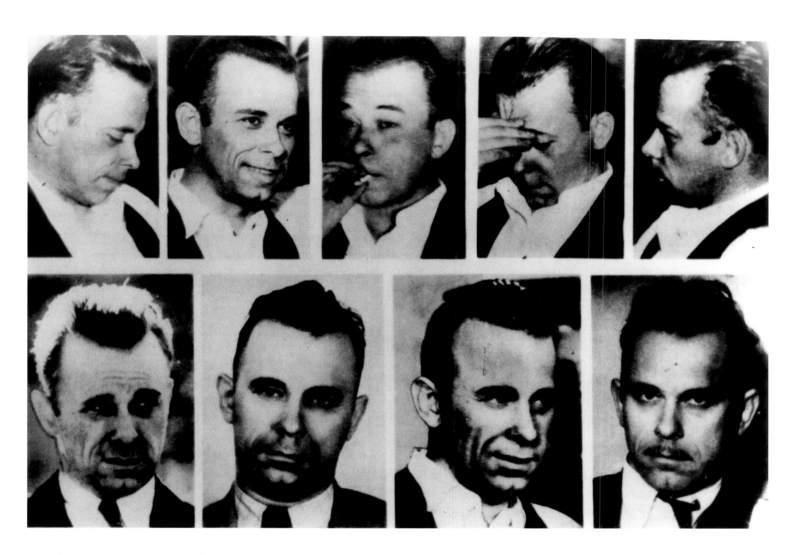

From September 1933 to July 1934, John Dillinger robbed ten banks, killed ten men, wounded seven others, robbed a police arsenal, and staged three jailbreaks. He eluded capture by constantly crossing state lines and slipping out of the local jurisdictions. On July 22, 1934, Dillinger walked out of the Biograph Theater. Special Agent Melvin Purvis gave a signal to close in, and Dillinger was surrounded. *FBI*

John Dillinger was gunned down outside the Biograph Theater. Hoover's opportunity to capture Dillinger came in early March 1934, when Dillinger broke out of an "escape-proof" jail in Indiana. In the process, he had stolen the sheriff's car and driven across the state line, upping the crime to a federal offense and into the gun sights of the Bureau. Special Agent Melvin Purvis believed that Dillinger, Hamilton, and Sage would take the same way back to Sage's apartment when they left the Biograph Theater. Purvis stationed himself near the theater entrance with the plan to light a cigar to signal when Dillinger and his companions passed.
Library of Congress

Purvis watched the Biograph from an automobile down the block. At approximately 8:15 p.m., Dillinger, his girlfriend Polly Hamilton, and Anna Sage walked up to the ticket booth, purchased tickets, and entered the theater to watch *Manhattan Melodrama* (a gangster movie, of course).

Purvis purchased a ticket and entered the theater. Unable to find the three in the darkness, he left the packed theater and waited for members of the Chicago Police Department to arrive.

When the crowd poured from the theater, Purvis spotted Dillinger, Hamilton, and the lady in red. (Purvis said in a 1959 article that she was actually wearing an orange skirt, and he did not recall the color of the rest of her outfit.) Dillinger was between the two women. "He looked into my eyes; surely he must have seen something more than casual interest in them, but apparently he didn't recognize me, and I struck the match and lit my cigar," Purvis recalled.

Dillinger was surrounded. Purvis stated, "I was about three feet to the left and a little to the rear of him. I was very nervous; it must have been a squeaky voice that called out, 'Stick 'em up, Johnnie, we have you surrounded.' "

Dillinger ran into an alley while reaching into his pants pocket to draw his pistol. Officers were on top of him and fired, dropping him halfway into the alley. They turned him over, but he was dead.

The successful conclusion to the Dillinger manhunt was the beginning of the end of the gangster era and a cornerstone in the evolution of the Bureau. What was lost in translation was that the end for Dillinger stemmed from a paid informer, the celebrated lady in red, rather than from clever police work.

A re-creation of Chicago's Biograph Theater on the FBI Academy's grounds gives new agent trainees a place to learn how to take down criminals as a team. *Henry M. Holden*

"Ma" Barker and the Karpis Gang

Kate "Ma" Barker (birth name Arizona Clark) was a legendary and alleged criminal. The actual degree of Barker's involvement in criminal activity, however, has been questioned. Her sons Herman, Lloyd, and Fred were clearly criminals, and the Karpis-Barker Gang committed a spree of robberies, kidnappings, and other crimes between 1931 and 1935. It appears, however, that the popular image of her as the gang's leader and criminal mastermind is more myth than fact.

In Ken Jones' book, *The FBI in Action,* Hoover is quoted as saying, "Ma Barker and her sons, and Alvin Karpis and his cronies, constituted the toughest gang of hoodlums the FBI ever has been called upon to eliminate. Looking over the record of these criminals, I was repeatedly impressed by the cruelty of their depredations . . . murder of two policemen . . . machine gun murder of an innocent citizen who got in the way during a bank robbery . . . kidnapping and extortion . . . train robbery . . . and the protection of high police officials bought with tainted money."

Alvin "Old Creepy" Karpis wrote in his autobiography, *The Alvin Karpis Story,* "The most ridiculous story in the annals of crime is that Ma Barker was the mastermind behind the Karpis-Barker gang . . . the legend only grew up after her death . . . to justify how she was slaughtered by the FBI. She wasn't a leader of criminals or even a criminal herself. There is not one police photograph or fingerprint of her taken while she was alive . . . she knew we were criminals but her participation in our careers was limited to one function: when we traveled together, we moved as a mother and her sons. What could look more innocent?"

When Hoover wrote about Ma Barker, he used harsh but not accusatory language: "It has been said that Ma Barker trained her sons in crime . . . certainly she became a monument to the evils of parental indulgence . . . there is hot-eyed, hard-featured Ma Barker in a jealous rage berating her boys. Then she is the

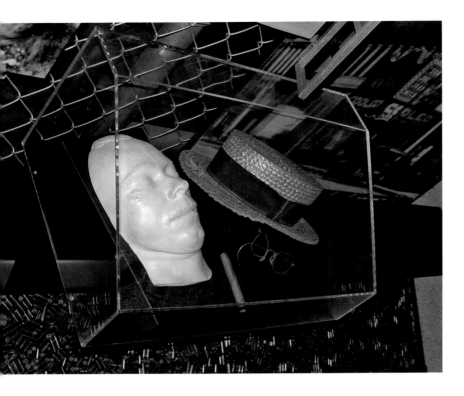

John Dillinger's death mask, straw hat, glasses, and a cigar found on his body. In his book, *American Agent,* Melvin Purvis said: "Probably I will never forget, although I would like to, the morbidness displayed by the people who gathered around the shooting . . . craning necks of curious persons, women dipping handkerchiefs in Dillinger's blood. Neighborhood business boomed temporarily. The spot where Dillinger fell became the Mecca of [the] morbidly curious." *FBI*

motherly individual, smoothly settling details of the rent with an unsuspecting landlord for an apartment hideout."

Hoover was in his favorite New York City hangout, the Stork Club, when he got a call that Karpis was in New Orleans. Karpis had threatened to go to Washington and kill Hoover, so Hoover chartered a plane to New Orleans to arrest Karpis personally. The scene was, however, a jumbled mess. Karpis came out of his surrounded house before Hoover had finished setting up, which startled Hoover. Karpis was even more startled. Confused, he almost fainted with fright. He easily submitted to arrest, but no one had handcuffs. Agents used the neckties of Karpis and another agent to secure Karpis' wrists. Since the feds did not know the neighborhood, Karpis had to give them directions back to the airport. The arrest got a lot of publicity, and Hoover decided it was a good move for him to show up at high-profile raids.

Hoover had built a solid reputation with the capture and elimination of these rural bandits through good police work and some hyperbole. The real damage would later come from the more highly organized gangsters.

Murder Inc.

Murder Inc. originated as a group of mostly Jewish hit men, "founded" by Benjamin Siegel and Meyer Lansky. In the early 1930s, Murder Inc. was the most efficient way to deal with "problems." The Bureau investigated Benjamin "Bugsy" Siegel for numerous crimes and implicated him in at least thirty murders. Born in 1906, Siegel was running his own primitive protection racket by the age of nine and setting fire to vendor pushcarts on the streets of Brooklyn. At fifteen, he had already earned the sobriquet "Bugsy," a name hinting he was crazy. He hated the nickname and severely beat anyone who called him Bugsy. At some point, Siegel met Charles "Lucky" Luciano and Meyer Lansky, two men who would become the keystone in his career.

The first time Bugsy and Lansky killed together, it was payback for a rat that sent Luciano to jail. The murder went according to plan, but a witness thought she could blackmail Siegel. Bugsy found her in a local bar, dragged her outside, and raped her behind a parked car. When Lansky added a threat to drench her face with acid, she became convinced she saw nothing.

Soon, Lansky and Bugsy took over the Lower East Side of Manhattan. Things began to heat up when Joe "the Boss" Masseria, who controlled all organized crime in New York City, saw Lansky and Siegel moving in on his turf. Siegel and Lansky began hijacking Masseria's illegal booze shipments and selling the liquor. During one hijacking, the two shot three of Masseria's men dead. Masseria sent word out to "get the two Jews."

Lucky Luciano and Vito Genovese had been working with Masseria. When Masseria put out a hit on Siegel, it did not sit well with Luciano, since he and Genovese were Siegel's good friends. On April 15, 1931, Luciano set up a "going-away" dinner for Masseria. As dinner was ending, Luciano excused himself to the men's room. Then Vito Genovese, Frank Livorsi, and Joe Stracci burst into the restaurant

Hoover's authoritarian style and personality was ingrained into everything associated with his Bureau. Just as he had changed his own name to the more distinctive J. Edgar (leaving it the old way, "John Edgar," on his official letterhead), he also had a long-standing problem with the name of the Bureau. A long-running radio program had featured (with the Bureau's approval) a fictitious special agent code-named "K-5." In 1934, a comic strip about the BOI appeared in the Hearst newspapers (without Bureau approval) titled "Special Agent X-9." Hoover had the cartoonist and the writer investigated; their lucky for them, their backgrounds came up clean.

The confusing alphabet soup that the public associated with the Bureau pushed Hoover to search for a new name for the organization, something distinctive, easily recognizable, and catchy in both the name and initials. Hoover ordered his senior agents to submit ideas. Edward Tamm, an assistant director and close friend of Hoover, came up with Federal Bureau of Investigation. Hoover was unconvinced at first, but Tamm told him the initials FBI would also stand for the qualities that best exemplified the Bureau and its agents: fidelity, bravery, and integrity. This appealed to Hoover's chivalric sense, and he was finally persuaded. On July 1, 1935, the Bureau of Investigation was officially renamed the Federal Bureau of Investigation.

Following the name change, G-man radio shows, bubble gum cards, comic strips, magazines, and movies flooded America. Hoover took advantage of the situation by supporting only those reporters and producers who would portray the Bureau in the most positive terms. Hoover made sure his FBI would glow in a carefully controlled limelight.

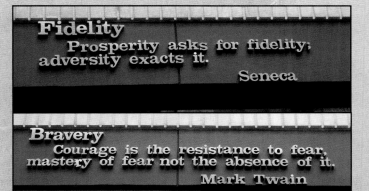

Fidelity
Prosperity asks for fidelity;
adversity exacts it.
Seneca

Bravery
Courage is the resistance to fear,
mastery of fear not the absence of it.
Mark Twain

Integrity
Integrity without knowledge is weak and useless,
and knowledge without integrity is dangerous and dreadful
Samuel Johnson

These three quotes on the walls of the FBI Academy summarize what the Bureau is about. *Henry M. Holden collection*

and shot Masseria out of his chair with a hail of bullets. It was a scene right from *The Godfather* movie, which would not appear on the screen until forty years later.

Prohibition was the mother's milk for the mafia. The mafia began to grow into a large, organized, criminal enterprise. Luciano and Lansky formed the National Crime Syndicate, bringing all the bosses from the major U.S. cities under one organization. However, at that time, the FBI still had little jurisdiction.

Siegel's murder machine was working overtime, and Bugsy was the number one killer-for-hire. In 1934, at the request of Dutch Schultz, Bugsy killed Bo Weinburg, a gangster who had moved in on Schultz's turf while Schultz had been jailed for tax evasion. Siegel pistol-whipped Weinburg to death in a stolen car and then pushed the vehicle into the East River. A year later, Bugsy ordered Dutch Schultz eliminated to tie up the loose end.

Louis Capone (not related to Al Capone), left, and Emanuel "Mendy" Weiss were hit men for Murder Inc. In late 1941, Weiss and Capone stood trial for the first-degree murder of a Brooklyn candy storeowner. The smiling convicted killers are surrounded by detectives during their railroad ride "up the river" to the Sing Sing prison death house. On March 4, 1944, Weiss and Capone died in the electric chair for the Brooklyn murder. *Library of Congress*

The Eighteenth Amendment prohibited the manufacture, sale, or transportation of intoxicating liquors within, the importation thereof into, or the exportation from the United States and all territory subject to the jurisdiction thereof for beverage purposes. The Eighteenth Amendment was repealed with the Twenty-first Amendment on December 5, 1933. These three mob gangsters were arrested for racketeering during the prohibition era. The criminals are (left to right): Irving Wexler (a.k.a. "Waxey Gordon"), Hymie Pincus, and Albert Aront. The photograph was taken in New York City on May 21, 1933. *Library of Congress*

During prohibition, the public often confused the Bureau of Investigation with the Prohibition Bureau. Here, federal agents of the Prohibition Bureau stand before the largest illegal still ever captured. Later, the Prohibition Bureau merged briefly with the Bureau of Investigation. Eliot Ness, made famous through television, was the head of a group of Treasury Department agents who targeted mobster Al Capone and his gang. Neither Ness nor his colleagues were FBI agents, although television gave that impression. Ness was a prohibition agent. He handpicked a small band of agents, who became known as the "Untouchables" because of their reputation for integrity. Ness made front-page news when he used a reinforced truck to break his way into one of Capone's breweries. *Library of Congress*

Bugsy had grown up with George Raft, who went on to become a Hollywood actor, and in 1933, Bugsy moved to Hollywood. Raft introduced Bugsy to all the big stars. His good looks and suave attitude made him a hit with the ladies. While at a Hollywood party, Bugsy got a phone call. He drove across town and sent "Big Greenie" Greenbaum on a one-way trip to never-never land. Bugsy returned to the party and bragged about what he had done, inviting the ladies to smell the gunpowder on his hands. A day later, the police arrested Siegel and charged him with the murder. He was out of jail within hours. The newspapers had a field day. Headlines and newsboys barked, "Bugsy Siegel Free!" An urban legend claims he shot the first newsboy he saw holding up the headline.

Siegel took over the screen actors' union and the Los Angeles dockworkers' union. He staged actors' strikes to cripple the filmmakers. Then he took payoffs from the filmmakers to get the actors back to work.

With the help of the Chicago mob, Siegel moved in on the telephone gambling operations on the West Coast. His wire service could report on horseracing results across the country, netting the Syndicate millions of dollars a year. He was the mob's golden boy until he came up with a wacky idea involving a remote desert town called Las Vegas.

In 1946, using mob money, Siegel built a luxurious hotel and casino called The Flamingo, his pet nickname for his mistress, Virginia Hill. Hill was a notorious blackmailer. She was a predator, and she thrived in Hollywood. Hill also spied on Siegel for the Chicago mob. Chicago controlled everything west of the Mississippi, and the Chicago group came to resent Siegel's control of both Los Angeles and his new Las Vegas casino. He was not playing, or paying, according to their rules, but he was untouchable because of his friend Meyer Lansky.

When The Flamingo opened, it was a flop. Despite the investment of over $5 million mafia dollars, not many people wanted to drive over the mountains from California to a desert wasteland to gamble.

Luciano called Bugsy in December 1946 to discuss The Flamingo's floundering financial performance. Bugsy ignored the phone message—an unforgivable sign of disrespect. Even Lansky, who was the number one financial officer of the Syndicate, could not save Bugsy.

On June 8, 1947, the mob told Virginia Hill to fly to Paris. She was a money courier and often flew to Europe to wash the Syndicate's money. She left for France, telling Siegel she was getting some wine for The Flamingo. Bugsy, who was up to his neck in the mess of his casino, couldn't care less.

On June 19, 1947, a hit man walked around behind Virginia Hill's Beverly Hills home. He fired nine bullets through a window into Hill's house. Two bullets caught Bugsy in the face. One blew his left eye across the room. Bugsy was history, but his Las Vegas vision would bloom and after his death bring the mob millions.

Charles "Lucky" Luciano

Charles Luciano's nickname, "Lucky," arose after he survived a gangland ride in 1929 in which he was beaten, stabbed with an ice pick, had his throat slashed, was thrown from a car, and was left for dead. Luciano had an extensive arrest record, and in June 1936, he had been convicted on sixty-two of ninety counts of compulsory prostitution. He was sentenced to thirty to fifty years in prison. On February 8, 1943, an application was filed asking for the suspension of his sentence. The application alleged that Luciano had performed a valuable wartime service for the navy during the early days of World War II.

About six months into World War II, Luciano, who was in jail, had been reading the papers and talking to Meyer Lansky about how vulnerable the waterfronts were to spies. German U-boats could sink U.S. ships right in the harbor. Luciano had a plan to get himself out of jail on the pretext of helping the war effort.

He had a jailhouse visit from mob boss Frank Costello. Lucky told Costello that Albert "The Mad Hatter" Anastasia had met with people from Naval Intelligence, and they had talked about dock security. All the war supplies and ships were spread over a wide area. They knew the supplies stored along the Hudson piers, the docks, and the ships were vulnerable. Anastasia's idea was to give the navy something real to worry about.

Anastasia and his brother, "Tough Tony," had talked of sinking a ship on the west side of Manhattan's port. The targeted French luxury liner, the SS *Normandie*, was to become a troop ship. Luciano thought it would get the attention of the navy and would not truly affect the war effort, since the ship had not yet been converted. A day later, the SS *Normandie* was ablaze and wrecked. To Naval Intelligence, it was obvious that German spies had done this.

The government began Operation Underworld. Naval Intelligence officers went to Joseph "Socks" Lanza, the czar of the Fulton Fish Market, for help. But Socks could offer no help. The docks belonged to Anthony "Tough Tony" Anastasia, who worked for Luciano. Luciano knew the naval officers would have to come to him for help. He agreed to help in return for a reduction in his sentence. Since it was a matter of national security, Luciano had the navy in a corner. Thomas E. Dewey, the New York prosecutor, agreed to the deal, but only if Luciano agreed to be deported to Italy. Luciano agreed to the terms, knowing he would at least be free.

All along the docks, the dockworkers agreed to help the Naval Intelligence officers secure the harbor against any German spies or U-boats, all on the say-so of Lucky Luciano. ■

From its earliest days, the American Communist Party received substantial funding from the Soviet government. In January 1920, the Communist International supplied communist journalist John Reed with about $2 million dollars in gold, silver, and jewelry to foster communism in America. The party also received a constant stream of Soviet political directives that it implemented without question. Not long after World War II ended, the FBI found its mandate was hunting Soviet spies within the government. In February 1946, Stalin gave a speech where he implied that future wars were inevitable until communism replaced capitalism worldwide. Americans feared communist expansion was not limited to Europe. By 1947, evidence existed that procommunist individuals had infiltrated the American government. FBI

Chapter 4

BLACKLISTS, BLACKMAIL, AND McCARTHYISM

Nazism, fascism, and communism threatened American democratic principles in the latter half of 1930s. With world war on the horizon, the FBI put the remnants of the gangster era on the back burner and found a new set of challenges. Hoover directed all his special agents in charge (SACs) to report any information related to subversive activities on the part of any individual or organization, regardless of the source from which the information came. The SACs were cautioned not to initiate any investigations without Hoover's approval.

The Depression had provided a fertile environment for radicalism in the United States as it had in Europe. European Nazis and fascists had their counterparts and supporters in the United States in the German-American Bund, the Silver Shirts, and similar groups. Because of the Nazi-Soviet Pact of 1939, the American Communist Party and its sympathizers posed a double-edged threat to American interests.

THE LOYALTY FILES

President Truman probably forestalled more draconian legislation when he, rather than Congress, took the lead by issuing Executive Order 9835 on March 25, 1947, which beefed up the rooting out of subversives in government. Prior to the executive order, general file room staff at the FBI managed all the files on loyalty cases. After it went into effect, files bearing information on the loyalty of incumbent or applicant federal employees became so voluminous that two additional FBI agents were assigned permanently to the loyalty files to help keep pace. In subsequent years, the burden of proving loyalty shifted from the accuser to the accused, setting the stage for the witch hunts to follow.

Labor unrest, racial disturbances, and sympathy for the Spanish Loyalists presented an unparalleled opportunity for the American Communist Party to proselytize supporters. The FBI stepped up surveillance when it became more aware that these groups may have posed threats to American security.

Learning from the American Protective League's experience of World War I, J. Edgar Hoover ensured that the FBI did not repeat the problem of relying on volunteer citizen groups as World War II approached. Instead, he did three things: he hired large numbers of new agents and support personnel; he developed relationships with local and state law enforcement officials through the FBI's National Academy; and he withheld official authorization and established firm guidelines when the American Legion offered its services in a manner similar to that of the APL.

Authority to investigate these organizations came in 1936 with President Roosevelt's authorization through Secretary of State Cordell Hull. A 1939 presidential directive further strengthened the FBI's authority to investigate subversives in the United States, and Congress passed the Smith Act in 1940, outlawing advocacy of violent overthrow of the government.

The Dies Committee

Martin Dies (D-Texas) introduced a resolution in July 1937 to create a special committee to investigate communist subversion in the United States. After prolonged debate, the resolution passed in May 1938. The Dies Committee hearings did not begin until August 12. The major target of the committee was organized labor groups, particularly the Congress of Industrial Organizations. Dies met secretly and usually alone with friendly witnesses who accused hundreds of individuals of supporting communist activities. This tactic set a pattern for how the committee functioned until after World War II. The press sensationalized these accusations, but only a few of the accused were given the opportunity to defend themselves.

Because the Dies Committee was a special committee, its mandate had to be renewed by Congress every two years. However, in 1945, the House Un-American Activities Committee (HUAC) replaced the Dies Committee. Over the next five years, the HUAC investigated the motion picture industry, looking for communists. As an influential political force, HUAC used the threat of contempt citations as blackmail against those who refused to testify by taking the Fifth Amendment, the right against self-incrimination. In 1950, for example, the committee issued fifty-six contempt citations out of the fifty-nine citations voted by the House of Representatives.

On August 3, 1948, Attorney General Thomas Clark authorized the creation of the FBI's Secret Security Index program based on a 1946 proposal by Hoover. Under the program, the FBI was authorized to compile a list of potentially dangerous individuals to be detained in case of war or the threat of invasion. This act was essentially a mirror image of Hoover's custodial detention plan of the late 1930s. Clark bypassed the idea of seeking congressional legislation beforehand and instead decided to seek *ex post facto* congressional approval. Hoover assured Congress that

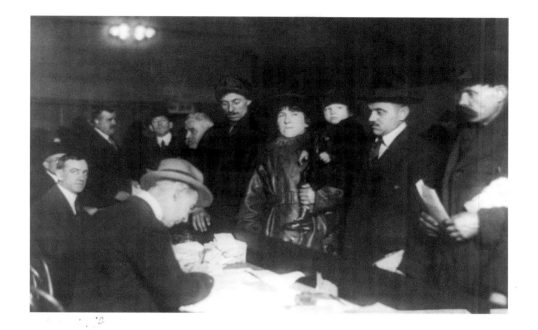

The 1940 Alien Registration Act (commonly known as the Smith Act) was a by-product of the Dies Committee and made it illegal for anyone to advocate, abet, or teach the appeal of overthrowing the government. The law required all alien residents over fourteen years of age to file a statement of their personal and occupational status and a record of their political beliefs. The objective was to undermine the American Communist Party and other left-wing political groups. First invoked against the Socialist Workers Party (Trotskyites) in 1940, it broadened the FBI's investigative authority. By the end of 1940, almost five million aliens had registered. *Library of Congress*

the FBI was ready to arrest fourteen thousand dangerous communists in the event of war with the Soviet Union.

Hollywood Blacklists

By 1947, a symbiotic relationship had developed between Hoover and the House Un-American Activities Committee. When HUAC announced that it was investigating communist influences in the American movie industry, Hoover provided a list of individuals who belonged, or once belonged, to the Communist Party or to communist front organizations, as well as a list of cooperative witnesses.

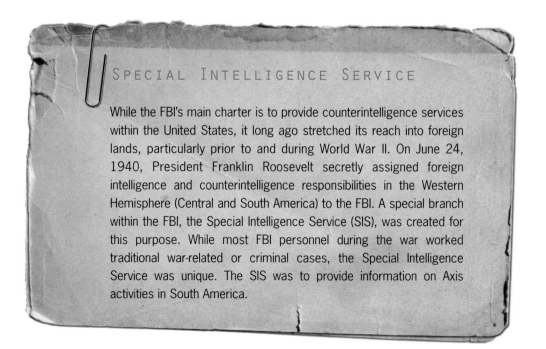

SPECIAL INTELLIGENCE SERVICE

While the FBI's main charter is to provide counterintelligence services within the United States, it long ago stretched its reach into foreign lands, particularly prior to and during World War II. On June 24, 1940, President Franklin Roosevelt secretly assigned foreign intelligence and counterintelligence responsibilities in the Western Hemisphere (Central and South America) to the FBI. A special branch within the FBI, the Special Intelligence Service (SIS), was created for this purpose. While most FBI personnel during the war worked traditional war-related or criminal cases, the Special Intelligence Service was unique. The SIS was to provide information on Axis activities in South America.

WB055 DL PD

RENO NEV FEB 11 1139A   The White House
                              Washington
THE PRESIDENT

  THE WHITE HOUSE   1950 FEB 11 PM 7 31

  IN A LINCOLN DAY SPEECH AT WHEELING THURSDAY NIGHT
I STATED THAT THE STATE DEPARTMENT HARBORS A NEST OF
COMMUNISTS AND COMMUNIST SYMPATHIZERS WHO ARE HELPING TO
SHAPE OUR FOREIGN POLICY. I FURTHER STATED THAT I HAVE IN
MY POSSESSION THE NAMES OF 57 COMMUNISTS WHO ARE IN THE
STATE DEPARTMENT AT PRESENT. A STATE DEPARTMENT SPOKESMAN

...TLY DENIED THIS AND CLAIMED THAT THERE IS NOT A SINGLE
COMMUNIST IN THE DEPARTMENT. YOU CAN CONVINCE YOURSELF OF
THE FALSITY OF THE STATE DEPARTMENT CLAIM VERY EASILY.
YOU WILL RECALL THAT YOU PERSONALLY APPOINTED A BOARD TO
SCREEN STATE DEPARTMENT EMPLOYEES FOR THE PURPOSE OF
WEEDING OUT FELLOW TRAVELERS. YOUR BOARD DID A PAINS-TAKING
JOB, AND NAMED HUNDREDS WHICH IT LISTED AS "DANGEROUS TO
THE SECURITY OF THE NATION", BECAUSE OF COMMUNISTIC
CONNECTIONS.

  WHILE THE RECORDS ARE NOT AVAILABLE TO ME, I KNOW

S

  TATE DEPARTMENTS GIVING TO THE CONGRESS ANY INFORMATION
IN REGARD TO THE DISLOYALTY OR THE COMMUNISTIC CONNECTIONS
OF ANYONE IN THAT DEPARTMENT, DISPITE THIS STATE DEPARTMENT
BLACKOUT, WE HAVE BEEN ABLE TO COMPILE A LIST OF 57
COMMUNISTS IN THE STATE DEPARTMENT. THIS LIST IS AVAILABLE
TO YOU, BUT YOU CAN GET A MUCH LONGER LIST BY ORDERING THE
SECRETARY ACHESON TO GIVE YOU A LIST OF THESE WHOM YOUR OWN
BOARD LISTED AS BEING DISLOYAL, AND WHO ARE STILL WORKING
IN THE STATE DEPARTMENT. I BELIEVE THE FOLLOWING IS THE
MINIMUM WHICH CAN BE EXPECTED OF YOU IN THIS CASE

...ATELY THAT OF ONE GROUP OF APPROXIMATELY 300 CERTIFIED
TO THE SECRETARY FOR DISCHARGE, HE ACTUALLY DISCHARGED ONLY
APPROXIMATELY 80. I UNDERSTAND THAT THIS WAS DONE AFTER
LENGTHY CONSULTATION WITH ALGER HISS. I WOULD SUGGEST
THEREFORE, MR. PRESIDENT, THAT YOU SIMPLY PICK UP YOUR
PHONE AND ASK MR. ACHESON HOW MANY OF THOSE WHOM YOUR
BOARD HAD LABELED AS DANGEROUS, HE FAILED TO DISCHARGE.
THE DAY THE HOUSE UN-AMERICAN ACTIVITIES COMMITTEE EXPOSED
ALGER HISS AS AN IMPORTANT LINK IN AN INTER-NATIONAL
COMMUNIST SPY RING, YOU SIGNED AN ORDER FORBIDDING THE

---

  (1) THAT YOU DEMAND THAT ACHESON GIVE YOU AND THE PROPER
CONGRESSIONAL COMMITTEE THE NAMES AND A COMPLETE REPORT ON
ALL OF THOSE WHO WERE PLACED IN THE DEPARTMENT BY ALGER HISS,
AND ALL OF THOSE STILL WORKING IN THE STATE DEPARTMENT WHO
WERE LISTED BY YOUR BOARD AS BAD SECURITY RISKS BECAUSE OF
THE COMMUNISTIC CONNECTIONS.

  (2) THAT UNDER NO CIRCUMSTANCES COULD A CONGRESSIONAL
COMMITTEE OBTAIN ANY INFORMATION OR HELP FROM THE EXECUTIVE
DEPARTMENT IN EXPOSING COMMUNISTS.

  FAILURE ON YOUR PART WILL LABEL THE DEMOCRATIC PARTY OF
BEING THE BED-FELLOW OF INTER-NATIONAL COMMUNISM. CERTAINLY
THIS LABEL IS NOT DESERVED BY THE HUNDREDS OF THOUSANDS OF
LOYAL AMERICAN DEMOCRATS THROUGHOUT THE NATION, AND BY THE
SIZABLE NUMBER OF ABLE LOYAL DEMOCRATES IN BOTH THE SENATE
AND THE HOUSE

  JOE MC CARTHY U.S.S. WIS..

Senator McCarthy sent a telegram to President Truman on February 11, 1950, two days after the Wheeling speech. Senator McCarthy repeated his assertion that he had the names of fifty-seven communists who were working in the State Department and called upon the president to provide Congress with a full accounting of communist infiltration of the State Department, including the role of alleged communist spy Alger Hiss in protecting security risks. *National Archives*

Hoover would go after Hollywood again, but he would not focus on the films; instead, his targets were the individuals writing, acting, and producing the films who he suspected of having Communist Party affiliations. The investigation was a continuation of pressures first exerted in the late 1930s and early 1940s by the Dies Committee, which had charged that communists had established a foothold in the Hollywood entertainment industry. During that era, and before the slaughter of tens of millions by Premier Joseph Stalin had become common knowledge, the American Communist Party attracted large numbers of followers. Many were young idealists in the arts, entertainment, and academia—the same types of people Stalin would murder in his 1952 purge.

Films such as *Mission to Moscow* and *Song of Russia*, produced in the late 1940s, were considered pro-Soviet propaganda. Studio executives attempted to explain the context of the films by telling HUAC that the films had value when put in the context of the Allied war effort.

On the far right end of the spectrum were those who accused Hollywood communists of placing subversive messages into their films. Their further concern was that communists were in a position to place negative images of the United States in films that would have worldwide distribution. In reality, the evidence of these types of images in the films was at best slim.

The McCarran Act

The Internal Security Act of 1950, a.k.a. the McCarran Act, was one of the most contentious and least understood laws in U.S. history. The bill attempted to address national security and individual liberties. It required the registration of communist organizations in the United States and established the Subversive Activities Control Board to investigate persons thought to be engaged in activities considered to be "un-American." President Truman, who had imposed the Loyalty Order for federal employees in 1947, vetoed the bill. He said it "would make a mockery of our Bill of Rights, and would actually weaken our internal security measures." An eighty-nine percent Senate majority overrode Truman's veto. Senator Pat McCarran's Senate Internal Security Subcommittee worked closely with the FBI for the next seven years.

In the 1940s, the FBI developed a series of secret programs designed to collect intelligence about the communist infiltration in the United States, dubbed "COMINFIL." COMINFIL authorized the investigation of legitimate, noncommunist organizations that the FBI suspected were being infiltrated by communists.

In his book, *The Liberals and J. Edgar Hoover*, William W. Keller described COMINFIL: ". . . the theory behind Cominfil is that the Communist Party members seek to infiltrate or join the ranks of legitimate organizations, rise to positions of leadership, establish effective control of the organization, and ultimately convert it into a vehicle for mass communist revolution."

J. Edgar Hoover said, "The forces which are most anxious to weaken our internal security are not always easy to identify. Communists have been trained in deceit and secretly work toward the day when they hope to replace our American way of life

Draft

My dear Senator:

I read your telegram of February eleventh from Reno, Nevada with a great deal of interest and this is the first time in my experience, and I was ten years in the Senate, that I ever heard of a Senator trying to discredit his own Government before the world. You know that isn't done by honest public officials. Your telegram is not only not true and an insolent approach to a situation that should have been worked out between man and man but it shows conclusively that you are not even fit to have a hand in the operation of the Government of the United States.

I am very sure that the people of Wisconsin are extremely sorry that they are represented by a person who has as little sense of responsibility as you have.

Sincerely yours,

[HST]

In an undated (and apparently unsent) reply to McCarthy's seriously disrespectful telegram, President Truman stated that McCarthy was not fit to serve in the U.S. government, adding that the people of Wisconsin must be very sorry to be represented in the Senate by such a person. *National Archives*

Beginning informally in 1946, the FBI assisted HUAC in its investigation of subversive material and suspicious activities by those in the entertainment industry. The subsequent blacklist that arose not only damaged the daily lives, reputations, careers, and families of those who were subpoenaed by HUAC, but did incalculable damage to America's political system and national psyche. When faced with testifying, witnesses had three options: one, invoke immunity; two, capitulate by informing on oneself and others; or three, inform only on oneself. Perhaps there were, in the words of Dalton Trumbo, "neither villains or heroes," only shades of gray during this otherwise dark era in America's history. This chapter profiles a few of the notable writers, musicians, actors, and entertainers who found themselves forever altered in a nation coming to grips with the meaning of freedom and tolerance.

with a Communist dictatorship. They utilize cleverly camouflaged movements, such as peace groups and civil rights groups, to achieve their sinister purposes. While they as individuals are difficult to identify, the Communist party line is clear. Its first concern is the advancement of Soviet Russia and the godless Communist cause. It is important to learn to know the enemies of the American way of life."

Under COMINFIL, the FBI investigated the activities of the National Association for the Advancement of Colored People (NAACP) and its members, and specifically targeted Dr. Martin Luther King Jr. in attempts to neutralize his public appeal and power. The surveillance activity against Dr. King and the Southern Christian Leadership Conference (SCLC) spanned from December 1961 until King's death in April 1968.

The FBI investigation included wiretaps of Dr. King's home telephone, the homes and offices of some of his advisers, wiretaps of the SCLC's telephone, hidden microphones in Dr. King's hotel rooms, and the use of FBI informants. The Select Committee to Study Government Operations found the actions to discredit Dr. King included efforts to cut off SCLC's funding sources, disrupt his marriage, undermine his efforts with foreign heads of state, and discredit him with the clerical and

British film star Charlie Chaplin lived in the United States from 1914 to 1952 and maintained dual citizenship. During the 1950s, Chaplin was accused of "un-American activities." His procommunist statements nearly led him to become a suspected communist sympathizer. The FBI kept extensive files on Chaplin (almost two thousand pages). After he campaigned for a second European front in the war, in 1942, the FBI increased its surveillance of him. In a declassified FBI memo, Chaplin is quoted as saying: "We must be more tolerant of the Russian system. Let's stop all this nonsense and evasion and call it what it is: the Communist system. And that Communist system is a very convenient ally. . . ." In 1952, when Chaplin left the United States for a brief trip to England, Hoover urged the Immigration and Naturalization Service to revoke his re-entry permit. Chaplin decided to make his home in Switzerland. He briefly returned to the United States in April 1972 to receive an Honorary Oscar. *Library of Congress*

Motion picture actor Humphrey Bogart, seen here in a publicity shot from *The Big Sleep*, was the epitome of the handsome, cynical, and lonesome wolf. He never played an FBI agent, but he played tough private eye, Philip Marlowe, looking cool in his fedora with a cigarette dangling from the corner of his mouth. Bogart was never the subject of an FBI investigation; however, his name is referenced within the FBI files concerning other subject matters. Bogart appeared before the House Select Committee on Un-American Activities. Subsequently, the chairman of the committee, Martin Dies, declared that Bogart was never a member of, nor sympathetic to, the Communist Party. *Henry M. Holden collection*

Edward G. Robinson, like many prominent liberal Hollywood actors, appeared several times before the HUAC in the early 1950s to clear his name against anonymous charges that he was a communist sympathizer and even a Russian spy. He was eventually exonerated of communist affiliations and returned to a long and successful career on stage and screen. *Henry M. Holden collection*

academic communities as well as the media. The committee concluded that the investigation was "unjustified and improper."

The FBI investigated the Communist Party's infiltration of the motion picture industry from 1942 to 1958. A February 1943 declassified FBI memo states, ". . . there are thirty-nine labor unions in the motion picture industry. More than half are A. F. of L. [American Federation of Labor]; the others are independent unions. About half the unions appear to be controlled by the Communist or follow the Communist Party line for business purposes. . . . The so-called 'cultural groups' actors, actresses, and writers, appear to be under control and direction of the Communist party . . . . Quite a number of directors and executives are well-known Communists . . . . The Communists in Hollywood have set up so many Communist controlled front organizations which follow change dictated by the foreign policy of the Communist party . . . ." In 1947, motion picture personalities were subpoenaed before the HUAC.

In June 1947, members of the Senate Appropriations Committee sent a confidential report to Secretary of State George Marshall, in which they stated: "It is evident that there is a deliberate, calculated program being carried out not only to protect

THE FIFTH AMENDMENT

"No person shall be held to answer for a capital, or otherwise infamous crime, unless on a presentment or indictment of a grand jury, except in cases arising in the land or naval forces, or in the militia, when in actual service in time of war or public danger; nor shall any person be subject for the same offense to be twice put in jeopardy of life or limb; nor shall be compelled in any criminal case to be a witness against himself, nor be deprived of life, liberty, or property, without due process of law; nor shall private property be taken for public use, without just compensation."

McCarthy tried desperately to use legal technicalities to get around the use of this amendment by witnesses in his attempts to implicate them as communist spies.

Left: Paul Robeson was born in Princeton, New Jersey, on April 9, 1898, to a former slave, the Rev. William Robeson. Robeson had a successful career as a scholar, athlete, performer, and activist. He won an academic scholarship to Rutgers University, as the third African-American student accepted at Rutgers and the only black student during his time on campus. Robeson went on to study law at Columbia in New York and received his degree in 1923. He faced discrimination and soon left the practice because a white secretary refused to take dictation from him. He turned to his childhood love of drama and singing, and starred in musical plays and eleven movies. During the 1940s, Robeson continued to have success on the stage, in film, and in concert halls, but he faced prejudice and racism. Finding the Soviet Union to be a tolerant and friendly nation, he began to protest the growing Cold War hostilities between the United States and the USSR. Robeson questioned why African-Americans should support a government that did not treat them as equals. At a time when dissent was hardly tolerated, Robeson was looked upon as an enemy by his government. In 1947, he was named by the HUAC, and the State Department denied him a passport until 1958. Events such as these, along with a negative public response, led to the demise of his public career. *Library of Congress*

Right: Burl Ives was an Academy Award–winning actor, acclaimed folk music singer, and author. Ives was identified in the infamous 1950 pamphlet *Red Channels* as an entertainer with supposed communist ties. In 1952, he cooperated with the HUAC and named fellow folk singer Pete Seeger and others as possible communists. Forty-one years later, Ives and Seeger were reunited in a benefit concert in New York City. Ives' cooperation with the HUAC ended his blacklisting, allowing him to continue with his movie acting. *Library of Congress*

HUAC CONTINUES THE HUNT

One of many "ism's" that arose in the 1950s began with Senator Joseph McCarthy's investigations into communists in the government. The investigation overshadowed the work of the HUAC. Operating in the background, the committee did not suffer from McCarthy's eventual downfall. The HUAC would continue to pursue communists and other un-American activities until early 1960, when it shifted its focus to black militants, the antiwar movement, other radical youth groups, and terrorism. In 1968, the committee was renamed the Committee on Internal Security. It was abolished in 1975.

Ruth Gordon was an Academy Award–winning American actress and writer. She was perhaps best known for her film roles, including that as the over-solicitous neighbor in *Rosemary's Baby*. In 1947, the HUAC began to investigate actors, screenwriters, and others associated with Hollywood. Individuals could cooperate with the committee and name names (actor Larry Parks likened this to "crawl[ing] through the mud to be an informer"), or they could exercise their rights against self-incrimination and become known—to use a phrase popularized by Senator McCarthy—Fifth Amendment communists. Gordon was blacklisted but made *A Double Life* in 1947 and *The Actress*, in 1953. Although nominated for a Tony for Best Actress, for her portrayal of Dolly Levi in *The Matchmaker* in 1956, her next film was in 1965, when she had a role in *Inside Daisy Clover*. She managed to get some TV roles beginning in 1957. *Library of Congress*

Communist personnel in high places, but to reduce security and intelligence protection to [nil] . . . On file in the Department is a copy of a preliminary report of the FBI on Soviet espionage activities in the United States, which involves large numbers of State Department employees . . . this report has been challenged and ignored by those charged with the responsibility of administering the department." This statement would later become ammunition for Senator Joseph McCarthy.

The subpoenas were issued, and Hollywood decided to fight back. The first writers called refused to cooperate, instead taking the Fifth Amendment, or read statements into the congressional record condemning the committee. The sessions turned into wild and disruptive shouting matches, garnering bad press for Hollywood. On November 24, 1947, Congress cited ten screenwriters with contempt for refusing to give testimony to the HUAC. Others in Hollywood, recognizing the warning signs announced, "No Communists or other subversives will be employed by Hollywood."

The screenwriters cited with contempt, dubbed the "Hollywood Ten," had been at one time or another alleged members of the Communist Party. They were only the first of a list that would grow to cover actors, producers, directors, musicians, and others in the entertainment field. Most were denied employment because of their political beliefs and associations, real or suspected. Some were barred from Hollywood employment for more than a dozen years. Actor John Garfield was one of the more famous performers blacklisted by the studios because of the HUAC hearings. Mental and physical anguish was common. Clifford Odets never again wrote well, and the deaths of Garfield, Canada Lee, and half a dozen others have been linked to the anguish brought on by their committee appearances.

Following a series of unsuccessful appeals, the Hollywood Ten cases arrived before the Supreme Court. Defense attorneys filed an *amicus curiae* brief (friend of the court) on behalf of the Hollywood Ten, signed by writers and actors. Of the 204 who signed the *amicus curiae* brief, 84 were later blacklisted. After the court denied review, the Hollywood Ten began serving one-year prison sentences in 1950.

In September 1950, director Edward Dmytryk, one of the Hollywood Ten, announced that he had been a communist but no longer was one and would give evidence against the other nine, whom he claimed were communists. Dmytryk had financial problems because of a divorce. Encouraged by his new wife, Dmytryk decided to try to get his name removed from the blacklist by appearing before the

Celebrated writer Richard Wright was born in 1908 and attended public high schools, where he formed some lasting early impressions of American racism. As a young adult, Wright moved to Chicago and became active in the Communist Party–dominated John Reed Club. Wright edited the Communist Party magazine, *Left Front*. While Wright was initially made happy by the positive relations he established with white communists in Chicago, he was later humiliated by white communists in New York City who rescinded an offer to find temporary housing for him because of his race. He left the Chicago chapter of the Communist Party and moved to New York City in 1937 to become the Harlem editor of the *Daily Worker*. In 1942, frustrated by the party's theoretical rigidity disapproving of purges in the Soviet Union, Wright formally broke with the Communist Party. The Hollywood movie studios blacklisted Wright in the 1950s. He died in 1960. *Library of Congress*

The *New York Times* reported on December 3, 1954, that the Senate had voted sixty-seven to twenty-two to censure Senator Joseph McCarthy. Censure is a procedure for publicly reprimanding a public official for inappropriate behavior. It has no basis in the Constitution or in the rules of the Senate and House of Representatives. It derives from the formal condemnation of either congressional body of their own members. McCarthy was censured by the Senate for failing to cooperate with the subcommittee that was investigating him and for insults to the committee that was trying to censure him. *Henry M. Holden*

Dalton Trumbo was one of the top screenwriters of the 1940s, and a member of the Hollywood Ten, a group of Hollywood writers who refused to testify before the 1947 House Un-American Activities Committee about alleged communist involvement. Trumbo was convicted of contempt of Congress and was blacklisted, and in 1950, he spent eleven months in prison. After Trumbo was blacklisted, some Hollywood actors and directors, such as Elia Kazan and Clifford Odets, agreed to testify. *Courtesy the Trumbo Family*

HUAC and testifying. His testimony freed him from jail following his HUAC appearance. He described his brief membership in the party and answered all their questions, including naming twenty-six former members of left-wing groups. His career recovered. The other nine remained silent, and after their release from prison, most were unable to obtain work in the film and television industry. Less than 10 percent of those blacklisted returned to successful careers.

Adrian Scott, who had produced several Dmytryk's films, including *So Well Remembered*, was one of those named by Dmytryk. His next screen credit would not come for two decades, and he would never produce another feature film. Some of those blacklisted continued to write for Hollywood or the broadcasting industry surreptitiously, using pseudonyms or the names of friends who posed as the actual writers.

In 1960, Otto Preminger officially broke the blacklist by crediting Dalton Trumbo, an unrepentant member of the Hollywood Ten, with writing *Exodus*. He also credited Michael Wilson, who had written *The Bridge on River Kwai* (1957) and completed a script that would become *Lawrence of Arabia* (1962).

Private-sector blacklisters relied on a HUAC publication, the *Guide to Subversive Organizations and Publications*, which was promoted by the FBI even before it was first published as a handbook in December 1948. The guide listed 563 organizations and 190 publications considered subversive, and it was updated and expanded in 1951, 1957, and 1961. J. Edgar Hoover furnished each field office with copies and referred concerned citizens to the HUAC's convenient report so they might spot fronts and "not be fooled into giving them . . . support."

Langston Hughes was born in 1902 and became an American poet, novelist, playwright, and columnist. Hughes, like many black writers and artists of his time, was drawn to the promise of communism as an alternative to a segregated America. In 1932, Hughes became part of a group of blacks who went to the Soviet Union to make a film to depict the plight of blacks living in the United States at the time, but the film was never made. Hughes' poetry was frequently published in the CPUSA newspaper, and he was involved in initiatives supported by communist organizations. Hughes was also involved in other communist-led organizations, such as the John Reed Club and the League of Struggle for Negro Rights, even though he was more of a sympathizer than an active participant. He signed a statement in 1938 supporting Joseph Stalin's purges and joined the American Peace Mobilization in 1940, which worked to keep the United States out of World War II. When asked why he never joined the Communist Party, he wrote, "It was based on strict discipline and the acceptance of directives that I, as a writer, did not wish to accept." In 1953, he was called before McCarthy's committee. Following his appearance, he distanced himself from communism and was subsequently rebuked by some who had previously supported him. Over time, Hughes would distance himself from his most radical poems. *Library of Congress*

Orson Welles was an Academy Award–winning American director, writer, actor, and producer for film, stage, radio, and television. His famous Charles Foster Kane character is loosely based on parts of William Randolph Hearst's life. There is alleged evidence that Welles was blacklisted in Hollywood after years of the Hearst news empire labeling him a communist. During the McCarthy era, Welles observed of Hollywood radicals: "Friend informed on friend not to save their lives but to save their pools." *Library of Congress*

Academy Award–winner Lee Grant was blacklisted in 1951 by the House Un-American Activities Committee for refusing to testify against her husband, blacklisted playwright/screenwriter Arnold Manoff. Except for an occasional role, she did not work in film or television for almost twelve years. By 1966, she had resumed her acting career in the TV series *Peyton Place* (1964), for which she won an Emmy Award. *Henry M. Holden collection*

Red Radio

In his book, *Red Channels*, Vincent Hartnett, a former U.S. Naval Intelligence officer, made across-the-board accusations about the communist influence in the entertainment industry. Hartnett's charges led the HUAC to investigate radio broadcasting as a vehicle for communist propaganda.

The broadcast industry blacklist became public in June 1950 with the publication of *Red Channels*, an anthology of the alleged communist affiliations of 151 actors, writers, musicians, and other broadcast entertainers. The list was not accurate, but it was devastating. Within a year, none of the individuals in *Red Channels* could find employment in the broadcast field.

The HUAC was still in operation, and although it had been relatively quiet after the Hollywood Ten hearings, it quickly sprang back into action to prove its continuing value. In 1951, the HUAC began its second wave of show-business hearings, which far surpassed the 1947 wave in scope.

If anyone refused to name names when called to appear before the HUAC, they were added to the blacklist. Over 320 people were on a list that effectively stopped them from working in the entertainment industry, including major stars such as Leonard Bernstein, Charlie Chaplin, Aaron Copland, Dashiell Hammett, Lillian Hellman, Burl Ives, Arthur Miller, and dozens of others.

The entertainment industry's blacklist was the tip of the iceberg. Most of the politically motivated dismissals affected communists and ex-communists in industries

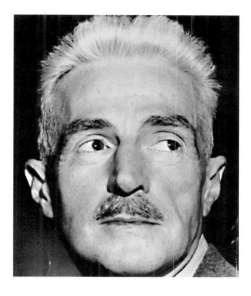

Lillian Hellman, left, was a successful American playwright, linked throughout her life with many left-wing causes. She was romantically involved for thirty years with mystery writer Dashiell Hammett, right. Hellman appeared before the House Un-American Activities Committee in 1952. At the time, HUAC was well aware that Hellman's longtime lover, Hammett, had been a Communist Party member. Asked to name names of acquaintances with communist affiliations, Hellman instead delivered a prepared statement, which read: "To hurt innocent people whom I knew many years ago in order to save myself is, to me, inhuman and indecent and dishonorable. I cannot and will not cut my conscience to fit this year's fashions." As a result, the Hollywood movie studios blacklisted Hellman for many years.

Dashiell Hammett was the author of hardboiled detective novels. Among the enduring characters he created are Sam Spade (The Maltese Falcon) and Nick and Nora Charles (The Thin Man). He also embarked on a thirty-year affair with Hellman. He was a strong antifascist throughout the 1930s, and in 1937, he joined the American Communist Party. Although a disabled veteran of World War I, he enlisted in the army during World War II. After the war, Hammett joined the New York Civil Rights Congress, a leftist organization. When four people who were related to the organization were arrested for being suspected communists, Hammett raised money for their bail bond. When the accused fled, he was subpoenaed about their whereabouts, and when, in 1951, he refused to provide that information, he was imprisoned for five months for contempt of court. During the 1950s, he was investigated by the HUAC. Although he testified to his own activities, he refused to cooperate with the committee and was blacklisted. Hammett died in 1961, and as a veteran of two World Wars, he was buried at Arlington National Cemetery. *Both images: Henry M. Holden collection*

where communist-led unions had been active, or middle-class intellectuals and professionals who had joined the Communist Party during a popular front movement. Teachers, union workers, lawyers, social workers, and journalists were all subject to the same kind of political dismissal and prolonged unemployment as show business people, and their experiences were just as devastating.

To counteract the negative effect the HUAC hearings were having at the box office, studios produced a number of anticommunist and anti-Soviet propaganda films and programs. Most, such as *The Red Menace* (1949), *I Married a Communist, I Was a Communist for the FBI* (1951), and *Walk East on Beacon!* (1952), were box office failures. However, they did placate the public and its threatened boycott of the industry.

FORTY-FOURTH STREET THEATRE

Prolific stage and screen actor Burgess Meredith (center) starred with Ingrid Bergman (left) on Broadway in 1940 in *Liliom*. Because of his widely publicized liberal views, Meredith found himself blacklisted in Hollywood for much of the 1950s. He returned to the Broadway stage acting in such seminal productions as *The Fourposter* (1952) and *The Teahouse of the August Moon* (1955). Ironically, Meredith played an informer in *Advise and Consent* (1962), who names Henry Fonda's secretary of state designee as a member of the Communist Party. Meredith's career was sidetracked until 1960, when Otto Preminger intervened. He is most remembered for his role in the *Rocky* series.

Elia Kazan (right), stage and film director of several films, including *A Streetcar Named Desire*, testified before the HUAC that he had been a member of the Communist Party for eighteen months in the mid-1930s, when there was "no clear opposition" between the United States and Russia. Kazan testified he joined the party in 1934 and later quit with a "deep and abiding hatred" of communist philosophy. Kazan identified some actors as members of the CPUSA and asked his friend, Clifford Odets, if he could name him. Odets said yes, and they both named names before the committee. Kazan said that he later regretted that he had influenced Odets to become a friendly witness, because it broke him psychologically. Odets was called before the HUAC and disavowed his communist affiliations. As a result, he did not share the fate of many of his colleagues who were blacklisted. *Henry M. Holden collection*

Arthur Miller was a prominent figure in American literature and film for over sixty years. He was often in the public eye and is most remembered for refusing to give evidence before the House Un-American Activities Committee. He was the recipient of the Pulitzer Prize for Drama, and is well known for marrying film star Marilyn Monroe. In 1952, Elia Kazan appeared before the HUAC and named eight people from the Group Theatre who had been members of the Communist Party. After speaking with Kazan about his testimony, Miller traveled to Salem, Massachusetts, to research the witch trials of 1692. In *The Crucible*, an allegorical play, Miller likened the situation with the House Un-American Activities Committee to the witch hunts in Salem. Though widely considered unsuccessful at the time of its release, today *The Crucible* is one of Miller's most frequently produced works. The HUAC took an interest in Miller himself not long after *The Crucible* opened and denied him a passport to attend the play's London opening in 1954. Miller and Kazan had been close friends throughout the late 1940s and early 1950s, but after Kazan's testimony to HUAC, the pair's friendship ended, and they did not speak to each other for ten years. *Henry M. Holden collection*

Zero Mostel, an outstanding comic actor, played Leopold Bloom in *Ulysses in Nighttown* (1958). Mostel's prolific career came to a halt during the 1950s. Seeing many of his show business friends blacklisted and forced to name names, it came as no surprise that he was named also. On January 29, 1952, Martin Berkeley identified him (and 159 others) to the HUAC as having been a member of the Communist Party. The accusation stopped Mostel's career even before he was subpoenaed to appear before the HUAC. Mostel famously remarked: "I am an actor of a thousand faces, all of them blacklisted." Mostel accepted the role in Burgess Meredith's *Ulysses in Nighttown*, a play based on the novel, *Ulysses*. The off-off-Broadway play was produced in a small theater, but Mostel received overwhelmingly favorable reviews, which propelled him back into the business. He later won over audiences with an uproarious portrayal of Max Bialystock in the Mel Brooks' film *The Producers* opposite Gene Wilder. *Library of Congress*

A panicked movie industry frantically sought good will with Congress and the public by launching its own communist hunt. Execs brought in ex-FBI agents to clean up their studios. The agents recorded anyone thought to possess suspicious political beliefs on a blacklist. Such individuals did not work for the movie studios again. Lena Horne was one of the many actresses listed in *Red Channels* and suspected of communist activities. In 1950, she appeared in *Duchess of Idaho*. Her next film was *Meet Me in Las Vegas* in 1956. She would not appear in another film until *Death of a Gunfighter* in 1969. Her singing career, however, did not suffer, and she went on to record albums beginning in 1955, and continued recording on almost a yearly basis until 1999. *Library of Congress*

American poet, author, and Pulitzer Prize winner Carl Sandburg was born in Galesburg, Illinois. In 1918, upon returning from Sweden, he had all his property of the Newspaper Enterprise Association (notebooks, and manuscripts addressing the Bolsheviks in the Soviet Union) confiscated by customs. Sandburg was a reputable correspondent, and his materials were released to him for publication. Sandburg was never the subject of an FBI investigative file, but his name appears in FBI documents. *Library of Congress*

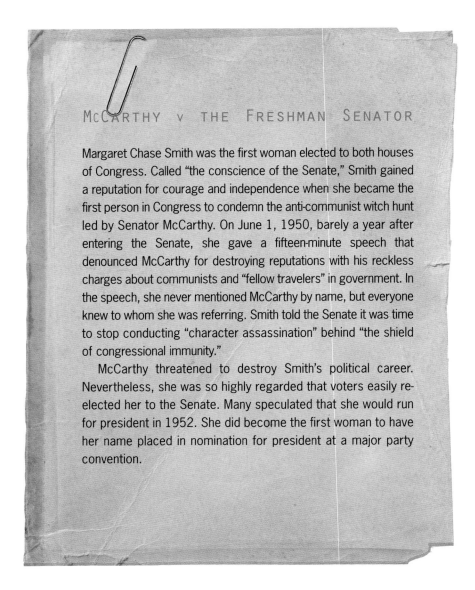

McCARTHY v THE FRESHMAN SENATOR

Margaret Chase Smith was the first woman elected to both houses of Congress. Called "the conscience of the Senate," Smith gained a reputation for courage and independence when she became the first person in Congress to condemn the anti-communist witch hunt led by Senator McCarthy. On June 1, 1950, barely a year after entering the Senate, she gave a fifteen-minute speech that denounced McCarthy for destroying reputations with his reckless charges about communists and "fellow travelers" in government. In the speech, she never mentioned McCarthy by name, but everyone knew to whom she was referring. Smith told the Senate it was time to stop conducting "character assassination" behind "the shield of congressional immunity."

McCarthy threatened to destroy Smith's political career. Nevertheless, she was so highly regarded that voters easily re-elected her to the Senate. Many speculated that she would run for president in 1952. She did become the first woman to have her name placed in nomination for president at a major party convention.

McCarthyism

The involvement of Senator Joseph McCarthy (R-Wisconsin) with the cultural phenomenon that would bear his name took place from 1950 to 1954. It was a period of intense suspicion, fear, and paranoia. The communist blockade of West Berlin had been broken, the Soviet Union had detonated an atomic bomb, and America was fighting a war of communist aggression in Korea. Anti-communist feelings at home were running high. During that period, the government was actively pursuing American Communist Party subversion. Eventually, people from all occupations, in the private sector and in government, became the subject of often-groundless accusations, aggressive witch hunts, and blacklisting, frequently based on inconclusive or questionable evidence. In his book, *Senator Joe McCarthy*, Richard H. Rovere said, "The late Joseph R. McCarthy, a United States Senator from Wisconsin, was in many ways the most gifted demagogue ever bred on these shores. No bolder seditionist ever moved among us—nor politician with a surer, swifter access to the dark places in the American mind."

Joseph McCarthy's vendetta-like campaign began with a speech he made on February 9, 1950, to the Republican Women's Club of Wheeling, West Virginia. He produced a piece of paper on which he claimed were names of known communists working in the State Department. McCarthy said, "I have here in my hand a list of two hundred five people that were known to the Secretary of State to be card-carrying communists and who, nevertheless, are still working and shaping the policy of the State Department."

When he spoke again in Salt Lake City, Utah, the number had dropped to fifty-seven. This speech resulted in a flood of press attention for McCarthy and set America on the path that would change the lives of countless citizens, leave an indelible impression on the American fabric, and eventually ruin McCarthy's career.

In his book, *Shooting Star, the Brief Arc of Joseph McCarthy*, Tom Wicker says, "[McCarthy] clearly loved the excitement, the aura of political power, the headlines that resulted from his every statement, his wildest charges, his most daring battles."

McCarthy's speech also caught Hoover's attention. In March 1950, Hoover began secretly advising McCarthy and passing on to him documents from FBI investigations. Hoover realized that McCarthy needed tutelage and dispatched agent Louis Nichols to counsel the senator. "Never use exact numbers, and never use the phrase 'card-carrying communist.'" Instead, Nichols instructed McCarthy to reference "loyalty risks."

From the viewpoint of McCarthy supporters, the identification of foreign agents and the suppression of radical organizations was necessary. McCarthy's supporters felt there was a subversive element that posed a grave danger to the security of the country, thereby justifying extreme measures.

Those accused in the McCarthy or HUAC hearings had little chance of exonerating themselves once their identities became public. Simple accusations of communist sympathies were sufficient to damage or end careers.

The 1952 election was full of sexual innuendo. The Democratic candidate, Adlai Stevenson, had been plagued with rumors of an arrest for homosexuality. His vice presidential choice, Senator Estes Kefauver, was allegedly a womanizer. Against the Republicans, the Democrats were rumored to have had a copy of General George C. Marshall's letter to Eisenhower admonishing him on his plans to divorce Mamie in order to marry his wartime driver, Kay Summersby. Hoover was one of the sources of the Stevenson and Kefauver material, but Pentagon files were the origin of the Eisenhower document.

Relationships between Hoover and the White House improved dramatically when Eisenhower won the presidential election. "Ike" respected and admired Hoover, and intended to give him his full support. Vice President Richard M. Nixon was already in Hoover's debt from his help in the Alger Hiss case. Herbert Brownell Jr., the new attorney general, got along well with Hoover. Brownell gave Hoover the approval to use microphone surveillance, but only in national security cases. From Brownell's point of view, "The methods were left to the discretion of the FBI." With a supportive president, an indebted vice president, and a trusting attorney general, Hoover had the best of all environments during the Eisenhower years. He had reached the height of his power.

WITCH HUNTS, OLD AND NEW

The Arthur Miller play and novel, *The Crucible*, written during the McCarthy era, used the Salem witch trials as a metaphor for McCarthyism in the 1950s. Miller used the trials as a mirror to reflect the anti-communist hysteria inspired by Senator Joseph McCarthy's "witch hunts" in the United States. The play suggested that the McCarthy tyranny could occur at any time.

For decades, the U.S. government has conducted information dissemination programs. One of the major (but not the only) vehicles for the dissemination of information has been the Government Printing Office (GPO). The FBI was just one of many government agencies that disseminated official and quasi-official information, but not through the GPO.

During its four active years from February 17, 1951, to March 1955, the Responsibilities Program identified certain radical affiliations. The program authorized "the dissemination of information to appropriate authorities on a strictly confidential basis concerning Communist or subversive elements in public service or semi-public service organizations." This program followed a 1951 Governor's Conference where Hoover met with a group representing the executive committee of the conference.

Hoover presumed the program's legality from the FBI's responsibility to safeguard the nation's internal security. Because public utilities and organizations served the public, the FBI was obliged to protect the facilities when information of a subversive nature was putting them in danger. Under the program, governors, civic leaders, and high-ranking members of police departments received FBI reports on suspected subversives employed in state agencies and in public or private educational facilities. Hoover shut the Responsibilities Program down in 1955, when a governor breeched Hoover's condition of confidentiality. The Bureau's role was not to be compromised; otherwise, a senior FBI official noted, "our standard claim that the files of the FBI are confidential would be threatened."

The FBI also extended its efforts to sharing information about homosexuals. In the mid-1930s, the FBI began collecting information on homosexuals but had not used it often. In June 1951, based on the notion that homosexuals were vulnerable to blackmail and thus possibly prone to betraying national security, Hoover authorized the Sex Deviates Program. Under the Sex Deviates Program, allegations concerning past or present federal employees were forwarded to designated officials in the executive, legislative, and judicial branches. In time, Hoover expanded these efforts to include information concerning sex deviates employed in educational and law enforcement agencies.

In 1939, Congress enacted the Hatch Act. It barred from federal employment anyone who belonged to a political party or organization that advocated the violent overthrow of the government. FBI

As Curt Gentry summarized in his book, *J. Edgar Hoover: The Man and the Secrets*: "Hoover's power did not stop at the majestic doors of the U.S. Supreme Court. All appointments to the Court were first cleared by the FBI, which conducted a full field investigation. During the Eisenhower years, the president filled four vacancies on the Court. Hoover approved all four. . . ."

In March 1953, President Eisenhower publicly began to question whether CPUSA members should be allowed to teach in public schools. J. Edgar Hoover, who supported Eisenhower's philosophy, ordered twenty-four field offices to begin compiling reports on subversive persons employed at fifty-six universities and colleges.

By the time McCarthy's vendetta ended, close to one hundred university academics had lost their jobs for refusing to cooperate with investigators. Many elementary and high school teachers also lost their jobs, sometimes after an appearance before HUAC or a failure to appear, or as the result of a local loyalty probe. Several hundred more were probably eased out under the FBI's Responsibilities Program.

In October 1953, McCarthy began investigating communist infiltration into the military. The Army-McCarthy televised hearings were the first nationally televised congressional inquiries and a cornerstone in the emergent nexus between television, American politics, and the public. Although Senator Kefauver's hearings preceded McCarthy and later political dog-and-pony shows, such as the Iran-Contra and Watergate hearings, the McCarthy hearings became the genre prototype for modern political theater.

The live, televised hearings allowed the public and press to see first-hand McCarthy's interrogations and contentious tactics. In one exchange, McCarthy reminded the army's attorney general, Joseph Welch, that he had an employee in his law firm who had belonged to an organization accused of communist sympathies. McCarthy insinuated that Fred Fischer, a young lawyer at Hale & Dorr, harbored communist sympathies. Welch responded with righteous indignation that hit all the hot buttons: "Until this moment, Senator, I think I never really gauged your cruelty or your recklessness. . . . Have you no sense of decency?"

When McCarthy tried to strike back, Welch cut him off and demanded the chairperson call the next witness. Pausing for just a moment, the hushed gallery erupted in applause. The uncomprehending McCarthy had been figuratively shot dead on live television. That exchange reflected the growing negative public opinion of Senator McCarthy. The Louisville *Courier-Journal* reported: "In this long, degrading travesty of the democratic process, McCarthy has shown himself to be evil and unmatched in malice."

Not long after the June 1953 executions of Soviet spies Julius and Ethel Rosenberg, the comfortable relationship between Joseph McCarthy and Hoover deteriorated. When Hoover saw McCarthy's tactics losing public support, he withdrew his own. In addition, damaging information began to leak about the senator. Reports about McCarthy's heavy drinking, fabricated military record, illegal campaign financing, and compulsive gambling were bad enough, but close friends of the senator were quoted as warning other friends not to leave McCarthy alone with young girls. An even more precipitous fall in McCarthy's influence followed these leaks.

On March 9, 1954, CBS reporter Edward R. Murrow aired a highly critical "Report on Joseph R. McCarthy," using footage of McCarthy himself to portray him as dishonest in his speeches and abusive toward witnesses.

Senator Joseph McCarthy's most famous and most often used question was, "Are you now or have you ever been a member of the Communist Party?" McCarthy's anticommunist speech on February 9, 1950, resulted in a flood of publicity for the senator and set America on a path that would leave an indelible impression on the American fabric and ultimately ruin McCarthy's career. Following McCarthy's charges, anxiety over domestic communism intensified. In 1950, the Supreme Court upheld the conviction of eleven top leaders of the Communist Party under the Smith Act. *Library of Congress*

By the spring of 1954, Hoover was complaining to the president that McCarthy was actually impeding the Bureau's investigation of communists. Some felt that McCarthy was trying to get himself elected president and simultaneously undermine the Eisenhower administration. McCarthy was out of control and had begun to criticize Eisenhower for being too soft on communists. McCarthy had become a liability to Hoover. Eisenhower was furious and realized that it was time to end McCarthy's activities.

The major criticisms of Senator Joseph McCarthy were well founded. His critics claimed he was ruining the reputations and lives of people by accusing them without credible evidence. McCarthy would counterattack by accusing his critics of communist sympathies. He argued against freedom of speech, and much of his rhetoric assumed that any discussion of communist ideas was dangerous and un-American.

Senator Ralph Flanders (R-Vermont), a strong critic of McCarthy, introduced the ultimately successful censure motion on December 2, 1954, to have McCarthy removed from his committee leadership. The Senate voted sixty-seven to twenty-two to censure McCarthy for his reckless accusations and fabrications, and for conduct unbecoming a United States Senator.

McCarthy's hunt for communists did not result in a single prosecution. Although it was illegal to advocate sedition or violent overthrow of the government, it was not illegal merely to be a communist. After the 1954 elections that brought a Democratic majority into Congress, his support dissolved, and McCarthy went into rapid political and physical decline. He died three years later, at the age of forty-nine, of an alcohol-related disease.

William Sullivan, one of Hoover's top agents, later admitted: "We were the ones who made the McCarthy hearings possible. We fed McCarthy all the material he was using."

Even at the height of the anticommunist tumult, the Hollywood blacklist, McCarthyism, and the anticommunist crusade in the United States would seem relatively mild when compared to Stalin's yet-to-be-revealed mass murders as a method of political repression of free speech. Although the U.S. anticommunist movement was not a deadly form of political repression, it was an effective one, as many of its victims would attest. The punishments were primarily economic. Without the participation by the private sector, where most people lost their jobs, McCarthy's tactics would not have worked. Many convictions were reversed on appeal, and only a few foreign-born radicals were deported. Only Julius and Ethel Rosenberg were executed; and of the roughly 150 people who went to prison, most were released within a year or two.

Senator McCarthy's political defeat did not normalize American politics. The anticommunist policies favored by the Eisenhower administration and the FBI continued the climate of suspicion. A series of Supreme Court rulings in 1956 and 1957, however, imposed restrictions on the FBI's attempts to make use of antiradical fears. The Supreme Court decisions limited the scope of permissible testimony by FBI informers and granted defense counsel greater access to pretrial statements that government witnesses had made to the FBI. The constitutionality of the Smith Act prosecutions also came into question. Yet in 1950, the Supreme Court upheld the conviction of eleven top leaders of the Communist Party under the Smith Act.

In April 1953, President Eisenhower signed an executive order expanding the loyalty program. However, the order failed to mention specifically the Dies Committee's less-than-accurate files and writings, such as those appearing in its publication *Communist Front Organizations*. Hoover continued to check the information collected by the committee and the HUAC in all federal employee security investigations. The Eisenhower loyalty-security program made it easier to fire potential security risks and any communists who had infiltrated the government, including any Roosevelt New Deal or Truman holdovers.

In June 1954, Attorney General Brownell advised Eisenhower that there were "some five hundred government employees on an FBI 'pickup list' in case of an emergency." At the HUAC's recommendation, the president amended the loyalty-security program, authorizing loyalty review boards to evaluate whether to retain a federal employee who had ever taken the Fifth Amendment before a congressional investigating committee.

The FBI also relied on the Dies Committee's publication, *Communist Front Organizations*, published in 1944. The publication was a collection of the committee's files, prepared by a subcommittee, when the Dies Committee's future was doubtful. It totaled seven volumes of two thousand pages, identifying some 250 groups as communist fronts. One volume had a twenty-two-thousand-name index. The full committee ordered it expunged from the record and all copies destroyed. The Library of Congress and government document rooms removed it; however, several sets had been sold to private subscribers and government agencies. Instead of destroying its copies, the FBI cross-indexed the publication with its other records. ■

Edward R. Murrow had gained a highly credible reputation during World War II as a newspaper correspondent. His television show in the early 1950s, *See It Now*, focused on a number of controversial issues, but it is best remembered as the show that criticized and contributed to the political downfall of Senator Joseph McCarthy. On March 9, 1954, Murrow and his news team produced a thirty-minute special entitled "A Report on Senator Joseph McCarthy." Murrow used excerpts from McCarthy's own speeches and proclamations to criticize the senator and point out where he had contradicted himself. Murrow and his coproducer, Fred Friendly, paid for their own newspaper advertisement for the program; they were not allowed to use CBS money for the publicity campaign or even the CBS logo. This thirty-minute TV episode contributed to a nationwide backlash against McCarthy and against the Red scare in general, and it is seen as a turning point in the history of television. *Henry M. Holden collection*

MISSING CALL FBI

THE FBI IS SEEKING INFORMATION CONCERNING THE DISAPPEARANCE AT PHILADELPHIA, MISSISSIPPI, OF THESE THREE INDIVIDUALS ON JUNE 21, 1964. EXTENSIVE INVESTIGATION IS BEING CONDUCTED TO LOCATE GOODMAN, CHANEY, AND SCHWERNER, WHO ARE DESCRIBED AS FOLLOWS:

ANDREW GOODMAN

JAMES EARL CHANEY

MICHAEL HENRY SCHWERNER

The turning point in federal civil rights actions occurred in the summer of 1964, with the murder of voting registration workers Michael Schwerner, Andrew Goodman, and James Chaney near Philadelphia, Mississippi. Only after 1966, when the Supreme Court made it clear that federal law could be used to prosecute civil rights violations, were seven men found guilty of violating the civil rights of the victims. FBI

Chapter 5

CIVIL RIGHTS, THE KKK, AND POLITICAL UNREST

During the turbulent 1960s and 1970s, the FBI mounted counterintelligence operations to penetrate and disrupt the activities of militant black and radical left-wing organizations, as well as right-wing organizations such as the Ku Klux Klan. Critics later contended that the FBI's campaign also targeted peaceful antiwar and civil rights protests.

The Invisible Empire

In 1898, the U.S. Supreme Court ruled in *Plessy v Ferguson* that separate-but-equal public facilities for blacks and whites were constitutional. This ruling led to more than half a century of institutionalized racism and murder of African Americans.

During the 1920s, the Klan was literally getting away with murder. A desperate Louisiana governor, John M. Parker, appealed to the assistant director of the BOI,

Colonel William Joseph Simmons sits during a House committee investigation of the Klan. Simmons founded the second Ku Klux Klan in 1915. Simmons had seen the film, *The Birth of a Nation*, remembered for the imagery of the burning cross, which had not existed in the original Klan and had been introduced with the film. *Library of Congress*

JUSTICE PREVAILS, PART I

In January 2007, former Ku Klux Klan member James Ford Seale was indicted in federal court on charges related to his role in the abductions and slayings of two young African-American men in 1964. Seale and his fellow Klansmen picked up the two men hitchhiking, drove them into the woods, and badly beat them. Henry Dee and Charles Moore were bound with duct tape and taken to the Old Mississippi River, where, while still alive, they were thrown overboard, weighted down by an engine block and railroad rails. Their decomposed bodies were found two months later during the search for three missing civil rights workers. The unsolved case was revived in 2005, when Charles Moore's brother, Thomas, and a documentary filmmaker discovered by chance that Seale was alive and living in Mississippi. Their legwork prompted the FBI to reexamine decades-old records and enlist the help of five retired FBI agents who investigated the original case in 1964. Seale was convicted in June 2007, and in August 2007 was sentenced to three life terms for his part in the murder of the two men.

J. Edgar Hoover, for help. "Due to activities of the Klan, men have been taken out and whipped. Two men have been murdered . . . they are likely to continue this rampage. These conditions are beyond the control of this state. The Klan has grown so powerful that it controls the northern half of the state," he wrote. But the BOI had no jurisdiction.

Parker petitioned President Harding to act under the constitutional guarantee that the federal government would protect the states from domestic violence. The president agreed, and the Bureau sent agents to investigate, even though it would likely have to turn any evidence over to state government to prosecute the cases.

After Bureau agents discovered the mutilated bodies of the victims, the legal system protected the Klan. A number of local law enforcement officers—acknowledged members of the Klan—were accused of murder. Two all-white grand juries, each containing known members of the Klan, heard overwhelming evidence, but neither jury brought indictments.

The Bureau, however, did find an Achilles heel in the form of Edward Young Clarke, an advertising executive and the Imperial Kleagle of the Louisiana Klan. He had a mistress whom he frequently took across state lines on trips. Bureau agents arrested him, and he pled guilty in federal court to violating the Mann Act.

The armed forces were segregated during World War II, although African Americans supported the war effort and had fought and died in battle. When those soldiers came home from the war, they came back to the continuation of institutionalized racism, violence, and murder.

On July 26, 1948, President Truman signed Executive Order 9981, desegregating the armed forces. But it was not until in 1954, in *Brown v Board of Education* (Topeka, Kansas), that the Supreme Court ruled that separate public school facilities

At this gathering of the Ku Klux Klan in 1923 in Mississippi, the FBI had no authority to intervene. The practice of cross-burning dated back to medieval Europe, an era the Klan idealized as morally pure and racially homogenous. In the days before floodlights, Scottish clans set hillside crosses ablaze as symbols of defiance against military rivals or to rally troops when a battle was imminent. Though the original Klan, founded in 1866, patterned many of its rituals after those of Scottish fraternal orders, cross-burning was not part of its initial repertoire of terror. *Library of Congress*

Members of the Ku Klux Klan are about to take off to drop recruiting literature in the suburbs of northern Virginia in 1922. In post–World War I America, the airplane was used for both legal and illegal commerce. Dropping leaflets was not illegal, but it put additional fear into African-Americans. *Library of Congress*

By the 1930s, the Ku Klux Klan was splintered but not dead. Communists and unions replaced Catholics and Jews on the top of the Klan's hate list, and the center of Klan activity shifted back to the South. The national Klan received a fatal blow in 1944, when the Internal Revenue Service placed a $650,000 lien against the Klan for back taxes. *Library of Congress*

This 1929 photo shows the twentieth annual meeting of the NAACP in Cleveland, Ohio. At that point, the Bureau of Investigation had little authority in the area of civil rights. *Library of Congress*

The Ku Klux Klan reached its apex not in the South, but in Indiana. In the 1920s, Klan membership in Indiana was 350,000. In a show of strength and to gain public support, Imperial Wizard Hiram Wesley Evans chose Washington, D.C., for the nation's largest parade. On August 8, 1925, Evans led forty thousand robed Klansmen down Pennsylvania Avenue. It would be one of the last shows of strength for the Klan. Negative press, scandals, and violence continued to diminish their ranks. From over 4 million in 1925, the national ranks fell to about 100,000 as the country entered the Great Depression. *Library of Congress*

were not equal and were unconstitutional. The separate conditions in which blacks lived were never equal, and blacks lived in a world of constant fear.

This landmark civil rights case began to unravel the cultural norm of racism. The case would lead to additional legislation that made racial segregation illegal, and it would empower the FBI with new authority. However, before there was equality of any kind, there would be much violence. *Brown v Board of Education* lit the fuse on the powder keg, leading to outbursts of violence and demonstrations throughout the South. Cross burning, beatings, and murders became the Klan's tactics of terror. As if to shore up the walls of segregation, young white men signed up to fight against black equality. Klan membership rose.

In 1961, the Congress of Racial Equality (CORE) tested the Supreme Court mandate of integrated bus stations by sending a busload of white and black riders on a trip throughout the South. At every station, the riders would attempt to use the "whites only" restrooms, lunch counters, and restaurants, and at every station, they were rebuked. When they got to Birmingham, Alabama, the powder keg exploded. A large hostile mob met them. The mob included twenty-five members of the Klan, who beat the riders with iron pipes and baseball bats. The police had made a deal with the Klan to call out sick in large numbers and did not interfere with Klan actions.

While peaceful demonstrations increased, so did the popularity of one civil rights leader, the Reverend Dr. Martin Luther King Jr. But King was also developing a virulent animus among some whites, the Klan, and J. Edgar Hoover. Birmingham became the epicenter of the civil rights struggle. It was the center of volatile feelings on

A House committee investigated the Ku Klux Klan in 1921. At the time, there were no federal laws related to depriving people of their civil rights through racially motivated murders, lynchings, and beatings. These were state crimes, and the Bureau did not have authority to investigate Klan activity. *Library of Congress*

both sides. There was a long history of unsolved bombings of black homes, and the city earned the nickname "Bombingham."

One of the most vicious acts perpetrated by the Klan occurred on Sunday, September 15, 1963. Klan members planted nineteen sticks of dynamite in the basement of the 16th Street Baptist Church. The church was at the center of the civil rights movement and served as a staging area for marches and other civil rights activities. It was a high-value target for the Klan.

Four teenage girls who had attended Bible class were in the basement putting on their choir robes. The girls died instantly in the blast, and twenty-two others were injured. Outrage over the bombing, and the grief that followed, helped ensure the passage of the Civil Rights Act of 1964. The bombers were initially acquitted of the murder charges in state court and convicted only of dynamite possession. An appeal overturned that verdict. In 1970, a newly elected state attorney general reexamined the case. Fifteen years after he had taken the lives of four innocent girls, a jury found Robert Chambliss guilty of murder, and he was sentenced to prison, where he died of illness.

In 1964, Mississippi was a closed society. Only six percent of the African-American population was registered to vote, and even fewer did. A coalition of several northern groups decided to start a voter registration drive. The coalition had over 1,000 young people willing to travel to Mississippi to inform black citizens and help them to register.

The turning point in the civil rights movement occurred in the summer of 1964, when civil rights activists Michael Schwerner, Andrew Goodman, and James Chaney were murdered near Philadelphia, Mississippi. The three had been arrested on a bogus charge and taken to the local jail, while the Klan assembled an execution team. At 10:30 that night, the sheriff released the three men. They were never seen alive again.

A nighttime parade of the Klan in a Virginia county bordering Washington, D.C., was often conducted to show a sign of unity and invoke fear in African-Americans. In 1946, over one thousand men gathered at Stone Mountain, Georgia, to hold a Klan revival. The organizer was forty-four-year-old Dr. Sam Green. Green had set the mold for future Klan groups—self-governing groups with no national affiliations. *Library of Congress*

Thurgood Marshall became chief counsel for the National Association for the Advancement of Colored People (NAACP). After amassing a record of Supreme Court challenges to state-sponsored discrimination, including the landmark *Brown v Board of Education* decision of 1954, President John F. Kennedy appointed Thurgood Marshall to the U.S. Court of Appeals. In that capacity, he wrote over 150 decisions, including support for the rights of immigrants, limiting government intrusion in cases involving illegal search and seizure, double jeopardy, and right to privacy issues. Before his nomination to the U.S. Supreme Court in 1967, Marshall won fourteen of the nineteen cases he argued before the Supreme Court on behalf of the government. Marshall represented and won more cases before the U.S. Supreme Court than any other American. *Library of Congress*

Dr. Martin Luther King Jr. is seen here with Malcolm X (born Malcolm Little). Malcolm X was a Muslim minister and national spokesman for the Nation of Islam (NOI). He was also founder of the Muslim Mosque, Inc. and the Organization of Afro-American Unity. Malcolm X went from being a drug dealer to one of the most prominent black leaders in the United States. He advocated black pride, economic self-reliance, and identity politics. Following a pilgrimage to Mecca in 1964, Malcolm converted to orthodox Islam. Less than a year later, he was assassinated on the first day of National Brotherhood Week, February 21, 1965. Three members of the NOI were convicted of his assassination (one confessed). *Library of Congress*

The plea for President Lyndon Johnson to go to Selma, Alabama, illustrated fear, outrage, and hope in the black community. In 1965, the SCLC joined a voting-rights protest march from Selma to Montgomery, more than fifty miles away. Police beat and tear-gassed the marchers just outside of Selma. The televised scenes of the violence resulted in an outpouring of support to continue the march. The SCLC petitioned for and received a federal court order barring police from interfering with a renewed march to Montgomery. *Library of Congress*

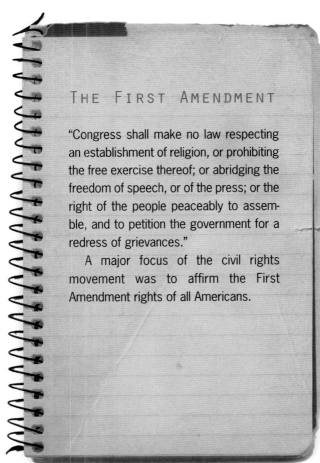

THE FIRST AMENDMENT

"Congress shall make no law respecting an establishment of religion, or prohibiting the free exercise thereof; or abridging the freedom of speech, or of the press; or the right of the people peaceably to assemble, and to petition the government for a redress of grievances."

A major focus of the civil rights movement was to affirm the First Amendment rights of all Americans.

The civil rights legislation of the 1960s would abolish this type of vicious segregation. Throughout the South, segregated facilities were uniformly inferior. Separate drinking fountains for whites and blacks, "Colored" restrooms, and seats in the back of the bus were the norm. Black restrooms and drinking fountains were poorly kept and unsanitary, often forcing black Americans to wait until they got home to use such facilities. In Mississippi and other southern states, it was illegal for a black person to marry a white person. *Library of Congress*

When word of their disappearance reached the White House, President Lyndon Johnson ordered J. Edgar Hoover to treat the incident as a kidnapping. The next day, FBI agents descended on Philadelphia, Mississippi. The following day, they found the burned-out shell of Schwerner's car. There was no sign of the three young men.

The discovery of the car ramped up the investigation. Within two weeks, more than 150 FBI agents were combing the woods around the car. But with no tangible results, the FBI began enlisting members of the Klan as paid informers. The tactic paid off. Within weeks, a tip led the FBI to a farm, where agents discovered the buried bodies of the three men. With information from informants and the confessions of two Klansmen, the FBI pieced together the puzzle. After the three men had left the jail, the Klan execution team and the deputy sheriff had followed them. The deputy ordered the car containing the three to stop and then ordered them into his patrol car. The deputy sheriff transported the men to a secluded farm and they were executed.

On Sunday, September 15, 1963, Ku Klux Klan members planted nineteen sticks of dynamite in the basement of the 16th Street Baptist Church. Marches and other civil rights activities had been staged from there. Special Agent William L. Fleming (left) and analyst Ben Herren helped bring Thomas E. Blanton Jr. to justice for the 1963 bombing in Birmingham. *FBI*

As attorney general, Robert Kennedy was a Hoover antagonist and wanted to remove him because of his political power. Kennedy immediately drew anger from Hoover when he insisted that all of Hoover's speeches and FBI press releases be submitted to him for approval. He had a direct telephone line installed between his office and Hoover's, bypassing Helen Gandy. No attorney general had ever put Hoover on such a leash. Kennedy saw the FBI as an arm of the administration, and Hoover as little more than a tired old warhorse that should be retired. Kennedy regularly violated the unwritten chain of command by going directly to special agents, bypassing the special agent in charge and others above him. No one had ever done this before, and it infuriated Hoover. *Library of Congress*

Legendary jazz musician Louis Armstrong was never the subject of an official FBI investigation; however, his name appears in numerous FBI files concerning other subject matters. Among these included a number of sources claiming he had Communist Party affiliations, and the not-so-surprising fact that he liked to smoke marijuana. One report quotes a source who worked at the famous Flamingo Hotel in Las Vegas as saying he occasionally "took care" of Armstrong by sending him "a bottle of scotch or a couple of reefers." *Library of Congress*

The FBI claimed there were eighteen members of the Klan involved, including the sheriff and his deputy. The state of Mississippi refused to charge any of the accused. The Klan had used complicit local law enforcement officers, which gave criminal jurisdiction to the federal government. The suspects were indicted for depriving the three men of their civil rights. In October 1967, the Klan's Imperial Wizard and six others were found guilty and sentenced to the maximum for the charge, ten years. The conviction of those men and the FBI's persistent investigation crippled that Klan group.

The depth to which the FBI infiltrated the Klan is demonstrated by another racial killing. On March 25, 1965, twelve thousand people gathered in Alabama after the successful conclusion of the Selma to Montgomery march for black voting rights. That evening, a white woman, Viola Liuzzo, was shuttling black marchers back to Selma. Four Klansmen spotted her and a black man together. They chased the car down, and shot and killed Liuzzo, but her passenger survived his gunshot wounds. Unlike previous investigations that took months to solve, if they were solved at all, President Johnson announced the next day that four Klansmen had been arrested

Nonviolent marches were the philosophy of Dr. Martin Luther King Jr. In this photo, he stands on the far left of a line of other civil rights leaders. Hoover's suspicions about the black civil rights leadership in the 1960s were rooted in pre-World War II beliefs. In August 1941, FBI Headquarters sent a request to the Oklahoma City field office for an investigation of "Communist Party domination" of the NAACP in connection with the development of "Nationalistic Tendency Charts." The field office report, dated September 19, 1941, concluded that based on an informant's reports, "There is a strong tendency for the NAACP to steer clear of Communistic activities. Nevertheless, there is a strong movement on the part of the Communists to attempt to dominate this group through an infiltration of communistic doctrines. Consequently, the activities of the NAACP will be closely observed and scrutinized in the future." *Library of Congress*

Civil rights leader Bayard Rustin organized the Journey of Reconciliation in 1947. This journey was taken by an integrated group of people who defied local ordinances banning them on public transportation in the South. Rustin was sentenced to a chain gang in North Carolina for his participation. The Journey of Reconciliation was the model for the Freedom Rides of the 1960s. Rustin was an instrumental advisor to Dr. King in organizing the SCLC and was the chief organizer and logistics person for a march on Washington for Jobs and Freedom in 1963. *Library of Congress*

Andrew Young was a civil rights activist, former mayor of Atlanta, Georgia, and the United States' first African-American ambassador to the United Nations. Young was jailed for his participation in civil rights demonstrations. He played a key role in events in Birmingham, Alabama, serving as a mediator between the white and black communities. In 1964, Young was named executive director of the SCLC, becoming, in that capacity, one of Dr. King's principal lieutenants. He was with Dr. King when King was assassinated in 1968. *Library of Congress*

for conspiracy to violate the civil rights of Mrs. Liuzzo. An FBI paid informant (in the killer's car) had fingered the men.

Three were indicted for murder, but an all-white, all-male jury could not reach a verdict. A second trial resulted in not-guilty verdicts. The Department of Justice brought charges of civil rights violations against the three, and in 1965, they were convicted and jailed. By the late 1960s, the confluence of unambiguous federal authority and local support for civil rights prosecutions allowed the FBI to play an influential role in enabling African Americans to vote, serve on juries, and use public accommodations on an equal basis.

COINTELPRO

Over the years, Hoover's obsessive hunt for communists was aided by a virtually unrestricted exercise of a broad range of covert measures known as Counter-intelligence Programs (COINTELPRO). The program began in 1956, in part because of Hoover's frustration with Supreme Court rulings that limited the government's power to proceed against dissident groups. By that time, Hoover was unable to distinguish between legitimate social protest, communist agitation, and subversion. The individuals and organizations to be neutralized ranged from the violent elements of the Black Panther Party to the Communist Party and the Ku Klux Klan. Advocates of violent revolution and peaceful supporters of social change alike were targeted by COINTELPRO. Even if a group or individual did not satisfy the "advocacy of violence" standard expressed in the Supreme Court's decisions, COINTELPRO investigated racial matters, hate organizations, and revolutionary-type subversives.

On August 28, 1956, Hoover authorized a program against the Communist Party USA to "harass, disrupt, and discredit the CPUSA." To promote dissension among its members, one program tactic included disseminating derogatory information about select CPUSA members to the press and selected public officials. As Internal Security Section Chief Alan H. Belmont noted in an August 1959 memorandum to Hoover, "The Counter-intelligence Program is one of the special programs that we have devised to disorganize and disrupt the Communist Party."

In January 1958, the FBI went to the U.S. Post Office to obtain approval for a mail surveillance program in an effort to identify membership in the CPUSA. Under the program, the FBI wanted to record the names and addresses of the sender and recipient of letters to and from the Soviet Union. However, the mail would remain unopened. The post office responded that it had been cooperating with the Central Intelligence Agency (CIA) in such a program for several years. In a surprising windfall for the FBI, and in an unusual move on the part of the CIA, the CIA provided the FBI with copies of the letters it had opened and copied.

In 1964, COINTELPRO was used against white hate groups such as the Ku Klux Klan and "other (White Supremacist) hate groups." One action set up a national Klan to drain the strength of and destabilize the United Klans of America.

COINTELPRO differed from earlier FBI activities because the FBI created a complete paper record of its actions in both the central COINTELPRO file at Bureau headquarters and in the field offices. Under the various counterintelligence programs, FBI agents submitted action and summary reports in writing. This recordkeeping would later damage the FBI.

COINTELPRO used the same techniques for suspected domestic enemies as used against foreign espionage agents. William C. Sullivan, a former assistant to the director of the FBI, testified before the Select Committee to Study Government Operations (a.k.a. the "Church Committee") in 1975 that, "This is a rough, tough, dirty business, and dangerous. It was dangerous at times. No holds were barred . . . . We have used [these techniques] against Soviet agents. They have used [them] against us . . . . [The same methods were] brought home against any organization which we targeted. We did not differentiate. This is a rough, tough business."

During the fifteen years of the COINTELPRO, more than two thousand disruptive actions against various groups were proposed.

Roy Wilkins was a prominent civil rights activist from the 1930s to the 1970s. Wilkins was named executive secretary of the NAACP in 1955. One of his first actions was to provide support to civil rights activists in Mississippi who were being subjected to a credit squeeze by members of the White Citizens' Councils. Under a plan, black businesses and voluntary associations shifted their accounts to the black-owned Tri-State Bank of Memphis, Tennessee. By the end of 1955, more than $280,000 had been deposited in Tri-State for this purpose. The money enabled Tri-State to extend loans to credit-worthy blacks denied loans by white banks. The FBI investigated alleged threats against Mr. Wilkins' life and proposed extortion plots. *Library of Congress*

Kennedy assassination

A national tragedy produced another expansion of FBI jurisdiction when Lee Harvey Oswald assassinated President John F. Kennedy on November 22, 1963, in Dallas, Texas. The crime was a local homicide at that time, and the FBI had no statutory authority. Nevertheless, newly sworn-in President Lyndon Johnson ordered the FBI to conduct the investigation. Congress then passed a law to ensure that any such act in the future would be a federal crime.

Oswald was arrested eighty minutes after the assassination for killing Dallas police officer J. D. Tippit, and that evening he was charged with the murders of Tippit and Kennedy. Oswald denied shooting the president and claimed he was being set up. Two days later, before the FBI could interrogate Oswald, Jack Ruby gunned Oswald down on live television while he was being escorted to an armored car for transport to the Dallas County Jail to await his trial.

Just hours after the murder of Oswald, Hoover allegedly said that he wanted "something issued so we can convince the public that Oswald is the real assassin." Oswald had been under surveillance by the FBI, or he was a confidential informer working for them, depending on which story one wants to believe.

In March 1963, Dallas FBI agent James Hosty was ordered to put Oswald under investigation. Hosty discovered that Oswald was purchasing *The Daily Worker*, the newspaper of the Communist Party USA. Hosty visited the home of Ruth Paine to see where Oswald was living. He spoke to both Paine and Oswald's wife, Marina. When Oswald heard about the visit, he went to the FBI office in Dallas. When told that Hosty was at lunch, Oswald left him a message in an envelope.

JUSTICE PREVAILS, PART II

On June 12, 1963, civil rights leader Medgar Evers was killed by an assassin's bullet. The FBI had gathered strong evidence against the accused killer, a white supremacist, Byron De La Beckwith. De La Beckwith stood trial twice in the 1960s, but in both cases, the all-white juries could not reach a verdict. Finally, in a third trial in 1994 (and thirty-one years after Evers' murder), Beckwith was convicted and sentenced to life in prison.

Three of the most powerful men in America in the 1960s were J. Edgar Hoover (left), President Lyndon Johnson, and Johnson's attorney general, Nicholas Katzenbach. On November 25, 1963, three days after President Kennedy's assassination and before any official investigation began, Katzenbach, then deputy attorney general, wrote to presidential assistant Bill Moyers. In a declassified FBI document, Katzenbach discusses a government coverup: "The public must be satisfied that Oswald was the assassin; that he had no confederates who are still at large; and that evidence was such that he would have been convicted at trial. . . . Speculation about Oswald's motivation ought to be cut off. . . . Unfortunately the facts on Oswald seem about too pat—too obvious. . . . We need something to head off public speculation or Congressional hearings of the wrong sort." According to the House Select Committee on Assassinations, Hoover told staff members on November 24, 1963, that he and Katzenbach were anxious to have "something issued so we can convince the public that Oswald is the real assassin." *Library of Congress*

November 25, 1963

MEMORANDUM FOR MR. MOYERS

It is important that all of the facts
surrounding President Kennedy's Assassination be
made public in a way which will satisfy people in
the United States and abroad that all the facts
have been told and that a statement to this effect
be made now.

1. The public must be satisfied that
Oswald was the assassin; that he did not have
confederates who are still at large; and that
the evidence was such that he would have been
convicted at trial.

2. Speculation about Oswald's motivation
ought to be cut off, and we should have some basis
for rebutting thought that this was a Communist
conspiracy or (as the Iron Curtain press is saying)
a right-wing conspiracy to blame it on the Communists.
Unfortunately the facts on Oswald seem about too pat--
too obvious (Marxist, Cuba, Russian wife, etc.). The
Dallas police have put out statements on the Communist
conspiracy theory, and it was they who were in charge
when he was shot and thus silenced.

3. The matter has been handled thus far
with neither dignity nor conviction. Facts have been
mixed with rumour and speculation. We can scarcely
let the world see us totally in the image of the
Dallas police when our President is murdered.

I think this objective may be satisfied
by making public as soon as possible a complete and
thorough FBI report on Oswald and the assassination.
This may run into the difficulty of pointing to in-
consistencies between this report and statements by
Dallas police officials. But the reputation of the
Bureau is such that it may do the whole job.

The only other step would be the appointment
of a Presidential Commission of unimpeachable personnel
to review and examine the evidence and announce its
conclusions. This has both advantages and disadvantages.
I think it can await publication of the FBI report
and public reaction to it here and abroad.

I think, however, that a statement that
all the facts will be made public property in an
orderly and responsible way should be made now. We
need something to head off public speculation or
Congressional hearings of the wrong sort.

Nicholas deB. Katzenbach
Deputy Attorney General

The two-page Katzenbach-to-Moyers memo regarding President
Kennedy's assassination. *FBI*

An individual working at the Dallas office alleged that
Oswald's message included a threat to "blow up the FBI and
the Dallas Police Department if you don't stop bothering my
wife." Hosty later claimed it said: "If you have anything you
want to learn about me, come talk to me directly. If you don't
cease bothering my wife, I will take appropriate action and
report this to the proper authorities."

Soon after Oswald's arrest, J. Gordon Shanklin, special
agent-in-charge of the Dallas field office, called Hosty into
his office. He asked what Hosty knew about Oswald. When
Oswald was shot dead two days later, Shanklin ordered Hosty
to destroy Oswald's letter.

The FBI discovered that Hosty's name and phone number
were in Oswald's address book, and Hoover worried that this information
would indicate that Oswald had been working with the FBI as an informant.
Instead of passing Oswald's address book on to the Warren Commission, the FBI
provided a typewritten transcription from which the Hosty entry was absent.

The FBI and Warren Commission each conducted investigations. On
December 9, 1963, just seventeen days after the assassination, the FBI issued its
report to the Warren Commission and remained on as the primary investigating
authority for the commission. The FBI reported that only three bullets were
fired—the first shot hit President Kennedy, the second shot hit Texas Governor
John Connally, and the third shot hit Kennedy in the head, killing him. The FBI
stated that Oswald was the lone assassin who fired all three shots. The commission's
report, published in September 1964, concluded that Lee Harvey Oswald was
the lone assassin. The Warren Commission agreed with the FBI investigation
that only three shots were fired. However, it disagreed on which shots hit
Kennedy and which hit Connally.

In 1979, the House Select Committee on Assassinations reviewed the FBI's investigation. The committee concluded: "The FBI effectively investigated Lee Harvey Oswald prior to the assassination and properly evaluated the evidence it possessed to assess his potential to endanger the public safety in a national emergency." According to the committee, the FBI conducted a thorough and professional investigation into the responsibility of Lee Harvey Oswald for the assassination, but it failed to investigate adequately the possibility of a conspiracy.

The FBI has received additional examination of its role in the investigation from researchers due to the actions of FBI agent James Hosty. When Hosty testified before the Warren Commission, he did not disclose his connection with Oswald or the existence of the letter. In 1964, Dallas FBI agent Will Griffin claimed that Oswald was an FBI informant. This statement undermined the testimony of Shanklin and Hosty.

The letter that Oswald gave to the FBI office in Dallas remained a secret until 1975. It became public knowledge when someone in the FBI tipped off a journalist as to its existence. The Select Committee on Intelligence Activities and the Select Committee on Assassinations then examined Oswald's relationship with James Hosty. Hosty admitted that he had misled the Warren Commission by not advising them of the letter from Oswald. Shanklin denied knowing about the letter, but the testimony of Hosty and William Sullivan, the assistant director of the FBI, contradicted Shanklin.

King assassination

Dr. Martin Luther King Jr. had a mutually antagonistic relationship with the FBI and J. Edgar Hoover. The FBI began monitoring King and the SCLC in 1961. The FBI's investigation had been largely superficial until 1962, when it learned that one of King's most trusted advisers, New York City lawyer Stanley Levison, had been involved with the CPUSA since the late 1940s, and another key King associate, Hunter Pitts O'Dell, was also linked to the CPUSA by sworn testimony before the HUAC. The Bureau placed wiretaps on Levison and King's home and office phones, and bugged King's rooms in hotels as he traveled across the country.

Attorney General Robert Kennedy and President Kennedy both unsuccessfully tried to persuade King to dissociate himself from Levison. On October 18, 1963, Robert Kennedy approved Hoover's request to wiretap the headquarters of the SCLC. For his part, King adamantly denied having any connections to communism, stating in a 1965 *Playboy* article, "There are as many communists in this freedom movement as there are Eskimos in Florida." Hoover responded by calling King "the most notorious liar in the country."

Seen here with President Lyndon Johnson is Nobel Prize–winner Dr. Martin Luther King Jr., one of the principal leaders of the American civil rights movement. His nonviolent challenges to segregation and racial discrimination helped convince many white Americans to support the cause of civil rights. *Library of Congress*

The declassified files of the FBI revealed a memo from J. A. Sizoo to W. C. Sullivan, dated December 1, 1964, which spoke of a proposed blackmail attempt that had been considered against Dr. King:

> [Name deleted] stated to DeLoach that he was faced with the difficult problem of taking steps to remove King from the national picture. It is, therefore, suggested that consideration be given to the following course of action: That DeLoach have a further discussion with [name deleted] and offer to be helpful to [name deleted] in connection with the problem of the removal of King from the national scene; That DeLoach suggest that [name deleted] might desire to call a meeting of Negro leaders in the country which might include, for instance, two or three top leaders in the civil rights movement such as James Farmer and A. Philip Randolph; two or three top Negro judges such as Judge Parsons and Judge Hasty; two or three top reputable ministers such as Robert Johnson, Moderator of the Washington City Presbytery; two or three other selected Negro officials from public life such as the Negro Attorney General from one of the New England states. These men could be called for the purpose of learning the facts as to the Bureau's performance in the fulfillment of its responsibilities under the Civil Rights statute, and this could well be done at such a meeting. In addition, the Bureau, on a highly confidential basis, could brief such a group on the security background of King [name deleted]. The use of a tape, such as contemplated in your memorandum, together with a transcript for convenience in following the tape, should be most convincing.

In 1968, Dr. Martin Luther King Jr. was assassinated in Memphis, Tennessee. At the time, the FBI lacked jurisdiction in what was considered a local crime. Attorney General Ramsey Clark ordered the FBI to investigate the shooting. Over three thousand special agents were eventually involved in tracking leads that led to the identity, arrest, and conviction of James Earl Ray. Ray received life in prison and died of illness behind bars.

The Black Panthers

J. Edgar Hoover once described the Black Panthers as "the greatest threat to the internal security of the country." In August 1967, the FBI initiated COINTELPRO against organizations that the Bureau characterized as black nationalist hate groups in order to "expose, disrupt, discredit, misdirect, or otherwise neutralize black nationalists or other militant civil rights organizations and their leadership, spokesmen, membership, and supporters."

The *New York Times* reported on September 8, 1968, that the Black Panther Party was "schooled in the Marxist-Leninist ideol-

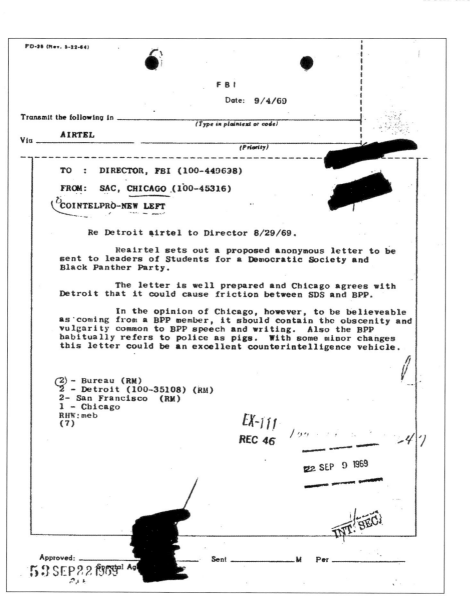

This FBI internal memo discusses the formulation friction between the Students for a Democratic Society and the Black Panther Party. The FBI considered both groups threats to domestic security. *FBI*

ogy, and the teaching of Chinese Communist leader Mao Tse-Tung. Its members have perpetrated numerous assaults on police officers and have engaged in violent confrontations with police throughout the country. Leaders and representatives of the Black Panther Party travel extensively all over the United States preaching their gospel of hate and violence not only to ghetto residents but to students in colleges, universities, and high schools as well."

The Weather Underground

In the 1960s, almost half of America's population was under eighteen years of age. This glut of adolescents set the stage for a crude attempt to revolt against the status quo: sexism, class struggle, and the Vietnam War. On campuses throughout the country, anger boiled over into violence.

As the 1960s unfolded, the Student Nonviolent Coordinating Committee (SNCC), an organization founded by Martin Luther King Jr. to promote nonviolent protest, became increasingly radicalized. Some within the group were dissatisfied with the level of militancy and splintered away to form the Weather Underground Organization (WUO). A line in the Bob Dylan song, "Subterranean Homesick Blues," inspired the group's name: "You don't need a weatherman to know which way the wind blows." The Weather Underground Organization (a.k.a. the Weathermen) was one of the most violent counter-culture groups the FBI encountered during the 1960s and 1970s. They boasted about the idealistic passion that drove them to "bring the war home."

Some of the WUO's former members cited the deaths of Black Panthers Fred Hampton and Mark Clark in December 1969, and a Chicago police raid, as flash points. They believed the actions were government-sanctioned killings to wipe out militant groups. In turn, the Weathermen would illustrate their philosophy by delivering the same violence they opposed.

Outraged by the Vietnam War and racism in America, the organization waged a violent, albeit low-level, war to overthrow

On April 11, 1968, President Lyndon Johnson signed the Civil Rights Act. The act expanded on previous legislation and prohibited discrimination concerning the sale, rental, and financing of housing based on race, religion, national origin, sex, and more. It also provided protection for civil rights workers. Just nine days later, in retaliation, Lemuel Penn, a black World War II veteran and colonel in the army reserve, was murdered. An all-white jury found the three Klansmen accused of the murder not guilty. The Justice Department appealed the ruling as a violation of Penn's civil rights. Two years later, the Klansmen were convicted of violating the veteran's civil rights. *Library of Congress*

Letter to SAC, Albany
RE: COUNTERINTELLIGENCE PROGRAM
BLACK NATIONALIST - HATE GROUPS

Dated 8/25/67

against the Communist Party and related organizations, or the program entitled "Counterintelligence Program, Internal Security, Disruption of Hate Groups," (Bufile 157-9), which is directed against Klan and hate-type groups primarily consisting of white memberships.

All Special Agent personnel responsible for the investigation of black nationalist, hate-type organizations and their memberships should be alerted to our counterintelligence interest and each investigative Agent has a responsibility to call to the attention of the counterintelligence coordinator suggestions and possibilities for implementing the program. You are also cautioned that the nature of this new endeavor is such that under no circumstances should the existence of the program be made known outside the Bureau and appropriate within-office security should be afforded to sensitive operations and techniques considered under the program.

No counterintelligence action under this program may be initiated by the field without specific prior Bureau authorization.

You are urged to take an enthusiastic and imaginative approach to this new counterintelligence endeavor and the Bureau will be pleased to entertain any suggestions or techniques you may recommend.

A COINTELPRO FBI memo urges special agents to take an "enthusiastic and imaginative approach" to counterintelligence programs of the Black Nationalists and other hate-type organizations. *FBI*

the government. They bombed the Capitol building and, according the WUO's Communiqué Number 4, had the "honor and pleasure" of breaking LSD guru Timothy Leary out of a California state prison. In Leary's book, *Confessions of a Hope Fiend,* he gives full credit to the WUO for the breakout and suggests that the money used to get him out, and safely to Algeria, came from illegal drugs. These, among other illegal acts, put the WUO on a trajectory to land on the FBI's Most Wanted list and, for a time, evade one of the largest FBI manhunts in its history.

FBI records show that between 1968 and 1974, WUO leader Mark Rudd and other members of the WUO had visited Cuba (dozens of times, often at the expense of Fidel Castro), the Soviet Union, the People's Republic of China, Algeria, and other communist-led countries for indoctrination and training. After Rudd's return from Cuba in 1968, he organized and led a student takeover of Columbia University that lasted seven days. He then went to Chicago to organize and lead the antiwar demonstrations that disrupted the 1968 Democratic National Convention (DNC).

The FBI linked the WUO to bombings and other attacks around the country, including a 1969 sniper attack on police headquarters in Cambridge, Massachusetts, and the bombing of several police cars in Chicago. In 1970, WUO members bombed a Detroit police station, killing one officer, and bombed a New York City police station, injuring three people.

Ironically, the WUO accidentally bombed itself and, in the process, reduced its membership by three. On March 6, 1970, WUO members leveled a luxury townhouse in New York City's Greenwich Village while assembling an antipersonnel bomb intended to be set off at a dance at a local army base. Eighteen members of the WUO were charged, and the FBI had to find them. Normally, the FBI had cooperation from citizens in tracking down serious and dangerous criminals. The WUO members were different. There was a cadre of hardcore sympathizers who aided and abetted the fugitives. "At every point, we were blocked by hostility from those we felt could give us leads, including the parents of the radicals," said Assistant FBI Director W. Mark Felt.

The FBI was also operating under new rules. In 1966, Hoover had imposed restrictions on some of the techniques used to penetrate clandestine conspiracies. He abolished black-bag jobs, restricted the number of wiretaps, and forbid the use of surreptitious entries (warrantless entries without the permission or knowledge of the occupants).

However, the chaos created a political hot potato; the White House pressured the FBI for action. Hoover met with President Nixon in the summer of 1970. Nixon wanted aggressive action. William Sullivan, who was in charge of all investigative operations in the FBI, later stated publicly that Hoover had told him in the fall of 1970 to use whatever means necessary to apprehend the fugitive Weathermen. Agents in the field who were hunting the bombers believed they were acting properly on instructions from Washington.

Mark Felt believed that Hoover's restrictions were not fully lifted until Hoover died and L. Patrick Gray III took over as acting director. "Domestic Intelligence chief Edward Miller

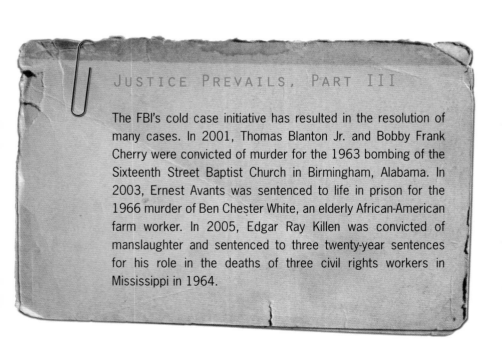

JUSTICE PREVAILS, PART III

The FBI's cold case initiative has resulted in the resolution of many cases. In 2001, Thomas Blanton Jr. and Bobby Frank Cherry were convicted of murder for the 1963 bombing of the Sixteenth Street Baptist Church in Birmingham, Alabama. In 2003, Ernest Avants was sentenced to life in prison for the 1966 murder of Ben Chester White, an elderly African-American farm worker. In 2005, Edgar Ray Killen was convicted of manslaughter and sentenced to three twenty-year sentences for his role in the deaths of three civil rights workers in Mississippi in 1964.

The Chicago Seven was a group of radicals blamed for disrupting the Democratic National Convention, during which policemen seeking to restore order clubbed protestors and twenty-one journalists covering the events. Protesters blamed Mayor Richard J. Daley and Police Superintendent James B. Conlisk Jr. for the beatings, claiming that they were trying to deter coverage of the events and restrict dissent. Authorities blamed the Chicago Seven for starting the melee (*New York Times*: August 28, 1968). More than a year later, in October 1969, the notorious Weather Underground began its "Days of Rage" to protest the trial of the Chicago Seven. Thousands of young sympathizers wearing football helmets and wielding pipes and bats cascaded through the streets of an upscale Chicago suburb. They smashed parked cars, broke shop windows, and attacked police following a rally in Lincoln Park.

and I sincerely believed," said Felt in his book, *A G-Man's Life*, "that Gray had authorized the use of these tools. . . . As I understood the standard, intelligence gathering that was not intended to result in criminal charges was not limited by the Fourth Amendment prohibition against 'unreasonable searches and seizures.' "

The WUO had foreign ties to hostile governments, and the FBI looked upon WUO leadership— with its links to Cuba, the Soviet Union, North Korea, and other countries—as agents for a foreign power. Felt and others believed that warrants to gather intelligence on foreign agents, as was sometimes the rule during World War II, were not necessary.

When a request came in from the field for a surreptitious entry, Miller would consult with Felt, and if the two agreed that the request was "completely justified in the interest of the United States," Miller would give permission to proceed. Miller would then send a confirming memo to Felt. Since Gray had given Felt complete operational control, Felt later testified before a grand jury that he had authorized seven black-bag jobs against the WUO without consulting Gray. These techniques were successful in removing the WUO from the population and stopping their terrorism.

Codename "Medburg"

On March 3, 1971, a radical anti-Vietnam war group called The Citizens Committee to Investigate the FBI broke into the FBI's residence office in Media, Pennsylvania, and stole thousands of documents that indicated there had been widespread civil liberties violations. The event permanently damaged the FBI's image in the mind of many Americans.

Hoover ordered an intensive investigation (codenamed "Medburg") to identify the burglars. The thieves waited two weeks to release the first documents that illustrated illegal behavior. Some in Congress demanded Hoover's resignation. The media went into a feeding frenzy. Several weeks passed, and just when the turmoil was quieting down, the thieves released additional documents. The Bureau had been attempting to explain the first set of documents, when the second release caught them short. All attempted explanations were unconvincing, as the latest release of documents showed further conspiracies and illegal activities.

In February 1972, a publication of the War Resisters League published all the stolen documents. The FBI may have had suspects, but no one was in custody, and the public believed the FBI would not solve the case. Nevertheless, there was a smoking gun—one that would further damage the FBI. A one-page memo among the documents had a mysterious word on it that caught a reporter's attention: COINTELPRO.

When Carl Stern, a reporter for NBC, could not get an explanation from the FBI as to what the word signified, he filed for access to the documents under the Freedom of Information Act (FOIA). The FBI denied his request. Stern successfully appealed to the U.S. Supreme Court in September 1973.

The media break-in compromised COINTELPRO, and Hoover shut it down on April 28, 1971. Five days later, he died.

The Church Committee

COINTELPRO was a prolonged headline-maker, and the public was eager to learn the depth of the alleged illegal behavior by the FBI. The Church Committee hearings on the FBI's role in COINTELPRO began in November 1975.

During its fifteen-month investigation, the Church Committee documented that the FBI had developed over five hundred thousand domestic intelligence files on Americans and domestic groups. The targets of the intelligence activities included organizations and individuals promoting revolutionary, racist, or otherwise extremist ideological viewpoints. But during the 1960s, it also included investigations of the civil rights, antiwar, and women's rights movements.

According to Church Committee documents, a General Accounting Office (GAO) review found that of 675 cases studied, 16 were referred for prosecution; of those, only 7

A TROUBLED PERIOD

By the late 1960s, Americans who objected to involvement in Vietnam or to other policies wrote to Congress or carried out demonstrations. The convergence of crime, violence, civil rights issues, and potential national security issues garnered the sustained attention of the FBI. Nevertheless, in 1970 alone, an estimated three thousand bombings and fifty thousand bomb threats occurred in the United States.

had actually been prosecuted, and only 4 convictions resulted. When the Church Committee presented its findings, Senator Frank Church described the committee's work evaluating the FBI's involvement in domestic intelligence in the following terms: "The Committee investigation's purpose is . . . to evaluate domestic intelligence according to the standards of the Constitution and the statutes of our land. If fault is to be found, it does not rest in the Bureau alone. It is to be found also in the long line of Attorneys General, Presidents, and Congresses who have given power and responsibility to the FBI but have failed to give it adequate guidance, direction, and control."

The Church Committee found that the FBI went beyond its investigative mandate and employed COINTELPRO to disrupt groups and discredit or harass innocent individuals. While the committee's final report did not question the need for lawful domestic intelligence, it concluded that the government's domestic intelligence policies and practices required fundamental reform.

Although the claimed purpose of the Bureau's COINTELPRO tactics was to prevent violence, some of the FBI's actions against the Black Panther Party appeared to encourage violence, and others could reasonably be expected to cause violence. For example, the FBI began a letter-writing campaign "to . . . intensify the degree of animosity between the two groups and occasion [name deleted] to take retaliatory action which could disrupt the Black Panther Party or lead to reprisals against its leadership."

One of many letters found in the Church Committee's report reads:

> Brother [name deleted]:
>
> I'm from the south side and have some Panther friends that know you and tell me what's been going on. I know those two [name deleted] and [name deleted] that run the Panthers for a long time and those mothers been with every 'black outfit going where it looked like they was something in it for them. The only black people they care about is themselves. I heard too they're sweethearts and that [name deleted] has worked for the man that's why he's not in Viet Nam. Maybe that's why they're just playing like real Panthers. I hear a lot of the brothers are with you and want those mothers out but don't know how. The Panthers need real black men for leaders not freaks. Don't give up brothers.

James Adams, deputy associate director of the FBI's Intelligence Division, testified before the Church Committee that: "None of our programs have contemplated violence, and the instructions prohibit it, and the record of turndowns of recommended actions in some instances specifically say that we do not approve this action because if we take it, it could result in harm to the individual."

While illegal domestic intelligence gathering was taking place, a more deadly activity was working to undermine the government . . . .

NEW CRIMES, NEW LAWS

In the 1960s, Congress gave the FBI new federal laws with which to fight civil rights violations, racketeering, and gambling. These new laws included the 1961 Crimes Aboard Aircraft Act, an expanded Federal Fugitive Act, the Sports Bribery Act of 1964, the Civil Rights Acts of 1960, 1964, and 1968, and the Voting Rights Act of 1965.

NATIONAL FIREARMS ACT

William Taylor Harris

Date photographs taken unknown
FBI No.: 308,668 L5
Aliases: Mike Andrews, Richard Frank Dennis, William Kinder, Jonathan Maris, Jonathan Mark Salamone, Teko
Age: 29, born January 22, 1945, Fort Sill, Oklahoma (not supported by birth records)

Height: 5'7"	**Eyes:** Hazel
Weight: 145 pounds	**Complexion:** Medium
Build: Medium	**Race:** White
Hair: Brown, short	**Nationality:** American

Occupation: Postal clerk
Remarks: Reportedly wears Fu Manchu type mustache, may wear glasses, upper right center tooth may be chipped, reportedly jogs, swims and rides bicycle for exercise, was last seen wearing army type boots and dark jacket
Social Security Numbers Used: 315-46-2467; 553-27-8400; 359-48-5467
Fingerprint Classification: 20 L 1 At 12
S 1 Ut

Emily Montague Harris

Date photographs taken unknown
FBI No.: 325,804 L2
Aliases: Mrs. William Taylor Harris, Mary Hensley, Joanne James, Anna Lindenberg, Cynthia Sue Mankins, Dorothy Ann Petri, Emily Montague Schwartz, Mary Schwartz, Yolanda
Age: 27, born February 11, 1947, Baltimore, Maryland (not supported by birth records)

Height: 5'3"	**Eyes:** Blue
Weight: 115 pounds	**Complexion:** Fair
Build: Small	**Race:** White
Hair: Blonde	**Nationality:** American

Occupations: Secretary, teacher
Remarks: Hair may be worn one inch below ear level, may wear glasses or contact lenses; reportedly has partial upper plate, pierced ears, is a natural food fadist, exercises by jogging, swimming and bicycle riding, usually wears slacks or street length dresses, was last seen wearing jeans and waist length shiny black leather coat; may wear wigs
Social Security Numbers Used: 327-42-2356; 429-42-8003

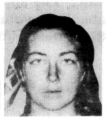

NATIONAL FIREARMS ACT; BANK ROBBERY

Patricia Campbell Hearst

FBI No.: 325,805 L10
Alias: Tania
Age: 20, born February 20, 1954, San Francisco, California

Height: 5'3"	**Eyes:** Brown
Weight: 110 pounds	**Complexion:** Fair
Build: Small	**Race:** White
Hair: Light brown	**Nationality:** American

Scars and Marks: Mole on lower right corner of mouth, scar near right ankle
Remarks: Hair naturally light brown, straight and worn about three inches below shoulders in length, however, may wear wigs, including Afro style, dark brown of medium length; was last seen wearing black sweater, plaid slacks, brown hiking boots and carrying a knife in her belt

Jan., 1971   Feb., 1972   Dec., 1973

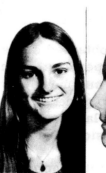

THE ABOVE INDIVIDUALS ARE SELF-PROCLAIMED MEMBERS OF THE SYMBIONESE LIBERATION ARMY AND REPORTEDLY HAVE BEEN IN POSSESSION OF NUMEROUS FIREARMS INCLUDING AUTOMATIC WEAPONS. WILLIAM HARRIS AND PATRICIA HEARST ALLEGEDLY HAVE USED GUNS TO AVOID ARREST. ALL THREE SHOULD BE CONSIDERED ARMED AND VERY DANGEROUS.

Federal warrants were issued on May 20, 1974, at Los Angeles, California, charging the Harrises and Hearst with violation of the National Firearms Act. Hearst was also indicted by a Federal Grand Jury on June 6, 1974, at San Francisco, California, for bank robbery and use of a weapon during a felony.

This is a wanted poster for Patty Hearst and two other members of the Symbionese Liberation Army (SLA). The SLA kidnapped Patty Hearst, kept her blindfolded and nude in a closet for several months, sexually assaulted her, and deprived her of food and sleep. Eventually, her abductors freed her and showed compassion. When they did, she joined their bank robbery escapades. Accounts of Hearst committing bank robberies seemed to portray a young woman who enjoyed her crimes as she acted under her own free will. Others say she was the victim of Stockholm Syndrome. When apprehended, Hearst was imprisoned for almost two years before President Jimmy Carter commuted her sentence. *FBI*

Change in Philosophy

When Jimmy Carter's administration took office, things at the FBI changed. Attorney General Griffin Bell's prosecutors felt that the WUO and its members, whose behaviors included terrorism and subversion, were political activists and, because they were American citizens, should be provided the protections of the Fourth Amendment.

Felt retired in 1973 and, within months of his retirement, he found himself in the spotlight in several investigations. The Church Committee called him five times about his actions during Watergate, but it was his actions against the WUO and the surveillance techniques that would create years of anguish for Felt.

In April 1978, the attorney general brought charges against Felt, Miller, and Gray for authorizing seven illegal break-ins of the homes and relatives of the WUO. He cited thirty-two overt acts of abusing "the rights of the Weathermen relatives and acquaintances to be secure in their homes, papers, and effects against unreasonable searches and seizures." The statute was a sixty-year-old law that had been used almost exclusively in the South to prosecute Ku Klux Klansmen.

The prosecution dropped its case against Gray for lack of evidence, but Felt and Miller were convicted in November 1980. The judge did not sentence them to prison but fined Felt $5,000 and Miller $3,000. In March 1981, President Ronald Reagan pardoned both men, stating that the convictions "grew out of their good-faith belief that their actions were necessary to preserve the security interests of our country." Reagan continued, "The record demonstrates that they acted not with criminal intent but in the belief that they had grants of authority reaching to the highest levels in government." ■

THE COUNTERINTELLIGENCE FILES

Twelve counterintelligence programs yielded over 52,600 pages of documentation in the FBI's files.

a. Black Extremist Hate Groups, 6,106 pages (1967–1971)

b. COINTELPRO Espionage Programs, 482 pages

c. CPUSA, 30,743 pages (1956–1971)

d. Cuban Matters (Pro Castro), 59 pages

e. Disruption of White Hate Groups, 5,457 pages (1964–1971)

f. Hoodwink (To Cause Dispute Between CPUSA and LCN), 60 pages

g. Mexican Communist Party Matters (Border Coverage Program), 122 pages

h. New Left, 6,244 (1968–1971)

i. Puerto Rican (Groups Seeking Puerto Rican Independence), 1,190 pages

j. Socialist Workers Party, 688 pages (1961–1969)

k. Special Operations (Nationalities Intelligence), 1,450 pages

l. Yugoslav (Violence Prone Yugoslav Emigres in U.S.), 84 pages

John Gotti Sr. and an unidentified associate discuss business in this surveillance photo. When mobsters fear they are bugged, they find other ways of communicating. Gotti knew his Ravenite Social Club on Mulberry St. in lower Manhattan was bugged, so he conducted business outside. The FBI electronically monitored Gotti's Ravenite Social Club, and between November 30, 1989, and January 24, 1990, Gotti spilled enough of the family's secrets to finally bring him down. The fall of the godfathers has not meant La Cosa Nostra went away. The families are still around, and they are morphing into new enterprises—bank fraud, cyber crime, unapproved airplane parts, and other contraband trade, as well as the old reliable, gambling. FBI

Chapter 6

BRINGING DOWN THE SYNDICATE
Investigating Organized Crime and Political Miscreants

The Eighteenth Amendment banned the sale and transportation of alcohol and created the era of prohibition, which ran from 1920 to 1933. It also spawned the modern American mafia.

La Cosa Nostra

The Sicilian mafia was a crime organization that held vast power in Italy in the 1870s and, some say, even today. The infamous American offshoot of the Sicilian mafia, La Cosa Nostra (LCN; literally "our thing"), considered itself a part of the Sicilian mafia until the early 1930s. With the emergence of Al Capone, it became a more inclusive Italian outfit. No crime organization in the twentieth century has ever come close to the organizational power and capabilities of the American mafia.

Organized crime in the early years of the twentieth century exploited poor and ill-educated immigrants in the overcrowded cities of New York, Boston, Chicago, and other urban areas in many ways, including child labor. Surprisingly, the Supreme Court intervened when Congress tried to crack down on these activities, which it viewed as immoral. In 1918, the Court struck down laws that forbade shipping goods across state lines if they were made by children in factories. *Library of Congress*

About four million Italians came to the United States between 1885 and 1926. Within that mass of people were members of the mafia in the form of the terrorist Black Hand group, which ruled the Italian-American communities until the birth of prohibition.

The bitter infighting and killing of rival mafiosi for the first two decades of the twentieth century left Salvatore Maranzano as *capo de tuti capo*, the "boss of bosses." Maranzano made Lucky Luciano his second in command, and Luciano thanked him by having him assassinated by four Jewish gunmen of Murder Inc. With the last of the traditional Sicilian mafia gone, Luciano and a handful of Italian-American and Jewish-American gangsters established a loose national crime syndicate in 1931. With the likes of Maranzano, who believed in ancient vendettas, secret rituals, and the concepts of honor and shame, now dead, modern Americanized gangsters, such as Luciano and Meyer Lansky, reshaped the mafia and severed the links to the Old World.

Unlike the 1930s and 1940s, the media had no prominent gangsters to popularize during the 1950s. The FBI focused on the Communist Party and its threat. However, in 1957, the infamous Apalachin conclave got the FBI's attention. The embryo that had incubated for 20 years had hatched into a giant, well-organized, multi-headed hydra.

Today, combating transnational and national criminal organizations such as LCN is one of the FBI's top priorities. In the past, however, involvement of the FBI in organized crime investigations was hampered in part by the lack of federal laws. During the 1940s and 1950s, Hoover had been reluctant to move against the growing crime organization because the Nazis and communists were his primary focus.

The Kefauver Committee

The first Senate hearings into organized crime occurred in May 1950. Senator Estes Kefauver (D-Tennessee) was the chairman of the Special Committee on Organized Crime in Interstate Commerce, a.k.a. the Kefauver Committee. The televised hearings drew between twenty and thirty million viewers. More than six hundred witnesses testified. The focus was on gambling, and the witnesses included law enforcement officers, politicians, governors, gamblers, and racketeers. Most of the mobsters took the Fifth Amendment. One mobster, Tony Accardo, took the Fifth one hundred fifty times.

Many of those who refused to talk were held in contempt of court, but the charges were later dismissed as unconstitutional. Because of the hearings, the FBI investigated and the Department of Justice prosecuted 138 people for labor racketeering. Kefauver said in his report that "there is a sinister criminal organization known as the Mafia operating throughout the country in the opinion of this committee." That, however, did not convince Hoover a mafia existed. According to some, Hoover was indebted to the mob. Others said Hoover understood power and the effort needed to bring the mob down, and he did not have the resources.

According to Bill Bonanno, son of the crime family boss, "It was a 'you scratch my back, I'll scratch yours.' You know, 'live, and let live.' "

Attorney General Robert F. Kennedy, seen here with President Lyndon Johnson, believed that Hoover did not move aggressively on organized crime. This opinion was partially true; until Congress began passing organized crime–specific legislation in the 1960s, the FBI could only gather information through informants and electronic surveillance of the mobsters. On February 15, 1963, Kennedy ordered an intensified investigation of organized crime leaders. *Library of Congress*

In 1966, the FBI launched an operation called "Hoodwink" to cause animosity between La Cosa Nostra and the Communist Party USA. This memo describes some of the details. *FBI*

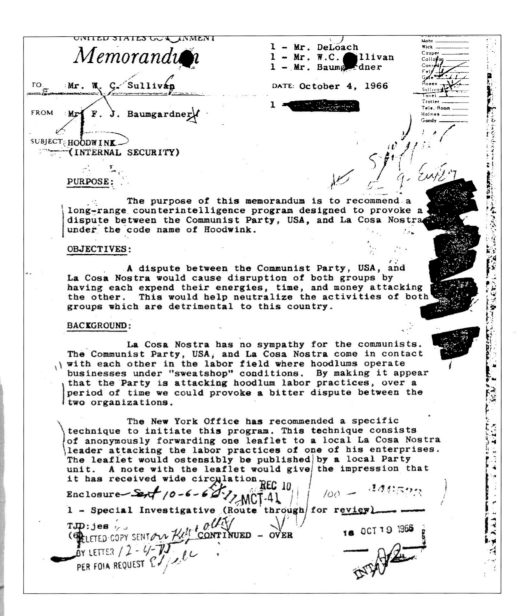

PIZZA CONNECTION

The Pizza Connection was one of the largest FBI criminal investigations in United States history. The prosecution, which took place between October 24, 1985 and March 2, 1987, centered on a mafia plot to distribute heroin and launder the proceeds using a chain of pizza parlors as a front. It is estimated that $1.6 billion worth of illegal drugs were brought into the United States between 1975 and 1984, when a number of the key drug traffickers were arrested in a Palermo, Italy, airport trying to smuggle in huge amounts of cash. The arrest resulted in a major crackdown primarily involving the FBI and New York City Police, with cooperation from Italian police. In 1984, the FBI closed the net; thirty-eight people were arrested and twenty-two stood trial. Later, many received prison sentences of up to forty-five years. The lead prosecutor was future FBI director, Louis Freeh.

The Apalachin Mob Convention

Some say the notorious Apalachin mob convention was organized by Vito Genovese in order to mend fences within LCN. The meeting took place after a long and deadly killing spree. The mob usually settled disagreements by killing the opposition. When Vito Genovese attempted unsuccessfully to assassinate fellow mobster Frank Costello, Genovese became a marked man. Albert Anastasia hated Genovese and put a contract out on him. With Genovese gone, Anastasia would become the boss of bosses. Genovese, however, decided the best defense was a good offense, and he struck first. He discovered that one of Anastasia's soldiers was eager to get rid of his boss. On the morning of October 25, 1957, Anastasia was gunned down in a barber's chair. The hit men were never identified, although it was alleged they were two of the underworld's most dangerous men, Joseph (Crazy Joey) Gallo and his equally crazy brother Larry. Carlo Gambino moved into Anastasia's slot, and Genovese remained boss of bosses. Genovese solidified his position by calling the meeting in upstate New York.

UNRECORDED COPY FILED IN

UNITED STATES GOVERNMENT

Memorandum

TO : DIRECTOR, FBI (100-446533)

DATE: 7/31/68

FROM : SAC, NEW YORK (100-159407) (C)

SUBJECT: HOODWINK
(INTERNAL SECURITY)

ReBulet to New York, dated 6/11/68, in which the Bureau requested the New York and Philadelphia Offices to submit recommendations and observations as to whether this operation should continue.

A review of captioned matter by the New York Office (NYO) reflects that since the Fall of 1966, the Bureau has been endeavoring to implement a long-range counterintelligence operation, the general objective of the operation being to disrupt the Communist Party, USA (CP,USA) by setting it against the La Cosa Nostra (LCN) and other organized criminal elements. Part of the objective would also be to cause subversive and criminal elements to expend their energies attacking each other.

The NYO recommends that this operation be discontinued at this time for the following reasons:

1. Since the Fall of 1966 a variety of counterintelligence actions have been undertaken in this program, however, none have produced substantial tangible results.

2. The NYO knows of no present issues which might precipitate a clash between the CP,USA and LCN.

3. Historically, the CP,USA is not interested in reformism and it does not take a stand on civic issues which do not lend themselves to exploitation consistent with CP aims and objectives.

4. Over the past several years, the CP,USA has not seen fit to undertake public criticism of labor elements which

(3) - Bureau (RM)
   (1 - 92-6054) (LCN)
1 - Philadelphia (100-49252) (INFO) (RM)
2 - New York (41)
   (1 - 92-2300-Sub P) (LCN) (221)

1o AUG 2 1968

JJE:ptp
(6)

57 AUG 8 1968

INT SEC

Buy U.S. Savings Bonds Regularly on the Payroll Savings Plan

Two years after Hoodwink was launched, the FBI's New York office recommended shutting it down. This declassified memo explains why. *FBI*

Umberto's Clam House in Little Italy, where "Crazy" Joe Gallo ate his final meal. The war in Vietnam and the violent political atmosphere of the 1960s bled itself into the 1970s, as various crime families in gangland went to war against each other. Like their 1930s fathers, the modern mob saw an advantage to media coverage and began vying for headlines and television. Two mortal enemies, Gallo and Joseph Colombo, became New York City media targets. Both flashy killers would meet brutal and well-publicized endings. After Crazy Joe Gallo was shot dead in Umberto's Clam House, his sister vowed the streets would flow with blood. Over the next few weeks, at least twenty-seven people were shot, some of whom were believed to be innocent bystanders. *Henry M. Holden*

At the 1957 Upstate New York meeting of the crime families, Buffalo was represented by Steve Magaddino. The mob was getting careless and becoming more public. In 1952, federal agents noted a meeting of mafiosi in the Florida Keys. In 1954, federal agents reported another mafia gathering in Los Angeles, one outside Chicago, and another in Mountainside, New Jersey. In May 1956, a mafia meeting in New York drew thirty-five known criminals. In October 1956, another meeting of mafiosi took place in Binghamton, New York. On November 10, 1957, another meeting took place in Livingston, New Jersey. Then, just four days later, the big one took place in Apalachin, New York. *Library of Congress*

Sixty mafiosi from around the country attended the convention at the home of Joseph Barbara in Apalachin, New York. An alert New York State Police trooper noticed the influx of Cadillacs. The large number of mobsters from all over the United States got the FBI's attention. The local police were so fascinated by the flood of limousines into the small town that they collected license plate numbers and set up a roadblock as the mafiosi were leaving. Police rounded up, identified, and searched the gangsters as they attempted to leave the Barbara property. More may have attended but escaped police by fleeing through a wooded area. In November 1960, an appeals court nullified earlier conspiracy convictions against twenty men who attended the 1957 meeting.

The police presence at the Apalachin conference destroyed the credibility of Genovese in the eyes of the other mobsters. He suffered further disgrace when the government put him away for fifteen years on narcotics violations. In the wake of the conference, the FBI identified all the individuals in attendance at the meeting. It confirmed the existence of a national organized-crime network. At that time, Hoover looked to the Hobbs Act of 1951 for federal authority to combat racketeering.

Hoover ordered his field offices to develop information on crime bosses in their areas of jurisdiction. This "Top Hoodlum Program" produced a wealth of information about organized crime activities. In a 1960 letter to all law enforcement officials, Hoover wrote, "If we must, let us learn a lesson from the barons of the underworld who have shown that cooperative crime is profitable—cooperative law enforcement can be twice as effective."

A July 1958 monograph on the mafia, prepared by the FBI, stated that the mafia "is a highly clandestine operation, most difficult to penetrate by informants . . . . The present day Mafia controls crime to the extent that it dominates certain criminal operations wherever it can, pushing crime to the limit beyond which further trespass would mean destruction of the productive society upon which it feeds or a popular rising against it in a wave of reprisals that would encompass the destruction of its elements." In this kind of environment, Hoover's paid informant strategy would not be enough.

Joe Valachi Rats Out the Mob

It was not until the FBI persuaded mob insider Joseph Valachi to testify that the public learned firsthand of the nature of LCN. Valachi was a mafioso from the 1930s. He took part in the November 1930 assassination of two mafiosi of an opposing family and was involved in gambling, loan-sharking, and other crimes, including drug running. In the mid-1950s, he was arrested several times on drug running but managed to avoid serious penalties. However, on November 19, 1959, Valachi's luck ran out. He was sentenced to fifteen

BLACKMAIL

The term "blackmail" comes from the extortion letters sent to prosperous members of the Italian-American community. The letters were usually "signed" by the imprint of a hand in black ink.

Paul Castellano made two fatal errors. He failed to show up for the funeral of his underboss, and he named his driver as underboss, leapfrogging more-senior gangsters. This gave John Gotti the motive and support to get rid of Castellano. Castellano had just arrived at Sparks Steakhouse in New York City, but unlike many of his predecessors, he did not enjoy a last meal. He was shot down along with his new underboss outside the restaurant on December 16, 1985. John Gotti, who was supposed to meet Castellano there, watched the execution from across the street. The public double murder sent a message to other mobsters. It was a bold bid for power, and it said mobsters could die anytime and anywhere. *Henry M. Holden*

years in prison. In 1962, he received another twenty-five years in prison for a related drug conviction.

Valachi, approaching age sixty, expected to spend the rest of his life behind bars. He was determined to be a stand-up guy until the mafia turned on him.

Also serving time in the same prison was Vito Genovese. Genovese suspected someone had ratted him out. His suspicions eventually focused on Valachi. Genovese reportedly ordered Valachi killed. Officials believe Valachi was tipped off through the prison grapevine, but Valachi says it was by a Genovese kiss of death. Believing he was acting in self-defense, Valachi killed another prisoner in June 1962. He pleaded guilty to the homicide and sought protection from federal authorities.

The Department of Justice assigned his case to the FBI. After a number of interviews and briefings on current Justice Department information on mafia networks outside of New York, Valachi appeared before the McClellan Committee. In 1962, Valachi became a major media star. After turning informant, the Justice Department used him to communicate the details of LCN to the American public. Valachi's testimony before the Senate committee outlined the events of the so-called Castellamarese War of the early 1930s and Valachi's own dealings with mafia families in New York.

Valachi set a precedent by becoming the first "made" member of LCN to cooperate with law enforcement. Valachi testified that he was a soldier in what he referred to as the "Genovese Family." In September 1963, Valachi revealed that Vito Genovese was the boss of bosses of the American mafia. In doing so, he had violated one of the mafia's basic laws—*omertá*—keeping silent about the mob's business. To violate this law was a certain death sentence. Valachi returned to

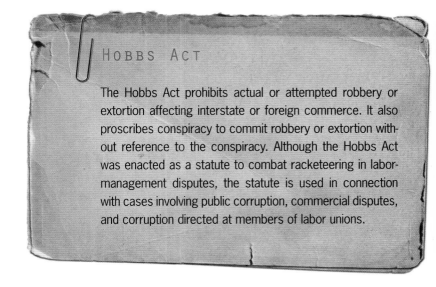

HOBBS ACT

The Hobbs Act prohibits actual or attempted robbery or extortion affecting interstate or foreign commerce. It also proscribes conspiracy to commit robbery or extortion without reference to the conspiracy. Although the Hobbs Act was enacted as a statute to combat racketeering in labor-management disputes, the statute is used in connection with cases involving public corruption, commercial disputes, and corruption directed at members of labor unions.

FBI undercover agent Joe Pistone never rose above the lower ranks of the mafia organization, but he caused it serious damage. When he retired from undercover work in 1981, he had collected enough information to dispatch 120 mafiosi to prison for life. His story became the Hollywood movie *Donnie Brasco*. Left to right: Special Agents Jerry Loar, Joseph Pistone, Jerry McEttee, Edgar Robb, and Doug Fenci. *FBI*

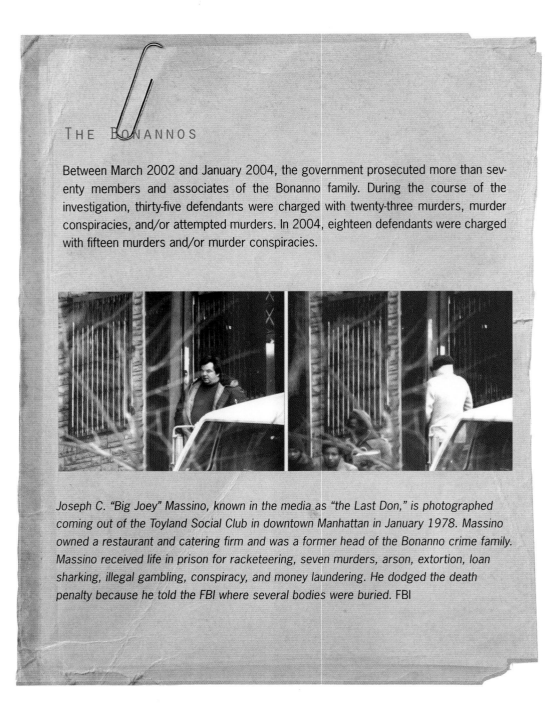

THE BONANNOS

Between March 2002 and January 2004, the government prosecuted more than seventy members and associates of the Bonanno family. During the course of the investigation, thirty-five defendants were charged with twenty-three murders, murder conspiracies, and/or attempted murders. In 2004, eighteen defendants were charged with fifteen murders and/or murder conspiracies.

Joseph C. "Big Joey" Massino, known in the media as "the Last Don," is photographed coming out of the Toyland Social Club in downtown Manhattan in January 1978. Massino owned a restaurant and catering firm and was a former head of the Bonanno crime family. Massino received life in prison for racketeering, seven murders, arson, extortion, loan sharking, illegal gambling, conspiracy, and money laundering. He dodged the death penalty because he told the FBI where several bodies were buried. FBI

Frank Coppa (left), a Bonanno captain, had an arrest record in New York State ranging from 1962 to 2000. On March 1, 2000, a grand jury indicted Frank Coppa and eighteen others on counts of racketeering, conspiring to commit securities fraud, and money laundering. On September 24, 2001, Coppa pled guilty to securities fraud conspiracy. "Big Joey" Massino was not as lucky; he's in for life. Massino was upset with Gotti's flamboyance, and informants testified that he remarked, "John set this thing of ours back a hundred years." *FBI*

BUGGING THE MOB

The mafia, the FBI discovered, was difficult to penetrate using undercover operatives. The undercover agent had to be of Sicilian descent and speak the dialect to be accepted. Thus, the FBI turned to another surveillance technique: wiretapping.

Invasive surveillance, planting bugs, and electronic surveillance may be the most dangerous jobs for an FBI agent, next to undercover work. In a criminal or terrorist investigation, the likelihood is that everyone under surveillance is carrying a gun. If the agent is caught in the act, he or she may be shot as an intruder, since the suspect does not know the person is an agent. If the agent's identity is revealed, he could still be shot for being an FBI agent, since the criminal would look upon him as the enemy.

Invasive surveillance takes thorough planning. It relies on confidential informants and knowing not only the habits of the residents of the building under surveillance but also of the surrounding neighborhood. It begins with weeks of external passive surveillance, weeks of photographing the suspects and their visitors, and keeping accurate logs of all who come and go.

When the FBI is reasonably certain the location is safe at a certain time or day, an agent must obtain a court order, usually restricted to a specific length of time, often thirty or sixty days. The FBI can enter and leave the premises anytime during that period to plant or remove the bugs and to retrieve audio or video recording devices. After the court order expires, agents are not allowed to continue the surveillance or enter the premises unless a judge has signed a new warrant.

While there are rules for surveillance, the methods are usually dictated by the location and the target. In general, advance teams of spotters have surrounded the targeted location to determine it is clear of suspects. The entry team will use various methods to enter the premises and plant the monitoring devices. The agents inside and outside are all in radio communication. When all the bugs are in place, the entry team will exit the premises if it is safe to do so. This type of surveillance was instrumental in bringing down John Gotti.

FBI agents planted an eavesdropping device in this statuette of Alvin (inset photo), a cartoon rodent from the fictional children's recording group, "The Chipmunks." The agents correctly reasoned that the mob would look under and inside telephones, table lamps, and light fixtures, but never inside this child's toy. FBI

A John (Junior) Gotti photo taken by an FBI surveillance team. John Gotti received life in prison without the possibility of parole. He served only ten years before succumbing to head and neck cancer on June 10, 1992. True to the mafia code, he never asked for favors and never bargained with information. In the end, his ego and carelessness led to his downfall. In his place, it is alleged that his son, John Jr., became boss. The government tried Junior Gotti twice on various charges, but the juries failed to convict him. *FBI*

THE GAMBINOS

Since John Gotti's conviction, the FBI has helped prosecute more than 225 Gambino family members who have been convicted and sent to jail, including eleven bosses and top lieutenants.

This Federal Bureau of Investigation mugshot of John Gotti was taken December 11, 1990. In 1986, the FBI estimated that the mafia families across the United States included 1,700 made members and many thousands of soldiers. The mafia still remains the dominant force in the American organized crime syndicate. It continues to draw its membership from those of Italian descent, but affiliated organizations include gangs and individuals of every ethnic background. *FBI*

federal prison in protective custody and died of a heart attack on April 3, 1971.

On the heels of Valachi's disclosures, Congress passed two laws to strengthen federal racketeering and gambling statutes. The Omnibus Crime Control Act of 1968 provided for the use of court-ordered electronic surveillance in the investigation of certain specified violations. It was followed by the Racketeer Influenced and Corrupt Organizations (RICO) Act in 1970.

RICO Act

Passed on October 15, 1970, RICO is a federal law that provides for extended penalties for criminal acts performed as part of an ongoing criminal organization such as La Cosa Nostra. One of its main tools for successful prosecution is wiretapping.

Using RICO, the FBI now plans long-term surveillance of entire organizations rather than specific individuals, as local law enforcement would do. "We pursue targets which have direct ties to significant national and international criminal enterprises, and systematically take those enterprises apart," said one agent. "We also have to remain flexible enough to pursue regional organized crime groups who are conducting significant racketeering activity; and we must ensure that our targets are permanently dismantled, or significantly disrupted."

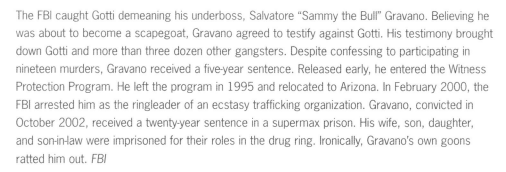

The FBI caught Gotti demeaning his underboss, Salvatore "Sammy the Bull" Gravano. Believing he was about to become a scapegoat, Gravano agreed to testify against Gotti. His testimony brought down Gotti and more than three dozen other gangsters. Despite confessing to participating in nineteen murders, Gravano received a five-year sentence. Released early, he entered the Witness Protection Program. He left the program in 1995 and relocated to Arizona. In February 2000, the FBI arrested him as the ringleader of an ecstasy trafficking organization. Gravano, convicted in October 2002, received a twenty-year sentence in a supermax prison. His wife, son, daughter, and son-in-law were imprisoned for their roles in the drug ring. Ironically, Gravano's own goons ratted him out. *FBI*

(left to right) Vito Rizzuto (known as the John Gotti of Canada), Gerlando Sciacca, Giovanni Ligammari (subject of the Pizza Connection, all Bonanno family captains) and Joseph Massino, outside the Capri Motor Lodge in Whitestone, Queens (New York) on May 6, 1981. This photo was taken the day after the triple murder of three Bonanno family captains. The murder was featured in the film *Donnie Brasco*. Sciacca was shot dead in March 1999. The bodies of Ligammari and his thirty-seven-year-old son, Pietro, were found hanged. The killers left no note, and investigators ruled it a double suicide. As of 2007, Rizzuto awaits trial in New York City, and Massino is in for life. *FBI*

The RICO Act allowed prosecutors to go after organized crime groups for all of their diverse criminal activities, without the crimes being linked by an individual or an all-encompassing conspiracy. RICO allowed the FBI to develop cases that, in the 1980s, put almost all the major traditional crime family heads in prison.

John "Dapper Don" Gotti

By the mid-1980s, the FBI and other federal agencies, with the help of local law enforcement, began to dismantle organized crime families across the country. In the midst of their effort, John Gotti emerged and captured the public's attention in what seemed like the last chance for the flamboyant gangster to leave his mark in the annals of the American mafia. Gotti became a star of the media. He was an impeccable dresser, earning the nickname "Dapper Dan" for his expensive and fashionable attire and for being a gentleman to the ladies. Gotti was also known as the "Teflon

When the FBI had enough evidence on Paul Castellano and the other heads of the five New York families, agents arrested them. All made bail and later went on trial. "Big" Pauley Castellano's house on Staten Island, New York, was one of the FBI's big challenges. There was always somebody at home, either Castellano, his secretary, housekeepers, or others. Two vicious Dobermans patrolled the outside in the event that someone beat the electronic security system also surrounding the house. The FBI, unknown to Castellano, was watching an operation dubbed "the Pizza Connection." The FBI had identified Castellano as a major player in the operation. For three years, agents gathered evidence on his movement in heroin and cocaine, and spent four months "inside" his house. *FBI*

Anthony "Fat Tony" Salerno became the Genovese family's *capo* from 1981 to 1987. In 1976, Angelo Lonardo (underboss of the Cleveland LCN) and Jack Licavoli traveled to New York to pay respects to Tony Salerno. When Joe Nardi ordered the murder of Leo Moceri, Licavoli and Lonardo went to talk to Salerno to obtain his help in murdering Danny Greene and John Nardi. Nardi and Greene had made a trip to New York to see Paul Castellano about a meat business. Salerno agreed to speak to Castellano and to have Nardi and Greene murdered on their next trip to New York. Nardi and Greene never made a second trip to New York. Salerno was jailed in 1987 on racketeering charges and was replaced by Vincent "the Chin" Gigante. Salerno died in prison from natural causes on July 27, 1992, at age eighty. *FBI*

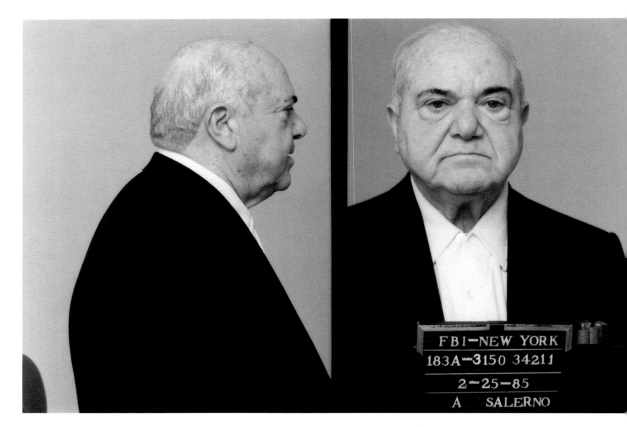

Don" because he escaped so many convictions due to hung juries. He became the icon of the American gangster and lived up to that status by being a cold-blooded killer. There were celebrity mobsters in the past, but few organized crime figures since Al Capone have captured the attention of the public as did John Gotti.

Gotti left behind a bloody trail of bodies and embarrassed law enforcement agencies. Putting him away became an obsession for federal prosecutors. With all the mafia chieftains away for long prison terms, federal prosecutor Rudy Giuliani found a new witness to testify against Gotti: Sammy "the Bull" Gravano. Gravano testified that he had helped Gotti set up the murders of Paul Castellano and his driver, Thomas Bilotti, and that he had watched it from across the street with Gotti.

Gotti was tried by a jury on April 2, 1992, for thirteen counts of murder, conspiracy to commit murder, loan sharking, racketeering, obstruction of justice, illegal gambling, and tax evasion. When the jury brought in a guilty verdict, the prosecutor said, "The Teflon Don is covered with Velcro—all the charges stuck."

Street Gang Warfare: El Rukins

The heavily damaged organized crime syndicate of the 1980s did not allow the FBI a breather. Instead, a new, and perhaps more deadly, gang structure arose: terrorist street gangs. In the mid-1980s, heroin and cocaine were flooding American cities. Dangerous street gangs had taken over large swaths of inner city neighborhoods. One in particular posed a grave danger for America, a vicious gang called "El Rukins." The FBI would team up with state and local police to bring them down. In the process, they discovered a frightening terrorist plot.

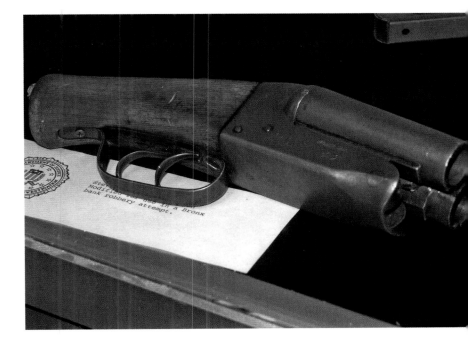

A favorite weapon of the mobster was the sawed-off shotgun. While some gangsters in the 1930s used machine guns, many preferred the *lupara*, a double-barreled shotgun originally carried by estate guards in Italy to shoot wolves. *FBI*

When John Gotti moved his operation to the Ravenite Social Club, it gave the FBI the opportunity to put a video surveillance team on him. They set up a $100,000 video camera in an apartment building two blocks away. They had a line-of-sight view right to the front door of the club and recorded the parade of mobsters in and out of the club. This activity proved a criminal organization was at work. On February 26, 1988, two FBI agents planted an audio bug inside the Ravenite. Eventually, the FBI caught Gotti on tape allegedly discussing a number of murders and other criminal activities. *FBI*

In the early 1990s, Vincent "the Chin" Gigante, the boss of New York's Genovese family, was indicted and charged with ordering six murders, including that of Gambino boss John Gotti (which failed), and conspiring in three others. Gigante was also charged with labor racketeering and extortion. He feigned mental illness by never changing out of his pajamas and robe and always mumbling to himself (earning him the nickname the "odd father"). Gigante had his trial postponed twice, but in June 1997, after being ruled mentally competent, his trial began. Gigante received twelve years in prison and three additional years for lying about his mental illness. Because of this investigation, twenty other LCN members went down, and $4 million in LCN assets were forfeited. Gigante died in prison in 2005 of complications from heart disease. *FBI*

The FBI formed the Organized Crime Drug Enforcement Task Force to break the deadly grip El Rukins had on Chicago. The FBI could not break the cycle of drugs and violence or get inside. Then, in May 1985, an informer gave agents a tip. Several El Rukins members, wanted for murder, had fled Chicago and were hiding in Cleveland. The FBI and Cleveland police raided the house and arrested several El Rukins members. Among them was a general named Anthony Summner. Jeff

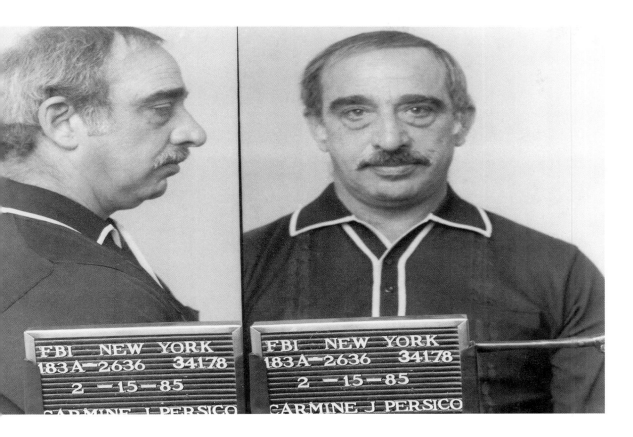

The New York–based Colombo family of LCN had approximately 120 made members and more than 450 associates. Following the shooting of boss Joseph Colombo in June 1971, Carmine "the Snake" Persico Jr. took over leadership of the group. Persico was able to lead the group until 1986, when a series of racketeering convictions resulted in his sentence to prison for 139 years. While in prison, he was found guilty of twenty additional counts and sentenced to another 100 years to run consecutively. *FBI*

WANTED BY THE FBI

RICO-PROPERTY CRIMES OF VIOLENCE; MURDER; HOBBS ACT-ARMORED CARRIER; BANK ROBBERY; ARSON

SURRENDERED

Photo taken 9/90   Photo taken 6/96

PAUL RAGUSA

DESCRIPTION

Born, December 25, 19__, Brooklyn, New York; Height, 5'10"; Weight, 160 pounds; Build, slender; Hair, brown; Eyes, brown; Complexion, medium; Race, White; Sex, male; Nationality, American (Italian); Recently had cosmetic surgery on his nose. Occupation, None known.

CAUTION

PAUL RAGUSA IS BEING SOUGHT FOR HIS PARTICIPATION IN AN ARMORED CARRIER ROBBERY IN WHICH TWO GUARDS WERE SHOT. RAGUSA IS BELIEVED TO BE A RINGLEADER OF A GROUP WITH TIES TO AN ORGANIZED CRIME FAMILY. RAGUSA IS PRONE TO VIOLENCE. RAGUSA HAS PREVIOUS ARRESTS ON WEAPONS CHARGES.

CONSIDERED ARMED AND EXTREMELY DANGEROUS

ADDITIONAL INFORMATION MAY BE FOUND ON THE FBI INTERNET PAGE http://www.fbi.gov.

FBI Ten Most Wanted Fugitive: September 1997.

Paul Ragusa was a bad boy associated with organized crime. He was on the FBI's Ten Most Wanted Fugitives list for five months. In spite of his armed-and-dangerous tag, he surrendered to face eighteen-month-old racketeering charges brought in June 1996 that included violent armed robberies. Law enforcement arrested his sister on drug charges and threatened to bring in other family members. To spare his family, Ragusa surrendered on January 30, 1998. *FBI*

Fort, the head of El Rukins, had set the gang up with twenty-one quasi-generals. If any one of the twenty-one generals tried a power play, the other twenty were in a position to let Fort know, and Fort would retaliate with deadly force. If the FBI could turn Summner, they may gain valuable intelligence on how the gang operated.

During questioning, Summner implicated himself in a double homicide in Chicago and would face serious charges. If the attorney general would reduce his charges, Summner would cooperate. What Summner revealed was shocking: the gang was well-organized and had hundreds of members and an arsenal of military-grade weapons.

The FBI thought it had taken Fort out of action with a long prison term, but according to Summner, Fort was coordinating and directing the gang's activities from a pay telephone in the prison. This information provided a major break for the FBI. Agents got a court-approved wiretap and listened in on his phone calls. If the phone conversations yielded probable cause, the FBI could raid the El Rukins headquarters. However, what they heard stunned them. Fort was talking in code—strings of words that made no sense. The agents believe Fort was discussing drug deals but had no frame of reference to understand what Fort and his

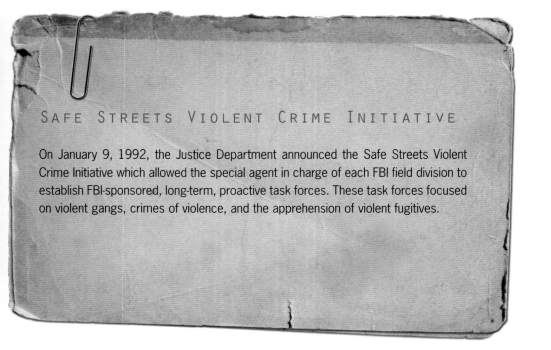

SAFE STREETS VIOLENT CRIME INITIATIVE

On January 9, 1992, the Justice Department announced the Safe Streets Violent Crime Initiative which allowed the special agent in charge of each FBI field division to establish FBI-sponsored, long-term, proactive task forces. These task forces focused on violent gangs, crimes of violence, and the apprehension of violent fugitives.

gang were talking about. Before the FBI could take down the gang, the agents had to break the code. Unfortunately, cryptologists at the FBI Laboratory were not having any luck.

The Chicago Police Department routinely made daily contact with the gang just to let them know they were being watched. The police decided to set a trap. A police officer would stop by, talk to the gang while Fort was on the phone, and see if the information was being passed on to Fort in real time and in a code. It was.

Breaking the code was a slow process. After two months, the FBI had barely scratched the surface. Agents realized that other phones in the gang's headquarters were part of the operation. When the FBI tapped the other phones, the agents discovered that the gang was using a new code.

Slowly, the agents pieced together phrases and discovered something strange. There were references to travel to Libya. That got everybody's attention. The United States believed Libya was sponsoring terrorism. A well-armed drug gang combined with foreign terrorists could present a deadly threat to national security.

The FBI went back over the tapes and discovered a plot to use Libyan money to destroy an airliner in the United States. The FBI called in the Joint Terrorism Task Force (JTTF). The JTTF took over and, together with Chicago police, set up surveillance to monitor the physical movements of the gang. They compared the movements with what they were hearing on the phones, enabling them to crack the new code. The calls, agents discovered, involved the gang's normal drug business and a plot between El Rukins and the Libyan government. The wiretaps revealed that several gang members had visited Libya. Based on the violent history of the gang, the FBI realized that an act of terrorism in the United States by the gang, financed from Libya, was a strong possibility.

On April 2, 1986, a bomb exploded on TWA Flight 840 between Rome and Athens. Four Americans were killed and nine injured. The FBI suspected President Mu'ammar al-Qadhafi of Libya was responsible.

The FBI had successfully translated the gang's code. Two days later, agents overheard Fort and one of his generals talking about bombing a plane in thirty days. Leo Mac Anderson and Rico Crenshaw, two of Fort's generals, were to travel to Libya to convince Qadhafi that they could do the same in the United States. Fort suggested that the two bring newspaper clippings of El Rukins' exploits to prove they were violent enough to commit acts of terror.

Fort instructed Mac Anderson and Crenshaw to meet the Libyan officials in Panama. On May 3, the two left for Panama, under the surveillance of the JTTF team. In Panama, the two were seen entering the Libyan Embassy. On May 10, the pair returned to the United States. The following day, the task force intercepted telephone conversations between Fort, Mac Anderson, and Crenshaw. They told Fort that the Libyans agreed to finance a terror operation and would deposit the money in a

Panamanian bank in the United States. Weeks went by, but the money did not appear. Fort decided the gang had to blow up an airplane or government building using a shoulder-fired missile to show the Libyans that they deserved respect.

The FBI finally had a way to take down the plot. Fort wanted to buy military-grade weapons, and the FBI would become El Rukins' supplier. An undercover agent made contact with one of El Rukins' generals from whom the agent had bought drugs in the past. They set up another drug buy at which point the undercover agent suggested he had a military weapons contact. The general was interested and told the agent what they needed: M70 Law Rockets capable of destroying a tank, a building, or a low-flying airliner. The FBI could not allow the gang to obtain the weapon on the open market, but it could build a dummy rocket to sell to the gang. The undercover agent negotiated a price of $1,800.

The Bureau of Alcohol, Tobacco, and Firearms (BATF) built a dummy rocket missing the explosive charge. It also had a radio transmitter that enabled the agents to track the device.

On July 29, 1986, the task force began the operation. The sale of the rocket would take place in a hotel outside Chicago. It was a dangerous operation. Surveillance teams formed an outer perimeter. The FBI SWAT team formed an inner perimeter in and around the hotel. On July 31, agents from the FBI, BATF, and DEA deployed to the hotel.

The three suspects approached the hotel, met the undercover agent, and the sale went down. The generals gave the dummy rocket to a third, low-level gang member to take back to El Rukins headquarters. Along the way, the surveillance teams had him in sight. Suddenly, his vehicle broke down, and he pulled off the road. The two El Rukins generals who had been following stopped, transferred the rocket to their vehicle, and then transported it to an apartment building a few miles from their headquarters.

A week went by. Fort was convinced that the buy was not a setup and decided to buy five more rockets and to test one. At that point, the FBI would take down the organization. If it waited, Fort might have told his generals to test the rocket they had, which would have revealed to the gang that they had been set up.

The raid was successful. All the major players except for one were captured without incident. The member who escaped remained at large for nine years. When he was finally captured, he was sentenced to three consecutive life terms. The FBI recovered the dummy rocket before the gang discovered it was a dummy. Agents also seized more than forty heavy weapons from the apartment location. Crenshaw and Mac Anderson were sentenced to more than fifty years each. Jeff Fort, who was already in prison, received an additional eighty-year term. This case was the first instance in the history of the country where American citizens were convicted of trying to commit a terrorist act for a foreign government.

This autographed jersey worn by New York Yankee Mickey Mantle sold for $25,000. The only problem was that it was a forgery. The FBI has a special squad, the White Collar Crime Squad, that investigates these sorts of crimes. *FBI*

The defendants in one case participated in a large cocaine-distribution ring operating from several locations in Chicago where the purchasers could freebase or use the cocaine. Employees of the dope house worked eight-hour shifts, covering three shifts a day. During the investigation, members of the organization paid $63,000 in bribes to Chicago police officers, and an FBI agent acting undercover, to protect their operation and to fix pending narcotics cases in court. The officers received various gold rope chains and a gold bracelet studded in diamonds worth about $24,000. *FBI*

The Supergang

In the early 1990s, under the FBI's Safe Streets Violent Crime Initiative, the FBI teamed up with the Newark Police Department to battle street crime and find fugitives. The FBI began to notice the emergence of supergangs, structured groups that demanded discipline from their members and promised strength in numbers. They had officers, codes, and networks for drugs, guns, and support. They had studied the California Bloods and adopted that gang's language and thirty-one rules. A gang member marked for punishment was called "food"; killing a rival gang member was called "puttin' in work"; and "pushed" was the code word for a murder. Because initiation into the gang was difficult, it was next to impossible to get a male undercover agent into the gang. Each prospective member had to endure thirty-one seconds of the worst beating the members could deliver, and most prospective members had tattoos covering most of the exposed parts of their bodies.

This military-like hierarchy gave the FBI a new opportunity. RICO, once reserved for mafia cases, allowed the FBI to pursue gangs as criminal enterprises. If the gang members acted like mobsters, the thinking was that they could be prosecuted as mobsters under the RICO statute. If prosecutors could bundle together crimes committed over a period of years, the gang members, because of the enhanced RICO penalties, would live behind bars probably for the rest of their lives. To do this, however, they would have to dismantle the business of the gang.

As a pseudo-military organization, the New Jersey supergang decided it needed a name. They called themselves "Double ii" to tie into both Inglewood, New Jersey, the gang's birthplace, and Illtown, the street nickname for East Orange, where they ruled.

The FBI had to rely on paid informants' authorized bugs in the Double ii's hangout to gain evidence against the gang. A recording of a low-level gang member's conversation gave them the first piece of the puzzle they needed for prosecution: the names, the leadership structure, and the discussion of criminal activity, including bragging about having pushed people. It was the foundation of a racketeering charge but only the first step. The FBI needed proof of specific crimes, eyewitnesses, and a lot of luck.

The FBI cultivated one informant who had been a former resident of East Orange. The young man, called "Smith" (not his real name), had been convicted of a federal crime in North Carolina and was heading to East Orange for one last visit before he began his sentence. The FBI agent in North Carolina suggested to Smith that he cooperate with the FBI in New Jersey. Smith agreed. Over the next few months, Smith recorded more than 100 meetings and conversations between gang members.

At the same time, local police combing through the records of guns confiscated from Double ii members noticed that three of the guns had been purchased in Ohio. The FBI traced all three guns to a student called "Jones" (not his real name) who lived in Newark and attended an Ohio college. Confronted by the FBI, Jones admitted to having other students act as straw men and purchase the guns. Jones admitted selling the guns to a man called "J-Rock," later identified as an officer in the Double ii.

An informant told agents that when J-Rock read of the shooting of an innocent nineteen-year-old in the newspaper, he wanted the credit. Two years later, twenty-five-year-old J-Rock would get the credit, and he would admit in federal

---

THE LATIN KINGS

From January of 1998 through September 27, 2005, the Milwaukee chapter of the Latin Kings engaged in a series of violent activity, including murder, attempted murder; drug trafficking, kidnapping, arson, drive-by shootings, and intimidation of witnesses. Following a lengthy Milwaukee FBI investigation, forty-nine members of the south-side gang were charged in federal court. The indictment contains specific allegations regarding four murders and thirty-eight attempted murders. According to FBI agents who infiltrated the gang, the Latin Kings had an established hierarchy, requiring the payment of membership and chapter dues from drug trafficking and robberies.

Drug kingpin Rayful Edmond III owned this diamond watch. Just before he was arrested in 1989, Edmond gave the watch to his attorney in an effort to hide it from law enforcement. In 1996, the attorney died, and the estate finally admitted to possessing the watch. Edmond purchased the watch in 1988 as a standard Rolex for approximately $5,000. He then had it encrusted in diamonds worth $65,000. *FBI*

Federal law permits the government to seize property purchased by drug dealers with the proceeds of their drug sales. This Alaskan Kodiak bear is believed to be one of the largest of its species. A drug dealer used drug profits to fly to Alaska, where he shot the bear and had it mounted. Since the trip and the taxidermy of the bear were financed with drug money, the bear was seized. The total value of the trip and the taxidermy was $22,000. *FBI*

court to racketeering, murder, and cocaine distribution. He would face thirty years in prison.

Before J-Rock and nine officers of the Double ii would march off to prison, teams of agents would monitor the gang. The police had the evidence of individual crimes they could prosecute at anytime, but the FBI needed the evidence of a criminal enterprise, and to do that it would have to get closer.

When the FBI learned that two of the gang members had a falling out with the gang, agents sent an informant to buy guns from them. Once the sale went down, they picked up the seller. He quickly cooperated with the FBI and told them where the gang bought its drugs, how they were distributed, and where they stashed the drugs.

The FBI had the pieces of a gun-and-drug enterprise. Agents still needed someone who could penetrate the Double ii's leadership. They began picking up individual members and charging them with gun or drug distribution, enough to isolate them from each other in prison.

Eventually the FBI found its insider. The informant, "Zak," was an officer in the Double ii and was in jail. He realized that he would either die in jail or die in the street gang. He wanted to live. The FBI released Zak, and he went back to the neighborhood and reclaimed his ranking status. At a meeting, the gang discussed moving to a new location. They suspected the current location was bugged. Zak said he had a cousin who had just moved to a small one-room apartment, and he thought she might let them meet there.

His so-called cousin (an undercover FBI agent) agreed. The apartment had a hidden camera, and the FBI was now on the inside. During one recorded conversation, J-Rock bragged about his killing of the nineteen-year-old. He was just trying out his new gun, he claimed. Other gang members bragged and admitted killing rivals or innocent people in the wrong place at the wrong time.

On October 19, 2004, a racketeering indictment charged nineteen members and associates of the New Jersey Double ii and their Ohio gun supplier with multiple murders, attempted murders, murder conspiracies, armed robberies,

Pulitzer Prize–winning cartoonist Herbert Block, whose pen name was "Herblock," was one of numerous political cartoonists who earned distinction with their illustrated commentaries on Nixon and the Watergate affair. *The Herb Block Foundation*

The Internal Revenue Service investigated Spiro T. Agnew, vice president of the United States, along with Baltimore, Maryland, political figures in the 1970s for tax evasion. The FBI entered the investigation when additional criminal offenses were uncovered. The FBI's investigation revealed bribery, extortion, conspiracy, corruption, and interstate transportation in aid of racketeering. Mr. Agnew resigned as vice president because of the investigation. *Library of Congress*

and a three-year-long heroin distribution conspiracy. The usual RICO penalties were enhanced to a maximum of life in prison for those charged. Many of the gang members will serve at least thirty years before being eligible for parole. Some of the informants and witnesses were relocated and given new identities.

The Double ii gang members in East Orange, New Jersey, were responsible for at least twenty-seven murders and countless shootings, assaults, and drug deals. The same racketeering statutes that brought down the mob brought down the gangs in northern New Jersey.

Watergate

FBI Director J. Edgar Hoover died on May 2, 1972, six weeks before the infamous Watergate break-in, where five men were arrested photographing documents at the Democratic National Headquarters in the Watergate Office Building.

Their arrest eventually uncovered a White House–sponsored conspiracy against political opponents. The trail of collusion would lead to some of the highest officials in government. Attorney General John Mitchell, White House Counsel John Dean, White House Chief of Staff H. R. Haldeman, White House Special Assistant on Domestic Affairs John Ehrlichman, and President Nixon were all involved.

Republican Party officials had authorized the break-in. Within hours, the White House began efforts to cover up its role, and the new acting FBI director, L. Patrick Gray III, was drawn into the mix. The FBI began its investigation of the break-in, and when all the culprits were thought to be identified, Gray's questionable personal

The New York Times

"All the News That's Fit to Print"

LATE JERSEY EDITION

General news, P. 37; sports, P. 30. North: Partly cloudy, mild today; fair and cool tonight. Temp range 65-78. South: Mild, chance of a few showers today and tonight. Temp. range 67-80. Details on Page 66.

VOL. CXXIII....No. 42,566   © 1974 The New York Times Company   NEW YORK, FRIDAY, AUGUST 9, 1974   30c beyond 50-mile radius of New York City except Long Island, Higher in all delivery mail   000069   15 CENTS

NIXON RESIGNS

HE URGES A TIME OF 'HEALING'; FORD WILL TAKE OFFICE TODAY

'Sacrifice' Is Praised; Kissinger to Remain

By ANTHONY RIPLEY
Special to The New York Times

WASHINGTON, Aug. 8—Vice President Ford praised President Nixon tonight for "one of the greatest personal sacrifices for the country and one of the finest personal decisions on behalf of all of us as Americans."

Mr. Ford, who will take office as the 38th President at noon tomorrow, vowed to continue Mr. Nixon's foreign policy and announced that Secretary of State Kissinger had agreed to stay on in the new Administration.

"I pledge to you tonight, as

I will pledge to you tomorrow and in the future, my best efforts in cooperation, leadership and dedication to what's good for America and good for the world," he said.

The Vice President, who never sought the nation's highest office and disclaimed any intention of seeking it after Mr. Nixon's term, will be sworn in a private ceremony at the White House.

Thus will he become the first man to serve as President without being chosen by the American people in an election. Tomorrow night he will address the nation on radio and television. It is expected that he will speak at 6 P.M.

All day today the signs of the historic change were in the air, sensed by the crowds that gathered along Pennsylvania Avenue near the White House. Applause rang out from the crowds when Mr. Ford appeared briefly.

SPECULATION RIFE ON VICE PRESIDENT

Some Ford Associates Say Selecting a Successor Could Take Weeks

By CHRISTOPHER LYDON

Vice President Ford meeting with newsmen last night
Associated Press

President Nixon on TV as he announced his resignation
United Press International

POLITICAL SCENE SHARPLY ALTERED

Text of Mr. Ford's remarks appears on Page 2.

Rise and Fall
Appraisal of Nixon Career

By ROBERT B. SEMPLE Jr.

JAWORSKI ASSERTS NO DEAL WAS MADE

Says Nixon Did Not Ask for

The 37th President Is First to Quit Post

By JOHN HERBERS
Special to The New York Times

WASHINGTON, Aug. 8—Richard Milhous Nixon, the 37th President of the United States, announced tonight that he had given up his long and arduous fight to remain in office and would resign, effective at noon tomorrow.

Gerald Rudolph Ford, whom Mr. Nixon nominated for Vice President last Oct. 12, will be sworn in tomorrow at the same hour as the 38th President, to serve out the 895 days remaining in Mr. Nixon's second term.

Less that two years after his landslide re-election victory, Mr. Nixon, in a conciliatory address on national

Text of the address will be found on Page 2.

television, said that he was leaving not with a sense of bitterness but with a hope that his departure would start a "process of healing that is so desperately needed in America."

He spoke of regret for any "injuries" done "in the course of the events that led to this decision." He acknowledged that some of his judgments had been wrong.

The 61-year-old Mr. Nixon, appearing calm and resigned to his fate as a victim of the Watergate scandal, became the first President in the history of the Republic to resign from office. Only 10 months earlier his first Vice President, Spiro T. Agnew, became the first man to resign the Vice Presidency.

Contrast in Tone and Content

Mr. Nixon, speaking from the Oval Office, where his successor will be sworn in tomorrow, may well have delivered his most effective speech since the Watergate

In March 1974, a grand jury indicted seven White House officials for their roles in the Watergate coverup and named Nixon as an "un-indicted co-conspirator." The following month, Jaworski requested and Nixon released written transcripts of forty-two tapes. The conversations revealed the White House tried to thwart the investigation. Three tapes revealed that on June 23, 1972, Nixon had ordered the FBI to stop investigating the Watergate break-in. The tapes also showed that Nixon had helped direct the coverup of the administration's involvement (*New York Times* front page: August 9, 1974)..

The CIA-led burglary of the headquarters of the Democratic National Committee, in the Watergate Hotel complex, led to a scandal that would engulf Nixon's administration. The abuse of power led to the largest FBI investigation since the assassination of President Kennedy, involving over three hundred agents and fifty-one field offices. On July 29–30, 1974, the House Judiciary Committee approved three articles of impeachment. Nixon resigned on August 9, 1974. *Library of Congress*

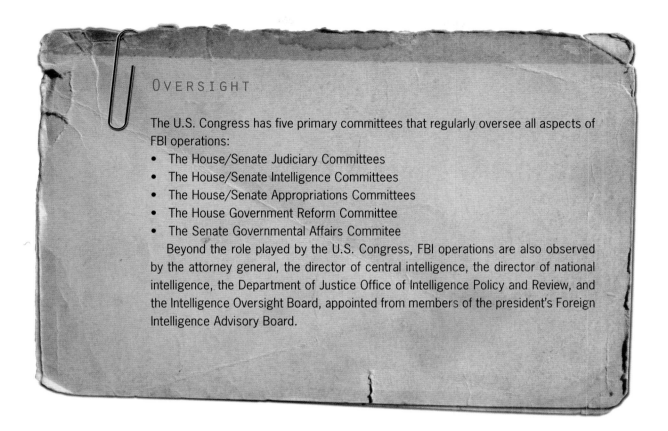

OVERSIGHT

The U.S. Congress has five primary committees that regularly oversee all aspects of
FBI operations:
- The House/Senate Judiciary Committees
- The House/Senate Intelligence Committees
- The House/Senate Appropriations Committees
- The House Government Reform Committee
- The Senate Governmental Affairs Commitee

   Beyond the role played by the U.S. Congress, FBI operations are also observed
by the attorney general, the director of central intelligence, the director of national
intelligence, the Department of Justice Office of Intelligence Policy and Review, and
the Intelligence Oversight Board, appointed from members of the president's Foreign
Intelligence Advisory Board.

role was revealed. President Nixon had nominated Gray as permanent director, but
his nomination was withdrawn after he admitted destroying documents given to him
by White House Counsel John Dean.

Deputy Attorney General William Ruckelshaus replaced Gray hours after he
resigned on April 27, 1973. Ruckelshaus remained until Clarence Kelley's appointment
as director on July 9, 1973.

In May 1973, a Senate committee opened hearings, and a series of startling
revelations followed. Dean testified that Mitchell had ordered the break-in and that
a major attempt was underway to hide White House involvement. Dean claimed the
president had authorized payments to the burglars to keep them quiet. Nixon's
administration denied this accusation.

Dean's testimony unlocked the entire investigation. On July 16, 1973, Dean told
the televised committee hearings that Nixon had ordered a taping system installed
in the White House to record all conversations, ostensibly to verify whatever was
said. Special prosecutor Archibald Cox subpoenaed eight tapes to confirm Dean's
testimony. Nixon refused to release the tapes, claiming national security issues. The
Federal District Court ruled against Nixon, and an appeals court upheld the decision.

On October 20, 1973, Nixon ordered Attorney General Elliot Richardson to
fire Cox. Richardson refused and resigned, as did his deputy, William
Ruckelshaus. Finally, the solicitor general, whose major function is to supervise
and conduct government litigation, fired Cox.

Nixon appointed another special prosecutor, Leon Jaworski, and gave the tapes
to District Court Judge John Sirica. Some subpoenaed conversations were missing,

President Gerald Ford appears at the House Judiciary Subcommittee hearings on his pardoning of former President Richard Nixon. On June 5, 1970, President Nixon ordered Hoover to assist House Minority Leader Gerald Ford's efforts to impeach Supreme Court Justice William O. Douglas. In 1953, Douglas had granted a temporary stay of execution to Ethel and Julius Rosenberg, the convicted atomic bomb spies. The basis for the stay was that the Rosenbergs had been sentenced to die by the judge without the consent of the jury. Chief Justice Fred M. Vinson took the unprecedented step of reconvening the Supreme Court before the execution date. The court ruled that the Rosenbergs' crime fell under the 1917 Espionage law, not the Atomic Secrets Act of 1946. The court set aside Douglas' stay. *Library of Congress*

and one tape had a mysterious gap of 18 1/2 minutes. Experts determined that the gap was the result of five separate erasures.

In May 1974, Jaworski requested sixty-four more tapes as evidence in the criminal cases. Nixon refused. On July 24, the Supreme Court voted 8–0 that Nixon must turn over the tapes.

Soon after the Watergate scandal hit the papers, the FBI uncovered a related group of illegal activities. Since 1971, a group called the White House Plumbers had conducted black-bag jobs for Nixon after Hoover had stopped such operations. A grand jury indicted Ehrlichman, White House Special Counsel Charles Colson, and others for organizing a break-in and burglary in 1971 to obtain damaging material against Daniel Ellsberg, who had published classified documents called the Pentagon Papers.

DEEP THROAT

Deep Throat is the well-known pseudonym for the secret source who leaked information about Nixon's role in the Watergate break-in. Deep Throat was an important source for *Washington Post* reporters Bob Woodward and Carl Bernstein, who together wrote a series of articles exposing the misdeeds of the Nixon administration. Some speculated that W. Mark Felt was Deep Throat, which Felt publicly confirmed on May 31, 2005.

At the time of Watergate, an internal FBI investigation in the midst of the scandal was unable to find evidence that Felt, an associate director of the FBI, had been a source for the *Washington Post*'s stories. Nixon and his aides were angered and frustrated by leaks from the FBI's investigation, and according to the White House tapes, they even discussed the possibility that Felt was the source.

Harold Bassett was the assistant director of the FBI's inspection division. Acting Director Gray had directed Bassett to investigate whether Felt or others in the FBI were leaking information. Bassett was unable to find any evidence to show that Felt was Deep Throat.

On June 10, 2005, Paul V. Daly, a former FBI executive, told the *Village Voice* newspaper that he had personal relationships with the people involved in the internal investigation. "These were men determined to protect the integrity of the FBI as an institution and to protect the integrity of a criminal investigation," he said. "I don't agree with what they did, but I believe they had a noble purpose."

Some of the people whom Deep Throat's revelations helped put in prison, such as Nixon's chief counsel Chuck Colson and G. Gordon Liddy, contended that Felt helped Woodward and Bernstein, at least in part, because Nixon passed over Felt in selecting a new head of the FBI after Hoover's death.

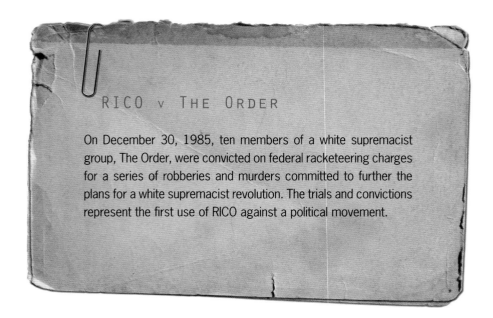

RICO v THE ORDER

On December 30, 1985, ten members of a white supremacist group, The Order, were convicted on federal racketeering charges for a series of robberies and murders committed to further the plans for a white supremacist revolution. The trials and convictions represent the first use of RICO against a political movement.

The FBI also discovered that the Nixon administration had solicited large sums of money in illegal campaign contributions to finance political espionage and to pay more than $500,000 to the Watergate burglars. White House aides testified that in 1972, they had falsified documents to make it appear that President John F. Kennedy had been involved in the 1963 assassination of President Ngo Dinh Diem of South Vietnam, and they had written false and slanderous documents accusing Senator Hubert H. Humphrey of sexual improprieties.

Gray and the FBI had failed to exercise political independence in the wake of the Watergate break-in. The Watergate hearings gave the media fodder for an anti-FBI campaign. A tape released in August, recorded only a few days after the break-in revelation, documented Nixon and Haldeman formulating a plan to block investigations by having the CIA claim (falsely) to the FBI that national security was involved.

The FBI's reputation would suffer collateral damage, a victim of the investigation. The *Washington Post* exposé of Watergate was a watershed. It destroyed the trust agreement by which the media kept quiet about sensitive information, such as the alleged sexual exploits of President John F. Kennedy and the alleged unethical dealings of President Lyndon B. Johnson.

The Watergate disgrace damaged the FBI and shook the faith of the American people in the presidency. It was also a supreme test of the Constitution. Throughout the ordeal, the constitutional system of checks and balances worked to prevent abuses, as the founding fathers had intended. Watergate proved that in a nation of laws, no one is above the law, not even a president.

ABSCAM

Director William Webster strengthened the FBI's response to white-collar crimes and attacked public corruption nationwide. The ABSCAM investigation in 1980 was an FBI sting that initially targeted trafficking in stolen property. It soon became a major operation of the FBI to trap corrupt public officials; up until 1970, only ten members of Congress had ever been convicted of accepting bribes. The investigation ultimately led to the conviction of a United States Senator, six members of the House of Representatives, the Mayor of Camden, New Jersey, members of the Philadelphia City Council, and an inspector for the Immigration and Naturalization Service.

The FBI set up Abdul Enterprises, Ltd. in 1978. FBI employees posed as Middle Eastern businessmen in videotaped talks with government officials where they offered money in return for political favors to a nonexistent sheik. A house in Washington, D.C., along with a yacht in Florida and hotel rooms in Pennsylvania and New Jersey, were used to set up meetings between various public officials and a mysterious Arab sheik named Abdul, who wanted to purchase asylum in the United States, involve them in an investment scheme, and help him in getting his money out of his country.

All of the ABSCAM convictions were upheld on appeal, although some judges criticized the tactics used by the FBI and lapses in FBI and Department of Justice supervision. In the wake of ABSCAM, Attorney General Civiletti issued *The Attorney General Guidelines for FBI Undercover Operations* on January 5, 1981. These guidelines were the first from an attorney general for undercover operations, and they formalized procedures necessary to conduct undercover operations. Congressional concern about sting operations persisted, creating numerous additional guidelines in the ensuing years: *The Reno Guidelines* (2001) and *The Ashcroft Guidelines* (2002). ■

The trial of the eight Nazi saboteurs was held behind closed doors in front of a military tribunal. The Long Island group had dressed in German marine uniforms but changed out of their uniforms and into civilian clothes before an unarmed coast guardsman discovered the group on the beach. The leader of the group attempted to bribe the sailor to forget what he had seen by giving him $260. The sailor accepted the bribe and returned to his station to sound the alarm. FBI

Chapter 7

SPYBUSTERS

Prior to World War I, the BOI had not investigated most suspected acts of domestic espionage and sabotage. As a result of the Soviet Nazi Pact of September 1939, a presidential directive instructed all FBI field offices to begin a review of their files for reliable contacts in order to prepare reports on "persons of German, Italian, and communist sympathies," as well as other persons "whose interest may be directed primarily to the interest of some other nation than the United States."

However, there is no evidence that either Congress in 1916 or Attorney General Harlan Stone in 1924 intended to authorize the establishment of a permanent domestic intelligence structure. In a memo dated October 20, 1938, Hoover advised the attorney general that the statute was "sufficiently broad to cover any expansion of the present intelligence and counter-espionage work which it may be deemed necessary to carry on."

Executive Order 9066 on February 19, 1942, created the internment of West Coast Japanese Americans. Because the FBI had arrested those whom it considered security threats, Hoover took the position that evacuating Japanese nationals and American citizens of Japanese descent from the West Coast to internment camps was unnecessary. The president and attorney general, however, supported the military assessment that internment was imperative. In 1942, the Roberts Commission revealed that the FBI was hampered in uncovering Japanese subversive activities. "The United States being at peace with Japan, restrictions imposed prevented resort [sic] to certain methods of obtaining the content of messages transmitted by telephone or radio telegraph over the commercial lines operating between Oahu and Japan." *Library of Congress*

When the president approved Hoover's plan for joint FBI–military domestic counterintelligence gathering, he was bypassing Congress and exercising what he felt was independent presidential power. Some people then and today would say he did not have that power.

A memo to Hoover from Clyde Tolson, dated October 30, 1939, indicated the FBI was also conducting confidential inquiries regarding "the various so-called radical and fascist organizations in the United States" for the purpose of identifying their "leading personnel, purposes and aims, and the part they are likely to play at a time of national crisis."

The FBI was homing in primarily on the Communist Party and the German-American Bund. The memo discussed the standard techniques of using informants, reviewing publications, and "soliciting and obtaining assistance and information from political émigrés and organizations which have for their purpose the maintenance of files of information bearing upon this type of study and inquiry," and "the attendance of mass meetings and public demonstrations."

A November 9, 1939, FBI memo made it clear that the FBI was beginning to prepare a list of specific individuals "on whom information is available indicating strongly that (their) presence at liberty in this country in time of war or national emergency would constitute a menace to the public peace and safety of the United States Government." The list included individuals "with strong Nazi tendencies" and "with strong Communist tendencies." Each person on the list had his citizenship status checked, and index cards were prepared summarizing the reasons for placing him on the list.

On December 6, 1939, Hoover issued a memo to all field offices instructing them to obtain information on such persons from "public and private records, confidential sources, newspaper morgues, public libraries, employment records, school records, et cetera." Agents were not to disclose the purpose of their investigation but only to say that the investigation was being made in connection with "the Registration Act requiring agents of foreign principals to register with the State Department."

The names were divided into two categories:

Category No. 1: Those to be apprehended and jailed immediately upon the outbreak of warfare between the United States and the government they serviced, supported, or owed allegiance to.

Category No. 2: Those to be watched at the start of hostilities and subsequent to the outbreak of hostilities because their previous activities indicated the possibility (but not the probability) that they would act in a manner against the best interests of the United States.

Hoover described this program as a "custodial detention" list. In a June 1940 memo, the field offices were reminded to furnish information on persons possessing "Communist, Fascist, Nazi, or other nationalistic backgrounds."

The potential targets included fifth column candidates for public offices, speakers at communist rallies, writers of communist books or articles, individuals "attending Communistic meetings where revolutionary preachings are given . . . demonstrations accompanied by violence, all members of the German-American Bund and similar organizations."

Attorney General Robert H. Jackson said in his address before the proceedings of the Federal-State Conference on Law Enforcement Problems of National Defense on August 5 and 6, 1940, that the primary targets of FBI intelligence surveillance

President Roosevelt signs a presidential directive on September 6, 1939. It read: "The attorney general has been requested by me to instruct the Federal Bureau of Investigation of the Department of Justice to take charge of investigative work in matters relating to espionage, sabotage, and violations of neutrality regulations. This task must be conducted in a comprehensive and effective manner on a national basis, and all information must be carefully sifted out and correlated in order to avoid confusion and irresponsibility . . . . All other law enforcement officers must promptly turn over to the nearest representative of the Federal Bureau of Investigation any information obtained by them relating to espionage, counterespionage, sabotage, subversive activities, and violations of the neutrality law." *Library of Congress*

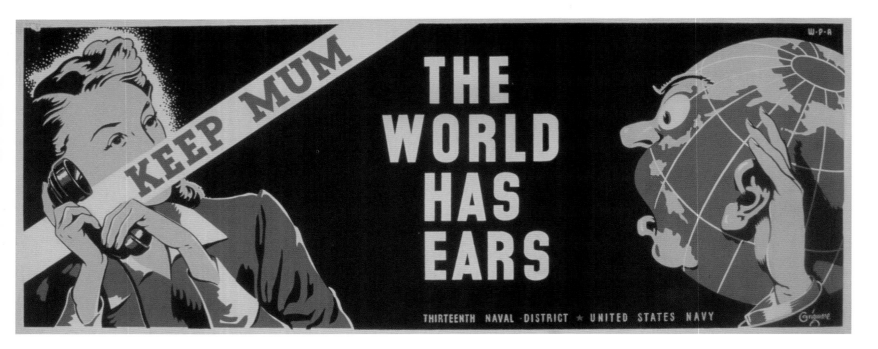

This poster urged any public or private agency or individuals with information about subversive activities to report it to the FBI. It warned Americans to "avoid reporting malicious gossip or idle rumors." Posters like this were distributed throughout the country. *Library of Congress*

under this program were active Nazis, fascists, and communists, but not legitimate business, labor, or religious activities.

Hoover summarized these subversive activities in a memorandum to the Justice Department on August 21, 1940: "The holding of official positions in organizations such as the German-American Bund and Communist groups; the distribution of literature and propaganda favorable to a foreign power and opposed to the American way of life; agitators who are adherents of foreign ideologies who have for their purpose the stirring up of internal strike [sic], class hatreds and the development of activities which in time of war would be a serious handicap in a program of internal security and national defense . . . ."

As a result, the Bureau gathered data about communist and fascist groups in its search for any subversive influence. At the opposite end of the political spectrum, the FBI reported the activities of numerous right-wing groups, such as the Christian Front and Christian Mobilizers (followers of Father Coughlin, a radical and prominent Catholic priest and spokesman on political and financial issues), the American Destiny Party, and others.

According to Don Whitehead, in *The FBI Story*, the scope of the information compiled through these investigations of alleged communist infiltration was enormous. The FBI estimated that by 1944, "almost 1,000,000 people knowingly or unknowingly had been drawn into Communist-Front activity."

The Duquesne-Sebold Case

On January 2, 1942, thirty-three members of a Nazi spy network headed by Frederick Joubert Duquesne received jail sentences totaling more than three hundred

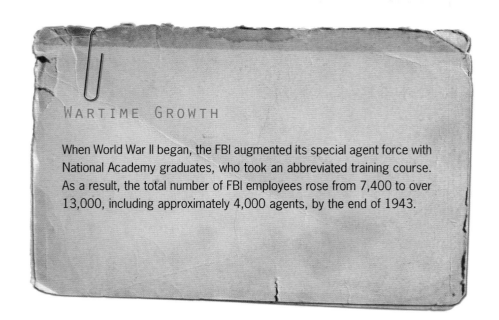

WARTIME GROWTH

When World War II began, the FBI augmented its special agent force with National Academy graduates, who took an abbreviated training course. As a result, the total number of FBI employees rose from 7,400 to over 13,000, including approximately 4,000 agents, by the end of 1943.

years. William Sebold, who had been recruited as a spy for Germany, was the key to the FBI's successful dismantling of the network through his work as a double agent for the United States. A native of Germany, Sebold served in the German army during World War I. He emigrated to the United States in 1921. In February 1936, he became a naturalized citizen. Sebold returned to Germany in February 1939 to visit his mother in Mulheim. When he arrived in Hamburg, a member of the Gestapo advised him that he would hear from them.

In September 1939, a Dr. Gassner visited Sebold in Mulheim and asked about military planes and equipment in the United States. He also asked Sebold to return to the United States as an agent for Germany. Subsequent visits by Dr. Gassner and a Dr. Renken—later identified as Major Nickolaus Ritter of the German Secret Service—persuaded Sebold to cooperate. He feared reprisals against family members still living in Germany.

Sebold claimed his passport had been lost, and he went to the American Consulate for a new one. While there, Sebold told Consulate personnel about his future role as a German agent and indicated he wanted to cooperate with the FBI.

According to Gestapo instructions, Sebold reported to Hamburg, where he learned how to prepare coded messages and microphotographs. He was given several microphotographs containing instructions for preparing codes and the type of information he was to transmit back to Germany. Sebold was to keep two of the microphotographs and deliver the others to German spies in the United States.

With the help of the FBI, Sebold established a residence in New York City under the alias "Harry Sawyer." The FBI established his cover as a consulting engineer in order to establish contacts with members of the spy ring. By selecting the office for Sebold, FBI agents could surreptitiously observe and film all meetings that took place there. In May 1940, a shortwave radio transmitter operated by FBI agents, posing as Sebold, established contact with a German shortwave station in Germany. This station served as a main channel of communication for

SUPERMAN...A SPY?

During World War II, everyone pitched in to the war effort. Even comic book characters like Bugs Bunny, Popeye, Captain America, Batman and Robin, and of course, Superman took up the fight. However, Superman also raised the suspicions of the FBI. On April 14, 1945, "The Science of Superman" ran in hundreds of nationally syndicated newspapers. It showed a science professor attempting to test Superman's powers using a cyclotron, or "atom-smasher." The scientist described the device as capable of bombarding "electrons at a speed of 100 million miles per hour and [was] charged with three million volts" of electricity.

Behind the scenes in government was the Manhattan Project, which developed the atomic bomb, and anything related to atomic energy was censored. By the time the government saw the comic strip, it was too late. The Secret Service stepped in to pressure DC Comics to pull the story. However, most papers had already published the strip. The FBI contacted Jerry Siegel, who they believed wrote the story. However, it was not Siegel but his ghostwriter, Alvin Schwartz, who wrote the story. Schwartz had learned of cyclotrons from a 1935 *Popular Mechanics* article. The War Department asked the newspaper syndicate to drop any stories related to atomic energy and requested that DC Comics monitor its own comic stories as well.

Afraid of capture, saboteurs George Dasch and Ernest Burger turned themselves in and assisted the FBI in locating the others. Attorney General Biddle and J. Edgar Hoover appealed to President Roosevelt to commute the death sentences of Dasch and Burger. Dasch received a thirty-year sentence and Burger received life. The remaining six were executed on August 8, 1942. In April 1948, President Truman granted executive clemency to Dasch and Burger on condition of deportation. *FBI*

FEDERAL BUREAU OF INVESTIGATION
UNITED STATES DEPARTMENT OF JUSTICE
J. EDGAR HOOVER, DIRECTOR

EIGHT GERMAN SABOTEURS

GEORGE JOHN DASCH   ERNEST PETER BURGER   RICHARD QUIRIN   HEINRICH HARM HEINCK

EDWARD KERLING   HERBERT HANS HAUPT   WERNER THIEL   HERMANN OTTO NEUBAUER

sixteen months. During that time, the FBI's radio station transmitted and received more than five hundred messages from Germany.

One of the German spies Sebold contacted was Frederick Joubert Duquesne. Duquesne was born in South Africa, immigrated to the United States in 1902, and became a citizen in 1913. Sebold established his first contact with Duquesne by letter and then met with him in Duquesne's office. During their initial meeting, Duquesne, who was concerned about the possibility of surveillance devices in his office, suggested they relocate to a nearby restaurant to exchange information about members of the espionage ring. Over the course of several months, Duquesne provided Sebold with information about the defense industry and the schedule of ships sailing to British ports, which the FBI altered and transmitted to Germany.

On one occasion, Duquesne provided Sebold with photographs and specifications for a new type of bomb being produced in the United States. He claimed he stole the material by breaking into a defense plant. Duquesne was eventually brought to trial, convicted, and served eighteen years in prison on espionage charges.

Nazi Saboteurs

One of the FBI's biggest counterintelligence victories came with the arrest of the Nazi saboteurs who landed on Long Island, New York, and Vero Beach, Florida. A clear sign of Germany's intention to engage in sabotage in the United States came with the apprehension of eight German saboteurs by the FBI. They were captured within two weeks of their landing from German submarines.

One group of four had landed on the beach at Amagansett, Long Island, on the night of June 13, 1942. A second group of four had landed on a beach a few miles below Jacksonville, Florida, on June 17, 1942.

Enemy Aliens in World War II

Declassified FBI records dated August 1, 1945, reveal that within seventy-two hours of the Japanese attack on Pearl Harbor, 3,486 Germans, Japanese, and Italian aliens were arrested and detained. These figures include 802 German and 1,271 Italian seamen who were apprehended before the United States entered the war.

There were 16,062 enemy aliens arrested during World War II. Of this number, 7,043 were German aliens—1,323 were released without a hearing; 1,225 were interned; 2,449 were paroled; 1,266 were released after a hearing; 691 were repatriated; and 47 died. Dispositions were unresolved in forty-two of the cases. The Japanese aliens arrested totaled 5,428. Of these, 1,532 were interned; 264 released without a hearing; 2,423 were paroled; 691 were released; 415 were repatriated; and 88 died. In fifteen of these cases, the dispositions were unresolved. The number of Italian aliens arrested was 3,567. Of this number, 367 were interned; 1,432 were released without a hearing; 861 were paroled; 805 were released after a hearing; 87 were repatriated; and 14 died. In one case, the disposition was unresolved.

In addition, twenty-four Hungarian, Bulgarian, and Romanian enemy aliens were apprehended. Of these, eight were paroled and fifteen were released. The disposition in one case was unresolved.

There were 25,881 searches of enemy-alien premises, where 3,127 shortwave radios; 2,240 sticks of dynamite; 4,626 firearms; 306,247 rounds of ammunition; and other items of contraband were seized.

The Florida group made its way to Jacksonville; then one pair went on to Chicago and the other pair to New York City. Their targets were hydroelectric plants, aluminum factories, and the locks on the Ohio River.

After narrowly escaping capture on the Long Island beach, one of the saboteur's resolve quickly diminished. George Dasch told Ernest Burger, another saboteur, that he wanted to turn himself in and confess. Dasch, using the code name "Pastorius," called the FBI's New York office, stating he had recently arrived from Germany and would call FBI Headquarters when he got to Washington, D.C.

On June 20, Dasch called the FBI in Washington, mentioned his code name, and furnished his location. The FBI quickly took him into custody. Dasch provided the saboteurs' names, details of their training, and their targets. Based on

Dasch's information, the FBI was able to arrest the remaining six saboteurs within days.

After the capture of the saboteurs, the German government made an effort via Swiss diplomatic channels to have the saboteurs treated as prisoners of war, which meant that they would remain in jail until the end of the war. The United States replied that they were not soldiers but spies and could be executed without a trial. President Roosevelt ordered a secret military tribunal to try the captured Nazis.

The eight went before a military commission comprised of seven U.S. Army officers appointed by President Roosevelt. All were found guilty and sentenced to death. President Roosevelt commuted the sentences of Dasch and Burger. Dasch received a thirty-year sentence, and Burger received life.

Hoover called the Department of Justice Building the "Seat of Government" or SOG, and it was home to the FBI until the Hoover Building opened in 1975. The trial of the eight German saboteurs took place in this building. During the trial, a petition was denied that sought trial by jury for the saboteurs. *Library of Congress*

An FBI agent sorts the evidence found on the beach after the Germans headed inland. In addition to a large amount of explosives, the saboteurs had $175,200 in currency to finance their activities. In two weeks, they had spent $612 on clothing, meals, lodging, and travel, and a bribe of $260. The swift capture of the saboteurs helped to allay fear of Axis subversion and bolster Americans' faith in the FBI. *FBI*

Judith Coplon

One spy case surfaced involving an employee of the Justice Department, through the brilliant code-breaking expertise of an Army Signal Intelligence Service (the predecessor of the National Security Agency) employee, Meredith Gardner. In 1943, Gardner was examining telegraph traffic involving the Soviet Union, which at the time was America's ally. The government, concerned that Stalin might make a deal with Hitler, began to monitor Soviet diplomatic communications.

In the fall of 1946, Gardner made an important breakthrough. He had been studying out-of-date Soviet codebooks when he figured out that the cipher text used for English letters allowed him to spell out proper names. Using the cipher, Gardner discovered the names of the scientists who worked on the atomic bomb inside America's most secret location, Los Alamos, New Mexico. Gardner and the other code breakers ultimately found cover names for more than three hundred Americans who spied for the Soviets during and after World War II. American counterintelligence was able to identify only about one hundred of these Soviet agents.

SABOTAGE ATTEMPTS FOILED

By war's end, the FBI had investigated more than sixteen thousand sabotage cases. Not one successful case of foreign-directed sabotage occurred during the war.

This German machine pistol is one of the weapons the FBI discovered on the beach where two spies landed. In late 1944, William Colepaugh and Erich Gimpel landed from a German submarine on the coast of Maine. The FBI apprehended them before they accomplished their mission. In February 1945, they stood trial before a military commission. The two were convicted of spying for Germany and were sentenced to hang. Three days before the execution, President Roosevelt died. President Truman commuted their death sentences to life in prison. The government released Colepaugh in 1955 and returned Gimpel to Germany. The postwar debriefing of German personnel revealed that Germany made no further attempts to land saboteurs in the United States by submarine. After the two failures, the naval high command would not risk a valuable submarine for another sabotage mission. *FBI*

The FBI arrested Rudolf Ivanovich Abel in June 1957. Although Abel refused to talk, his hotel room and office revealed a stash of espionage equipment. Abel went on trial in October 1957, and because he was uncooperative, he was sentenced to death. His lawyer argued that one day Abel might prove useful as a hostage, and his sentence was commuted to thirty years. On February 10, 1962, Abel was exchanged for the American U-2 pilot, Francis Gary Powers, who was a prisoner of the Soviet Union. *FBI*

The FBI was aware that one of the decoded secret messages indicated that a female spy was working in the New York office of the Justice Department in 1945 and later transferred to Washington, D.C. Only one person fit the profile: twenty-eight-year-old Judith Coplon. The FBI put her under surveillance.

Coplon graduated from Barnard College in 1943 and went to work for the Justice Department. A year later, she transferred to the Foreign Agents Registration section, where she had access to counterintelligence information. The KGB recruited her as a spy in 1944.

The FBI set up a sting. Agents planted pseudo-secret documents for Coplon to steal. In March 1949, she met with Valentin Gubitchev, a KGB agent employed by the United Nations. She was carrying the documents in her purse when the FBI arrested her. In 1949, a jury convicted Coplon of espionage. In another trial, in 1950, she and Gubitchev were found guilty of conspiracy. The crimes carried a cumulative sentence of twenty-five years but were overturned by an appeals court. One reversal was due to reasons related to the arrest. The warrant, which had been based on probable cause, was written incorrectly. It could not show probable cause based on meeting her Soviet contact. Therefore, the court ruled that the FBI had not properly obtained the warrant. The other reversal was because of attorney-client privilege. Conversations with her attorney had been recorded by an FBI wiretap.

Judith Coplon was one of the first major figures tried in the United States for spying for the Soviet Union. Her disclosures to the FBI were the first information on the large size of the counterintelligence operation against the United States.

February 22 1942

Dear Friend

You probably wonder what has become of me
as I havent written to you for so long.We
have had a pretty bad month or so.My little
nephew the one I adore so has a malignant
tomor on the brain and isnt expected to live
so we are all so crushed that we dont know
what we are doing.They are giving him exray
on the head and they hope to check it but
give us absolutely no hope in a complete cure
and maybe not even any relief.I am completely
crushed.
You asked me to tell you about my collection
a month ago I had to give a talk to an Art
Club so I talked about my dolls and figurines
The only new dolls I have are THREE LOVELY
IRISH dolls.One of these three dolls is an
old Fisherman with a Net over his back another
is an old woman with wood on her beck
and the third is a little boy.
Everyone seemed to enjoy my talk I can only
think of our sick boy these days.
You wrote me that you had sent a letter to
Mr. Mr.Shaw,well I went to see MR.SHAW
he distroyed YOUR letter,you know he has
been Ill. His car was damaged but
is being repaired now.I saw a few of his
family about.They all say Mr.Shaw will be
back to work soon.

I do hope my letter is not too sad.There
is not much I can write you about these
days.
I came on this short trip for mother for
business before I try to make out her income
report,that is also Why I am learning to
type/
Everone seems busy these days the streets
are full of people.
Remember me to your family sorry I havent
written to you for so long.

Truly

Mary Wallace

Mother wanted to go to Louville
but due to our worry the Louville plan
put out   our minds now.

In early 1942, five letters were written and mailed, by seemingly different people from different locations, to the same person at a Buenos Aires, Argentina, address. The letter had been postmarked New York City and referred to a Mr. Shaw who had been ill but would be back to work soon. This letter was written a short time after the Destroyer *Shaw* had its bow blown off at Pearl Harbor, was being repaired in a West Coast shipyard, and soon would rejoin the fleet. "THREE LOVELY IRISH" dolls were three warships being repaired at a West Coast naval shipyard; and "fish nets" meant submarine nets. Wartime censors had intercepted the letters and referred them to cryptographers at the FBI Laboratory. The FBI concluded that the letters were written in a code. *FBI*

Elizabeth Bentley

Elizabeth Bentley was an educated and well-traveled woman who joined the American Communist Party. She eventually became a courier for her Soviet agent/lover. Bentley had been passing information to the Soviets for years, and by 1944, pressures from her Soviet contacts led her into bouts of heavy drinking. Her Soviet handler suggested she immigrate to the Soviet Union, but she felt if she did, she would be executed, since she would be of no use to them over there.

Velvalee Dickinson's doll shop on Madison Avenue catered to wealthy doll collectors and hobbyists. However, she struggled to keep her business solvent. It turned out, too, that she had a close association with the Japanese diplomatic mission in the United States, and she had $13,000 in her safe deposit box traceable to Japanese sources. *FBI*

The Japan Society of San Francisco
FAIRMONT HOTEL ~ ROOM 128
SAN FRANCISCO
Telephone DOuglas 8800

June 16, 1937

Mrs. Lee Taylor Dickinson
Fairmont Hotel
San Francisco

Dues for year   to July 1, 1937
Patron Membership   ☐
Life Membership   ☐
Budget A Membership ☐
Budget B Membership ☐
Budget C Membership ☐
Sustaining Membership ☐
Regular Membership   ☒ $5.00

(Please make checks payable to The Japan Society)

"The object of the Society is to promote friendly relations between the peoples of the United States and of Japan and to diffuse among the American people a more accurate knowledge of the people of Japan, their ideals, arts, sciences, industries and economic conditions."—*Constitution*.

Among the evidence the FBI turned up was Mrs. Dickinson's membership in the Japan Society. Dickinson had been instructed by the Japanese naval attaché to use the code he provided to construct the letters. All of the letters came back stamped: "Return to Sender." The senders, according to the return addresses, were women who knew nothing about the letters and had not sent them. *FBI*

Bentley apparently knew the content of the documents she carried and the names of more than a dozen people in the spy network. Of the names she knew, seven had worked with the Office of Strategic Services (OSS), the forerunner of the CIA, and the others worked in the Treasury Department.

In August 1945, fearing she was out of control and that perhaps the Soviets would kill her, Bentley went to the FBI. She did not immediately defect, however. Instead, she seemed to probe the FBI to see if they were sincere. It would not be until November that she began to tell her full story.

When the FBI debriefed Bentley, she gave them over eighty names, including those of thirty-seven federal employees. The FBI already suspected some of the people she named, and an earlier defector, Whittaker Chambers, had named some of them, so the FBI believed her story was genuine. Most of the people accused by Bentley would later invoke the Fifth Amendment and refuse to answer questions. J. Edgar Hoover ordered the strictest measures to hide her identity and defection.

The FBI drew a lucky break because one recipient was a doll collector. She believed that a Madison Avenue, New York City, doll shop owner, Mrs. Velvalee Dickinson, was responsible. She said Mrs. Dickinson was angry because she had been late paying for some dolls she'd ordered. The FBI discovered the other women were also Dickinson's customers. *FBI*

Whittaker Chambers and Alger Hiss

Whittaker Chambers was an American writer, editor, former Communist Party member, and a spy for the Soviet Union. In the early 1930s, Chambers joined the Ware group, a secret communist cell in Washington, D.C. In 1936, Chambers became disillusioned with communism and started to question his beliefs when Stalin began his Great Purge. Chambers saw the 1939 Hitler–Stalin nonaggression pact as a betrayal of his communist values, and he feared the information he was supplying to the Soviets would find its way to the Nazis.

In September 1939, Chambers flew to Washington to meet with Assistant Secretary of State Adolf Berle, a meeting the FBI officially found out about in late 1942. Chambers named eighteen government employees as spies or communist sympathizers. Most of the people he named held minor posts or were already independently suspected by the FBI. A few names were surprising: Alger Hiss, Donald Hiss, and Lawrence Duggan, all midlevel and apparently unimpeachable officials in the State Department. A fourth, Lauchlin Currie, was a special assistant to Franklin Roosevelt. The White House did not think the information was credible and took no action.

In 1941, after Soviet defector Walter Krivitsky allegedly committed suicide in his hotel room, Berle thought the Soviets might try to kill Chambers too. He then informed the FBI of Chambers' confession. The FBI interviewed Chambers twice, but it was not until November 1945, when Elizabeth Bentley defected and corroborated much of Chambers' story, that the FBI took him seriously. In March 1945, Alger Hiss had been named acting secretary general of the United Nations, and if the allegations were true, the appointment would have serious consequences. The FBI began surveillance of Hiss and his wife, Priscilla. The surveillance included wiretaps, but no evidence of espionage was uncovered through these methods.

Mrs. Dickinson was indicted for violation of the censorship statutes, espionage, and violating the Registration Act. She pled not guilty and was held in lieu of $25,000 bail. In a plea deal, Mrs. Dickinson pled guilty to the censorship violation. On August 14, 1944, Dickinson was sentenced to ten years and a $10,000 fine. The court commented, "It is hard to believe that some people do not realize that our country is engaged in a life and death struggle. Any help given to the enemy means the death of American boys who are fighting for our national security. You, as a natural-born citizen, having a university education, and selling out to the Japanese, were certainly engaged in espionage. I think that the government has given you every consideration. The indictment to which you have pleaded guilty is a serious matter. It borders close to treason." *FBI*

Hoover secretly, and perhaps purposely, knowing it would leak, passed the identity of Elizabeth Bentley to the head of British intelligence, Sir William Stephenson. Word leaked to Kim Philby, a Soviet agent in Britain's MI6, who passed it on to Soviet intelligence. The Soviets immediately shut down virtually all of their U.S. espionage operations. *FBI*

According to Chambers, he and Hiss had developed a close friendship. In the fall of 1936, Hiss became an assistant to Assistant Secretary of State Francis Sayre. Hiss contended later that his relationship with Chambers ended in 1936. Chambers later testified that he began receiving secret State Department documents from Hiss in early 1937. If Chambers's claims were true, it would have been damaging for the United States. Hiss attended the Yalta Conference in 1945 and was responsible for negotiating the Soviet Union's three seats in the United Nations.

On August 3, 1948, Chambers, by then a strong anticommunist, testified before the HUAC that Alger Hiss was a member of the Communist Party and a spy for the Soviet Union. The two had met in August 1934, when Hiss allegedly started paying Communist Party dues. According to Chambers, Hiss began working with Soviet intelligence in 1935, when Chambers was a courier. Chambers testified that Hiss brought documents home nightly and retyped them for later transfer to Chambers.

When Hiss claimed he could not type, Chambers then said Priscilla Hiss had retyped the documents. Priscilla, Chambers claimed, then passed them on to the spy network. No one believed Chambers, since some of the original documents had been photographed and then passed on.

In December 1948, Hoover shared with Richard Nixon papers he believed Chambers had squirreled away. Congressman Nixon got a subpoena and, along with another member of the HUAC, took Chambers to his garden, where Chambers had hidden five rolls of microfilm in a hollow pumpkin (thus the nickname, the Pumpkin Papers). When developed, the microfilm produced classified State Department documents and four memos written by Hiss, which Chambers said Hiss had given him. The documents bore dates between January 5 and April 1, 1938.

Alger Hiss voluntarily appeared before the HUAC to deny Chambers' accusations. Some committee members had doubts about attacking Hiss, but Congressman Richard Nixon, who had been secretly fed information from Hoover, confidently encouraged the committee to continue the investigation.

The Pumpkin Papers were mostly classified trade regulations, not top-secret military intelligence. Both Chambers and Hiss denied any act of espionage in their testimony to Congress. The Pumpkin Papers, however, opened Chambers and Hiss to perjury charges.

Hiss went on trial on May 31, 1949, charged with two counts of perjury, since the statute of limitations on espionage had expired. Hoover was perplexed when the trial ended with a hung jury (8-4 to convict). Several months later, Hiss faced another trial on the same charges. That time, a known Soviet agent (Bentley) testified that she and Hiss had met in 1935. In January 1950, the jury convicted Hiss on two counts of perjury, and he was sentenced to five years on each count. He served less than four years total.

When the Soviet Union dissolved, Hiss petitioned the Soviet intelligence archives to release any relevant files. In the fall of 1992, the Russians reported that they had found no evidence that Hiss had been a spy for the Soviet Union. In 1995, ABC News reported that Russian President Boris Yeltsin said that KGB files had supported Hiss' claim.

According to an FBI internal memo dated May 15, 1950, the FBI had tentatively identified a spy code named "Ales" as Alger Hiss.

In 1995, the declassified Venona Project revealed more. Venona Project transcript No. 1822, dated March 30, 1945, revealed that Hiss had been a Soviet spy since 1935. In 1997, the bipartisan Daniel Patrick Moynihan Commission on

Alger Hiss denied that he knew Whittaker Chambers, pictured here, but when confronted by Chambers, Hiss claimed that he had known Chambers as "George Crosley." In 1984, President Ronald Reagan posthumously awarded Chambers the Presidential Medal of Freedom for his contribution to "the century's epic struggle between freedom and totalitarianism." Hiss maintained his innocence and fought his perjury conviction until his death in 1996. *FBI*

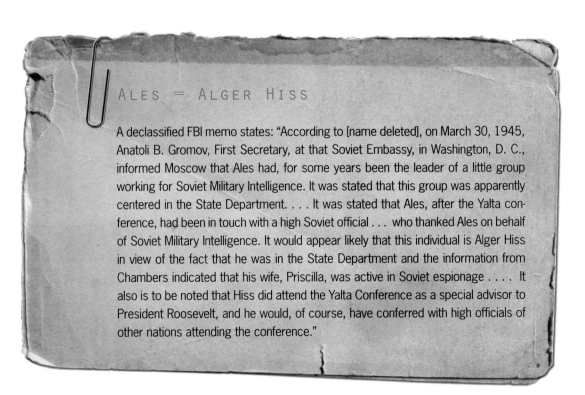

ALES = ALGER HISS

A declassified FBI memo states: "According to [name deleted], on March 30, 1945, Anatoli B. Gromov, First Secretary, at that Soviet Embassy, in Washington, D. C., informed Moscow that Ales had, for some years been the leader of a little group working for Soviet Military Intelligence. It was stated that this group was apparently centered in the State Department. . . . It was stated that Ales, after the Yalta conference, had been in touch with a high Soviet official . . . who thanked Ales on behalf of Soviet Military Intelligence. It would appear likely that this individual is Alger Hiss in view of the fact that he was in the State Department and the information from Chambers indicated that his wife, Priscilla, was active in Soviet espionage . . . . It also is to be noted that Hiss did attend the Yalta Conference as a special advisor to President Roosevelt, and he would, of course, have conferred with high officials of other nations attending the conference."

The headline announces the execution of the Rosenbergs (*New York Times* front page: June 20, 1953). In imposing the death sentence on the Rosenbergs, the judge made the following comment: "Your crime is worse than murder. Plain, deliberate, contemplated murder is dwarfed in magnitude by comparison with the crime you have committed. In your case, I believe your conduct in putting in the hands of the Russians an A-bomb, years before our best scientists predicted Russia would perfect the bomb, has already caused the Communist aggression in Korea with the resultant casualties exceeding 30,000—and who knows what millions more of innocent people may pay the price of your treason."

Government Secrecy stated in its findings: "The complicity of Alger Hiss of the State Department seems settled."

In his 1998 book, *Secrecy: The American Experience*, Moynihan writes, "Belief in the guilt or innocence of Alger Hiss became a defining issue in American intellectual life. Parts of the American government had conclusive evidence of his guilt, but they never told."

Julius and Ethel Rosenberg

In the summer of 1949, the U.S. Army's Venona program, a forerunner of the National Security Agency, revealed that the top-secret construction plans of the atom bomb had been stolen and turned over to a foreign power. In September, the White House announced that the Soviet Union had detonated an atomic bomb. The news shocked the nation and the world. With all the secrecy surrounding the bomb's development, how was this possible? Was it the hard work of Russian scientists, or were American traitors responsible?

Venona also revealed that Klaus Fuchs, a German born British atomic scientist, was involved. British authorities arrested Fuchs in February 1950, and he admitted his involvement in Soviet espionage. He was sentenced to prison. Fuchs claimed his American contact was code named "Raymond." The FBI could not locate Raymond until Fuchs's sister said she remembered meeting Raymond on several occasions. She said he mentioned something about chemistry and Philadelphia. "Raymond," through an extensive FBI investigation, was determined to be Harry Gold, a Philadelphia chemist. Gold confessed his espionage activity to the FBI.

Gold's confession led to David Greenglass, a U.S. Army enlisted man who had been assigned to the secret Manhattan Project at Los Alamos in 1944. Gold said he had picked up espionage material from Greenglass in June 1945 on instructions of "John," his Soviet handler. The FBI later identified "John" as Anatoli Yakovlev, a.k.a. Anatoliy Antonovich Yatskov, a former Soviet vice consul, in New York City, who had left the United States in December 1946. Under interrogation, Greenglass and his wife, Ruth, admitted espionage activities directed by Julius and Ethel Rosenberg, brother-in-law and sister of David Greenglass.

Code breaker Meredith Gardner discovered a reference to an agent code named "Liberal" in several messages. Gardner determined that the name was a code and contained three groups of letters, the first representing E and the third L. This was a new code for Gardner. In his August 2002 obituary in the *London Telegraph*, he was quoted once as saying, "Then I said, 'Ah, they anticipate sending a lot of English text, and the most common word in the English language is 'the.'" That realization led to the name Ethel, the wife of Julius Rosenberg.

Julius and Ethel Rosenberg were Americans and Communist Party members. Julius Rosenberg and Ethel Greenglass met at a meeting of the Young Communist League around 1932. They married in 1939. Julius had a bachelor's degree in electrical engineering.

In September 1940, Rosenberg went to work as a civilian employee and junior engineer with the War Department. During the war, Rosenberg transferred to the Army Signal Corps, and by 1943, he was passing information to Alexander Feklisov, who was then Klaus Fuchs' Soviet case officer. When Feklisov was transferred to London, Rosenberg made his hand-offs to Anatoli Yakovlev.

Information reached the FBI in March 1944 that Rosenberg was a member of the Communist Party. After the FBI verified the information, Rosenberg was fired in March 1945. Until his arrest in 1950, Rosenberg worked various jobs in electronic companies. Ethel had one stint in government service when she worked as a temporary clerk with the Census Bureau in 1940.

The Rosenbergs maintained that nothing was more important than the communist cause. Some say they were belligerent toward anyone who disagreed with their communist philosophy. They recruited many people, including all the adult members of Ethel's family.

Based on information provided by Rosenberg's co-conspirators, David Greenglass and others who were in custody, the FBI arrested Julius Rosenberg on July 17, 1950. In response to a subpoena, Ethel Rosenberg appeared before a federal grand jury on August 7. She was arrested, and both were charged with conspiracy to commit espionage on behalf of a foreign power between June 6, 1944 and June 16, 1950.

On August 17, the Rosenbergs, along with Anatoli Yakovlev, were charged with eleven (alleged) overt acts of espionage. Since Yakovlev had fled the country, he was charged in absentia. The Rosenbergs were arraigned on August 23 and held on $100,000 bail. On October 10, a superseding indictment charged the Rosenbergs, Yakovlev, Morton Sobell, and David Greenglass with conspiracy to violate the espionage statutes. The indictment read that the Rosenbergs, Greenglass, and Sobell had "communicated, delivered and transmitted to the Soviet Union, documents, writings, sketches, notes, and information relating to the national defense of the United States of America."

The Rosenbergs and Sobell pled not guilty. Greenglass pled guilty and admitted he had stolen information about the atomic bomb and turned it over to Rosenberg. He later testified that Julius and Ethel Rosenberg maintained two apartments in New York City, one of which was used as a photo lab for their espionage network. Alfred Sarant, who had leased one of the apartments to the Rosenbergs, feared that he may be called to testify and fled to Mexico and then to the Soviet Union.

When the trial began, the U.S. attorney severed Yakovlev and Greenglass (since Greenglass had pled guilty) from the trial. Julius and Ethel Rosenberg were found guilty and sentenced to death. Hoover opposed the death penalty for Ethel and rec-

THE HOLLOW NICKEL

1) WE CONGRATULATE YOU ON A SAFE ARRIVAL. WE CONFIRM
THE RECEIPT OF YOUR LETTER TO THE ADDRESS "V REPEAT V"
AND THE READING OF LETTER NUMBER 1. 2) FOR ORGANIZATION
OF COVER, WE GAVE INSTRUCTIONS TO TRANSMIT TO YOU THREE
THOUSAND IN LOCAL (CURRENCY). CONSULT WITH US PRIOR TO
INVESTING IT IN ANY KIND OF BUSINESS, ADVISING THE CHARACTER
OF THIS BUSINESS. 3) ACCORDING TO YOUR REQUEST, WE WILL
TRANSMIT THE FORMULA FOR THE PREPARATION OF SOFT FILM
AND NEWS SEPARATELY, TOGETHER WITH (YOUR) MOTHER'S
LETTER. 4) IT IS TOO EARLY TO SEND YOU THE GAMMAS
(MEANING HERE UNKNOWN, LITERALLY MUSICAL EXERCISES).
ENCIPHER SHORT LETTERS, BUT THE LONGER ONES MAKE
WITH INSERTIONS. ALL THE DATA ABOUT YOURSELF, PLACE
OF WORK, ADDRESS, ETC., MUST NOT BE TRANSMITTED IN ONE
CIPHER MESSAGE. TRANSMIT INSERTIONS SEPARATELY.
5) THE PACKAGE WAS DELIVERED TO YOUR WIFE PERSONALLY.
EVERYTHING IS ALL RIGHT WITH THE FAMILY. WE WISH YOU
SUCCESS. GREETINGS FROM THE COMRADES. NUMBER 1,
3RD OF DECEMBER.

Maki led the FBI to a dead drop, where FBI agents found a hollowed-out bolt with a typewritten message inside. Hayhanen helped investigators crack the code of the mysterious hollow coin and told them who his case officer was—a Soviet spy named Rudolf Abel. The FBI discovered Abel was operating without diplomatic cover and arrested him. *FBI*

On Monday, June 22, 1953, Jimmy Bozart, a delivery boy for the *Brooklyn Eagle*, made his collection rounds. After his collections, he walked down the stairs and dropped a coin. It fell apart! Inside was a tiny photograph—a picture of a series of numbers. The boy turned the nickel over to law enforcement. In examining the nickel, the FBI noted that the microphotograph had ten columns of typewritten numbers. The agents immediately suspected that they had found a coded espionage message. In 1957, the FBI got a break in the case when a Russian spy named Reino Hayhanen defected. Hayhanen was American-born Eugene Maki. *FBI*
INSET: Decoded message from the hollow nickel. *FBI*

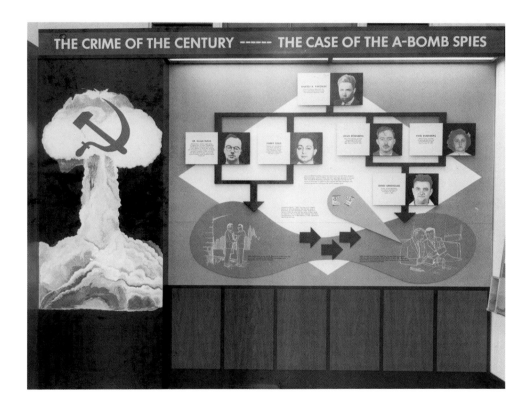

A display that once stood in the FBI tour at Headquarters called the Rosenberg treason the "Crime of the Century" and had the six major spies pictured: Dr. Klaus Fuchs, Harry Gold, Anatoli A. Yakovlev, Julius and Ethel Rosenberg, and David Greenglass. The Rosenbergs' trial and execution on June 19, 1953, have remained controversial, but at the time, it was a message to the world. The United States had seen a large part of Europe occupied by communist governments. The first flashpoint came when the Soviet Union blockaded all ground corridors into West Berlin from June 24, 1948, to May 11, 1949. The second came when the Soviets detonated the atom bomb on August 29, 1949. The third came when communist North Korea invaded democratic South Korea on June 28, 1950. The executions of the Rosenbergs sent a clear sign of the threat the United States considered communism. The FBI would investigate Soviet spies for the next forty years. *FBI*

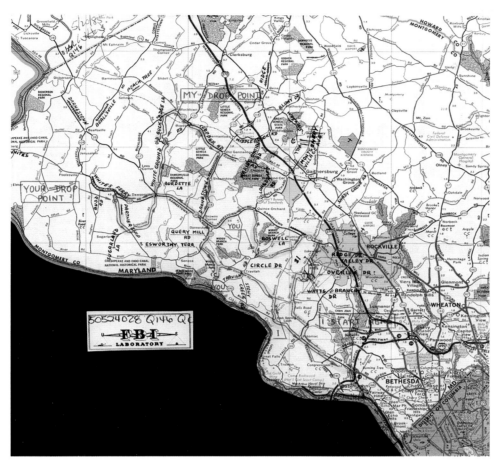

The map John Anthony Walker Jr. used for his dead drops. Walker's spy ring was the first major spy case since the Rosenbergs. His arrest north of Washington, D.C., in May 1985 was the inaugural event to what soon became known as "The Year of the Spy," during which seven more U.S. citizens would be accused of spying. Passing the information is the most dangerous part of espionage. The most common method is through a dead drop. The handler picks a public area that is secluded enough not to draw undue attention to any activity. Often, the information is concealed in an object that blends into the surroundings, such as a hollowed-out tree branch if the drop is in a park. *FBI*

This package of cigarettes concealed a hidden miniature camera, such as a Minox, used to photograph documents. A spy could pass the innocent-looking package of cigarettes, which contained the camera, in broad daylight. *FBI*

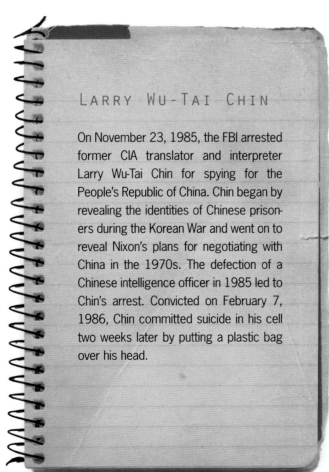

LARRY WU-TAI CHIN

On November 23, 1985, the FBI arrested former CIA translator and interpreter Larry Wu-Tai Chin for spying for the People's Republic of China. Chin began by revealing the identities of Chinese prisoners during the Korean War and went on to reveal Nixon's plans for negotiating with China in the 1970s. The defection of a Chinese intelligence officer in 1985 led to Chin's arrest. Convicted on February 7, 1986, Chin committed suicide in his cell two weeks later by putting a plastic bag over his head.

The Minox camera was a favorite spy camera and the most used camera during the Cold War. It was capable of photographing three hundred pages on one cassette and was used by John Walker. Walker, like all spies, was recruited because of his access, but he was not always good at spying. Walker photographed over 250,000 documents during his spy career, but he was sloppy. Spies are told to keep their information on undeveloped film (which can be destroyed easily) and not to keep hard copies. When the FBI searched Walker's house, many top secret documents were lying around in plain sight. Walker had saved most of his instructions from the dead drops, along with the containers and maps. *FBI*

In May 1985, the FBI dismantled John Walker's spy ring. Former navy personnel John Anthony Walker, Jerry Whitworth, Arthur Walker, and Michael Walker were convicted of, or pled guilty to, passing classified material to the Soviet Union since the 1960s. In debt, John Walker had walked into the Soviet Embassy and sold a U.S. Navy cipher card. Over the years, he recruited his wife and other family members. He retired from the navy in 1976 and set up a front as a private investigator while continuing to pass secrets to the Soviets. When he divorced and failed to pay his former wife, Barbara Walker, alimony, she went to the FBI and revealed the spy ring. Walker and his accomplices were convicted, and he received eighteen years in prison. *FBI*

ommended to the attorney general that she be given an extended prison term. The judge disagreed. The Rosenbergs went to their deaths without confessing to any crime or naming anyone in their network. Morton Sobell received a sentence of thirty years.

On April 6, 1951, the judge imposed a sentence of fifteen years on Greenglass. The judge stated he recognized the help given by Greenglass in bringing to justice "the arch criminals in this nefarious scheme." He pointed out that it took courage for him to testify and he had helped to "strike a death blow to the trafficking of our military secrets by foreign agents."

The Year of the Spy

The FBI solved so many espionage cases during the mid-1980s that the press dubbed 1985 "the year of the spy." The John Walker spy ring, Richard Miller, Jonathan Pollard, Ronald William Pelton, and Robert Hanssen, perpetrated the most serious espionage damage uncovered by the FBI.

Richard Miller

On October 3, 1984, the FBI arrested former FBI Special Agent Richard Miller, making him the first agent in FBI history arrested for espionage. In comparison to later FBI spies, Miller was a small-timer. He sold classified documents and an FBI counterintelligence manual to two Israeli spies.

Former FBI special agent and author Gary Aldrich described Miller: "Most agents assigned to Los Angeles during that time who knew Miller would probably agree that he should never have been hired in the first place. . . ." According to Aldrich, Miller was "one of the dumbest, most unkempt, most unpopular misfits the agency had ever hired. . . . The management should have watched Miller more carefully," he said.

On July 14, 1986, Richard Miller received two consecutive life terms and fifty years on other charges. The conviction was overturned in 1989, because the judge erred in admitting polygraph evidence during the trial.

On October 9, 1990, Miller was convicted on all counts of espionage for the second time, and on February 4, 1991, he was sentenced to twenty years in prison. The second time, a federal appeals court upheld his conviction. On May 6, 1994, Miller was released from prison following the reduction of his sentence by a federal judge.

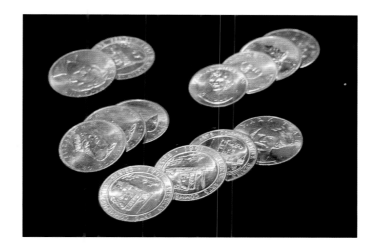

William Bell, an engineer employed at Hughes Aircraft Corporation was facing financial difficulties in 1980. Marian Zacharski, a Polish intelligence officer posing as a businessman, recruited Bell. Bell provided classified defense information to Zacharski. As payment, the Polish government gave Bell these gold coins, worth approximately $10,000. The FBI arrested Bell and Zacharski in 1981 for violations of the Espionage Act. Bell pled guilty and received eight years in prison. Zacharski was convicted and sentenced to life in prison. He was returned to Poland in 1985 as part of an East/West spy swap. *FBI*

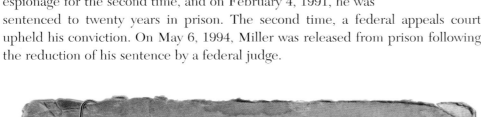

RONALD WILLIAM PELTON

On November 25, 1985, a major spy, former National Security Agency employee Ronald William Pelton, was arrested and charged with selling military secrets to the Soviets. He never passed any documents, but his colleagues claimed he had a photographic memory and was able to give a full accounting of the agency's activities. He received three life sentences.

Jonathan Pollard

In 1985, the Navy Field Operational Intelligence Office in Washington, D.C., grew suspicious of Jonathan Pollard, a navy intelligence analyst. Many classified documents unrelated to his work were found in his office. The FBI investigated and, on November 21, arrested Pollard for spying for Israel. Pollard attempted to flee arrest by requesting asylum at the Israeli embassy, as originally ordered by his Israeli handlers. The Israeli embassy refused, and the FBI later apprehended Pollard. In 1986, he received a life sentence.

Aldrich Hazen Ames

In the fall of 1999, the Berlin Wall fell. The following year, a mob of twenty thousand Germans stormed the East German Ministry of State Security (a.k.a. the Stasi) to burn its files. The Stasi had intruded on every East German's life and had documented all dissent against the government. Even after the crowd had been scattered, tens of thousands of files remained. Among the unburned files were documents revealing that every American-sponsored agent in East Germany had been compromised. Among them was the highest-ranking GRU officer ever to work for the United States intelligence. Lieutenant General Dimitri Polyakov, code name "Top Hat," had been working for the Americans since 1962. The FBI and CIA launched a joint operation called "Anlace" to uncover the mole within the American intelligence community. Anlace, followed by "Playactor" and "Skylight," failed to uncover the mole, but the FBI and CIA did not give up. Eventually, the FBI dug Aldrich Ames out of his hole. He was, at the time, considered one of the most damaging spies in U.S. history.

Ames began working for the CIA in 1962 in a low-level job. Over the years, he graduated from college and advanced through the ranks of the CIA while working in the Records Integration Division of the Operations Directorate.

In 1969, on his first assignment as a case officer, Ames was stationed in Ankara, Turkey, where his job was to target Soviet intelligence officers for recruitment. Ames was then assigned to the CIA's Europe Division counterintelligence branch, where he was responsible for directing the analysis of Soviet intelligence operations. He had access to the identities of U.S. assets in the KGB and Soviet military.

The Soviets paid Ames approximately $2.7 million, allowing him and his wife to live a lifestyle beyond the means of a normal CIA officer's family. Ames struggled with alcoholism and had no ideological allegiance to the USSR. Before he was caught, he was assigned the task of preparing the damage assessment of Jonathan Pollard's activities. The FBI believes he used the opportunity to attribute to Pollard some of his own acts of espionage.

On October 9, 1993, Attorney General Janet Reno authorized a warrantless search of Ames' residence. The search yielded a typewriter ribbon that contained impressions of a note Ames had written to his KGB contact regarding a meeting in Caracas, Venezuela, in October 1992. In February 1994, Ames was about

This photo is of the actual arrest of Aldrich Ames on February 21, 1994. Ames first began spying for the Soviet Union in 1985, when he walked into the Soviet embassy in Washington to offer secrets for money. He ultimately gave the Soviet Union the names of every American asset working in their country. The information Ames provided led to the compromise of at least one hundred U.S. intelligence operations and to the execution of at least ten U.S. assets. *FBI*

This magnetic key holder stored film at a dead drop. It could attach to anything metallic, such as the mailbox at 37th and R Streets, in Washington, D.C., identified as a drop site used by Aldrich Ames. The key holder contained microfilm of computer documents relating to Ames' relationship with the KGB, including information on clandestine communications, classified CIA operations, and classified CIA human assets. *FBI*

to fly to Moscow as part of his duties for the CIA. Fearing that he would defect, the FBI arrested Ames and his Colombian-born wife, Rosario, on February 21.

Ames and his wife were charged with espionage for the Soviet Union and its successor organization, the Russian Foreign Intelligence Service. Ames received a life sentence and, as part of a plea-bargain by Ames, his wife received a five-year prison sentence for conspiracy to commit espionage and tax evasion. Rosario Ames is believed to be living in South America.

Earl Edwin Pitts

Ex-FBI Special Agent Earl Edwin Pitts, who had been a counterintelligence officer, committed treason by spying for the Soviets for money. He had been assigned to the New York City field office.

The thirteen-year Bureau veteran was charged with espionage and communicating classified documents over a five-year period beginning in 1987. His crimes were far more extensive than the one count of passing classified information to Israel for which Jonathan Pollard was convicted. Nevertheless, Pitts' twenty-seven-year sentence was lighter than the life sentence given to Jonathan Pollard. Prosecutors had requested twenty-four years, but the judge told Pitts his crimes were especially severe and said Pitts had yet to apologize fully: "You betrayed your country; you betrayed your government, your fellow workers, and all of us, really. Every time you go by Arlington (National Cemetery) . . . every name you see on the Vietnam Memorial . . . you betrayed them especially."

Pitts gave the Russians the FBI's Soviet Administrative List, a listing of every Russian official in the United States and their connections with the intelligence community. He also gave the Russians a top-down-view assessment of the progress the United States was making in understanding the Soviet intelligence apparatus.

Robert Hanssen used this park as a dead drop. Dead drops are usually in play for minutes to perhaps hours. There is always a signal hiding in plain sight to tip the handler that the sight is active. Spy recruiters look for one of four vulnerabilities in a potential recruit. They use the acronym MICE: the person needs **M**oney; they are **I**deologically driven; they can be personally **C**ompromised; and they have a big **E**go. The FBI arrested Hanssen on February 18, 2001, and charged him with selling secrets to Moscow. Hanssen received more than $1.4 million in cash and diamonds over a fifteen-year period. Officials describe his treason as the "worst intelligence disaster in U.S. history." *FBI*

Pitts, the second FBI agent caught spying, pled guilty to conspiring and attempting to commit espionage. The plea spared Pitts a possible life prison sentence on the twelve charges he originally faced. Pitts collected $224,000 from the Soviets and was caught because of a sixteen-month undercover FBI sting.

Robert Philip "Greyday" Hanssen

Robert Philip Hanssen was a counterintelligence special agent of the FBI who was convicted of providing classified national security information to the Soviet Union and Russia. Between 1985 and 2001, Hanssen sold secrets to the Russians for cash and diamonds. His most damaging betrayal occurred in 1985, when he informed the Soviet KGB that two KGB officers were spies for the United States. Both men were executed.

Discovering Hanssen's deception was not easy. Both the CIA and the FBI were baffled by who "Greyday" could be. Louis Freeh, director of the FBI, and George Tenet, the CIA director, devised a plan—one that had never been tried before. They pooled their financial resources, and with other inducements, such as a new protected life in the United States, they would present an offer to a high-ranking KGB agent. The financial inducement was in the seven-figure range, which would get the attention of the new entrepreneurs of the old Soviet Union.

After studying the files of the CIA and FBI, Freeh and Tenet selected five senior KGB officials, all retired, who would likely have had access to Greyday's files. They would approach them individually.

The first KGB officer gave a direct and undiplomatic negative reply. The second was more friendly but failed to show up for a second meeting. The third wanted the cash, U.S. citizenship for himself, and relocation to the United States for his mother. The deal was done, and the FBI asked him to give up Greyday. The KGB officer said he could not. He only knew of him by his Soviet code name, "Ramon Garcia,"

The FBI Laboratory matched the typeface on the documents to the Hiss family's typewriter. There has been disagreement about the accuracy of this typewriter identification. Hiss contended that the typewriter introduced as evidence was not the Hiss family typewriter. The serial number allegedly indicated the sale of the machine took place after the Hiss family had purchased it. *FBI*

Robert Hanssen's arrest and search warrant (abridged) read: "He compromised numerous human sources of the United States Intelligence Community. Three of these sources were compromised by both Hanssen and former CIA officer Aldrich Ames, resulting in their arrest, imprisonment, and, as to two individuals, execution. . . ." *FBI*

but he said he had plenty of records from the infamous Lubyanka, the headquarters of the KGB. The FBI became disbelieving. Nobody gets anything out of Lubyanka. They decided to ask for samples of what he wanted to sell to the FBI.

In October 2000, the Russian officer and the FBI met in a neutral country. The agents took the documents back to the FBI Laboratory. The Lab said the documents were authentic. They listed dates, times of meetings, and amounts paid to Greyday, but none of the documents revealed Greyday's identity. Just when the CIA and FBI thought they had hit a stone wall, the Lab called. There were papers that revealed that even the Russians did not know who Greyday was. The papers revealed that they had been working with Greyday for more than two decades, and no one had ever met him or photographed him. The KGB, which considered itself the best spy organization in the world, could not identify Greyday. While they were unsuccessful in identifying Greyday, they inadvertently gave the FBI the clue they needed. The KGB had recorded a phone conversation with Greyday. On the tape was the unmistakable voice of Robert Philip Hanssen.

The FBI could not simply arrest Hanssen. The Bureau needed to catch him in the act of espionage. Agents bugged his phone, computer, car, home, and everything they thought he could use to communicate with his handler. Then the FBI waited. On the night of February 18, 2001, Hanssen made a drop in the woods in a local park in Vienna, Virginia. They arrested him on the spot.

Hanssen received life in prison. The 2007 film *Breach* tells a fictionalized account of this story. ■

If negotiations in an airline hijacking fail, the Hostage Rescue Team must swing into siege action and take control of the situation. FBI

Chapter 8

STANDOFFS GONE BAD
Confronting Ruby Ridge,
Waco, and Other Disasters

Human disasters and potential disasters come in many forms, from bombings and mass murders, to chemical, nuclear, and biological accidents, to armed standoffs. Over the years, the FBI has addressed many of these scenarios.

Between the 1990s and early 2000s, the FBI faced difficult challenges. Some critics say the FBI is at least partially responsible for the loss of life in armed standoffs at Ruby Ridge, Idaho, in 1992 and at Waco, Texas, in 1993. These two events would have a major impact on the FBI's policies, image, and operations.

Ruby Ridge

In August 1992, the FBI responded to the shooting death of Deputy U.S. Marshal William Degan, who was killed at Ruby Ridge, Idaho. He was part of a surveillance task force monitoring a federal fugitive named Randy Weaver. A tense and deadly confrontation took place between federal agents and Weaver's family. In the course of the standoff, Weaver's fourteen-year-old son, and forty-three-year-old wife were shot and killed by an FBI sniper.

FBI snipers took their positions around the Weaver cabin a few minutes after 5 p.m. on August 22. Newspapers widely reported that shots were fired at an FBI helicopter. Within an hour, every adult in the cabin either was dead or wounded—even though they had not fired a shot at any federal agent.

Weaver owned a twenty-acre property where he, his wife, three children, and family friend Kevin Harris lived. There was an outstanding warrant for Weaver's arrest for a firearms violation, and the U.S. Marshals had his house under surveillance. The family dog, a yellow Labrador retriever, noticed the marshals sneaking

In 1940, a small plane carrying twenty-five people, including two FBI employees, crashed, killing all on board. The FBI went to the crash site and used its fingerprinting expertise to identify eight of the twenty-five victims. The crash demonstrated a need for a national disaster squad, which would have experts ready to travel to a disaster scene to assist local authorities in identifying victims. During the 1990s, this elite group of experts assisted in the investigations of the bombings of the Oklahoma City federal building, the Khobar Towers in Saudi Arabia, and the crashes of ValuJet Flight 592, EgyptAir Flight 990, and TWA Flight 800. *FBI*

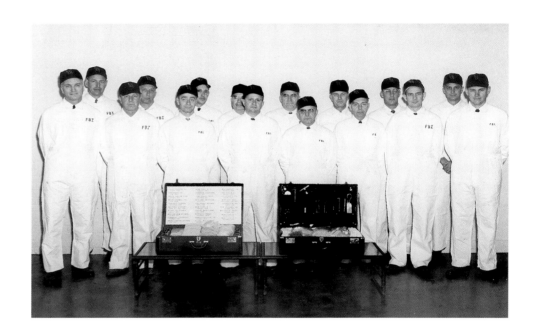

An airline hijacking is potentially disastrous for the passengers if the negotiations are not conducted a certain way. FBI special agent SWAT/hostage negotiators create realistic training scenarios that involve a simulated hijacking of a plane. *FBI*

On Friday, May 3, 2002, a series of improvised bombs was left inside mailboxes in rural areas of eastern Iowa and northwest Illinois. Accompanying each pipe bomb was a letter that rambled about life, death, pain, and the impact of government on the individual. By Monday, May 6, a total of eighteen bombs in five states had been found. The full resources of the FBI—including bomb-scenting dogs, the FBI Bomb Data Center, the FBI Laboratory, FBI aviation assets, and the FBI Behavioral Analysis Unit—were brought into the investigation. The efforts, resources, and hundreds of state and local law enforcement officers were coordinated and directed by the JTTF. The investigation resulted in the arrest of Lucas John Helder. *FBI*

Helder Mailbox Bomb

around in the woods and began barking. Randy Weaver, his fourteen-year-old son Sammy, and Harris grabbed their rifles, thinking the dog had come upon a wild animal. Sammy fired into the woods, and the marshals returned the fire. Sammy fell dead, and Weaver and Harris retreated to the house.

Randy Weaver, Harris, and sixteen-year-old Sara Weaver stepped out of their cabin a few minutes before 6 p.m. to retrieve Sammy's body. As Weaver, Harris, and Sara Weaver struggled to get back into the cabin, an FBI sniper shot Randy Weaver in the back. Vicki Weaver stood in the cabin doorway holding her baby. The sniper fired again. The bullet passed through a window in the door, hit Vicki Weaver in the head, killing her instantly, and then hit Harris in the chest.

The FBI faced widespread criticism, and Attorney General Janet Reno established a Department of Justice task force to investigate what had happened. National debates fueled antigun and government sentiments. Some say the bombing of the government building in Oklahoma City a year later by Timothy McVeigh was partially motivated by revenge for what happened at Ruby Ridge. After eleven days, the standoff ended with Harris and Weaver taken into custody.

The Justice Department's report said, "We have been told by observers on the scene that law enforcement personnel made statements that the matter would be handled quickly and that the situation would be 'taken down hard and fast.' The FBI issued rules of engagement that declared that its snipers 'can and should' use deadly force against armed males outside the cabin."

The report concluded that the FBI rules of engagement flagrantly violated the U.S. Constitution: "The Constitution allows no person to become 'fair game' for deadly force without law enforcement evaluating the threat that a person poses, even when, as occurred here, the evaluation must be made in a split second. The Constitution places the decision on whether to use deadly force on the individual agent; the Rules attempted to usurp this responsibility."

The Department of Justice task force expressed doubts about the wisdom of the FBI strategy: "From information received at the Marshal's Service, FBI management had reason to believe that Weaver and Harris would respond to a helicopter in the vicinity of the cabin by coming outside with firearms. Notwithstanding this knowledge, they placed sniper/observers on

The Strategic Information and Operations Center is the nerve center for all crises and disasters. The Justice Department report on Ruby Ridge noted: "The Strategic Information and Operations Center (SIOC) at FBI headquarters log indicates that shots were fired during the events of August 22 . . . . We have found no evidence . . . that shots were fired at any helicopter during the Ruby Ridge crisis. The erroneous entry was never corrected." *FBI*

FBI SWAT teams and snipers surrounded the Weaver home and, after an eleven-day standoff, Weaver surrendered. At his trial, the government claimed that Weaver and Harris were shot because they had threatened to shoot at an FBI helicopter. Because of insufficient evidence, the federal judge threw out the charge. The Idaho jury found Weaver and Harris innocent on almost all charges. *Department of Defense*

the adjacent mountainside with instructions that they could and should shoot armed members of the group, if they came out of the cabin. Their use of the helicopter near the cabin invited an accusation that the helicopter was intentionally used to draw the Weaver group out of the cabin."

The report also noted that a member of an FBI SWAT team from Denver "remembered the rules of engagement as 'if you see 'em, shoot 'em.'" The task force report said, "Since those rules which contained 'should' remained in force at the crisis scene for days after the August 22 shooting, it is inconceivable to us that FBI Headquarters remained ignorant of the exact wording of the rules of engagement during that entire period."

The task force was critical of the FBI sniper's second shot: "Since the exchange of gunfire [the previous day], no one at the cabin had fired a shot. Indeed, they had not even returned fire in response to the FBI sniper's first shot. Furthermore, at the time of the second shot, Harris and others outside the cabin were retreating, not attacking. They were not retreating to an area where they would present a danger to the public at large. . . ."

Regarding the sniper's killing of Vicki Weaver, the task force concluded, "By fixing his cross hairs on the door when he believed someone was behind it, he placed the children and Vicki Weaver at risk, in violation of even the special rules of engagement. . . . In our opinion he needlessly and unjustifiably endangered the persons whom he thought might be behind the door."

The Justice Department task force was suspicious that the adults did not receive any warning or demand to surrender: "While the operational plan included a provision for a surrender demand, that demand was not made until after the shootings. . . . The lack of a planned 'call out' as the sniper/observers deployed is significant because the Weavers were known to leave the cabin armed when vehicles or airplanes approached. The absence of such a plan subjected the government to charges that it was setting Weaver up for attack."

An Idaho state prosecutor brought manslaughter charges against the FBI sniper who shot Vicki Weaver. The FBI insisted it was capable of policing its own without outside interference. The Department of Justice sent the solicitor general to a federal appellate court to argue that the charges against the sniper should be dismissed. The solicitor general argued to dismiss the case even if the evidence supported the charges, because "federal law enforcement agents are privileged to do what would otherwise be unlawful

FBI SWAT teams are well trained and equipped to conduct dangerous, high-risk, search-and-arrest warrants. The equipment and weapons of the SWAT and Hostage Rescue Team are different from the usual weapons law enforcement uses on the street. Some of the weapons are more lethal, including automatic weapons and long-range, high-caliber rifles. Their uniform is selected to provide intimidation and create psychological fear when an assault takes place. *FBI*

The FBI will always attempt to use superior numbers when enforcing a search warrant. This was the case at Ruby Ridge, where the offenders were known to be heavily armed. *FBI*

Continued on Page B3, Column 4 | to isolate Iran and to dissuade it from | Continued on Page A10, Column 1

F.B.I. Shaken by Inquiry Into Idaho Siege

Officials at High Level Could Face Charges

By DAVID JOHNSTON
with STEPHEN LABATON
Special to The New York Times

WASHINGTON, Nov. 24 — The bloody standoff between the F.B.I.'s elite paramilitary force and a white separatist in Idaho has produced one of the largest and most wrenching internal inquiries ever conducted by the Justice Department, threatening some of the country's top law-enforcement officials with criminal prosecution.

The far-reaching inquiry, which has been under way for weeks but has remained largely unknown, centers on the operation at a remote ridge in August 1992 by the Hostage Rescue Team, the Federal Bureau of Investigation's unit trained to capture terrorists, hostage-takers and other violent criminals with minimal casualties.

Fatal Confrontation

The rescue unit was sent to the Idaho mountain after a confrontation between the white separatist, Randall C. Weaver, and Federal marshals in which one Federal agent and Mr. Weaver's 14-year-old son were killed. The next day a sniper from the rescue team shot and killed Mr. Weaver's wife, Vicki, who was in the doorway of their cabin holding their 10-month old daughter. She was not considered a threat, and the F.B.I. later acknowledged that she had been shot by mistake. After a 10-day siege, Mr. Weaver surrendered.

Deputy Attorney General Philip

B. Heymann, who is supervising the inquiry, described it as a top-to-bottom review of the case. People who have been interviewed by Government agents in the course of the inquiry said the focus was on whether officials misjudged the danger the agents faced and knowingly violated the agency's limits on the use of deadly force by killing Mrs. Weaver. The inquiry is also examining whether officials failed to consider less aggressive tactics and later closed ranks to avoid scrutiny of their actions.

Investigators from the Office of Professional Responsibility, the Justice Department's internal ethics unit, have warned top manag-

A Hostage Rescue Team member in a training exercise.

Top Paramilitary Unit Focus of the Review

ers, agents, prosecutors and former officials that they could face civil or criminal charges, including obstruction of justice and violations of civil rights law.

The Hostage Rescue team, with its black Ninja uniforms and body armor, its crack snipers and assault specialists, has achieved near heroic status within the F.B.I. and at the Justice Department. Team members have taken part in dozens of operations, including a 1991 case when they stormed a prison cell block to free hostages without firing a shot.

Another Assault

Earlier this year the team's performance was heavily criticized after it led the tear-gas assault on the Branch Davidian compound near Waco, Tex. It ended when the compound caught fire and at least 75 cultists died, including 25 children.

Now, after the two deadly incidents, agency officials are planning changes in managing crises.

The investigation of the Idaho siege has begun to reach the highest officials in the F.B.I. and the Justice Department in the Bush Administration, although investigators say many of the officials they interviewed are not likely to be charged.

Among those questioned is Larry A. Potts, head of the F.B.I.'s criminal investigative division, who is the most senior Washington

Continued on Page B16, Column 1

This newspaper headline claims high-level FBI officials might face charges in connection with the Ruby Ridge siege. Only a sniper was charged, and the charges were later dropped (*New York Times* front page: November 25, 1993).

if done by a private citizen." The appeals court rejected that argument as a license to kill. However, by the time that ruling came down, a newly elected local prosecutor announced that it was time to move on, and dropped the criminal case against the sniper.

In a statement read before the Senate Subcommittee on Terrorism, Technology, and Government Information on October 19, 1995, FBI Director Louis Freeh said, "At Ruby Ridge, the Hostage Rescue Team was operating in accordance with rules of engagement that were reasonably subject to interpretation that would permit a violation of FBI policy and the Constitution. Those rules said that, under certain circumstances, certain persons 'can and should' be the subject of deadly force. Those rules of engagement were contrary to law and FBI policy. Moreover, some FBI SWAT personnel on scene interpreted the rules as a 'shoot on sight' policy which they knew was inconsistent with the FBI's deadly force policy.

"According to Special Agent Lon Horiuchi, the HRT sniper who accidentally shot Mrs. Weaver, he fired two shots on August 22, 1992, both pursuant to the FBI's deadly force policy. He has testified that he did not shoot pursuant to the rules of engagement that I just mentioned. The shot that killed Mrs. Weaver was the second that Special Agent Horiuchi fired. He testified that it was not intended for Mrs. Weaver and was not fired at her."

In discussing Special Agent Horiuchi's second shot, Freeh said, "I am not saying that I approve of it. I am not trying to justify it . . . but final action must be based upon a full and accurate reporting of the facts."

FBI and other investigators examine damage caused by a 1984 explosion inside the Washington Navy Yard Officers Club, Building 101. Any violence occurring on government property brings the FBI into the investigation. The club was closed for business at the time, and there were no injuries. *Department of Defense*

Critics also slammed the FBI for promoting Acting Deputy Director Larry Potts. "Larry Potts," said Freeh, "was one of the twelve FBI employees included in my disciplinary decisions this past January. He received a letter of censure for failure to provide proper oversight with regard to the rules of engagement employed at Ruby Ridge. It should be noted that the administrative summary report recommended that neither Mr. Potts nor Mr. Coulson be disciplined. I disagreed with that conclusion based upon the facts as I found them.

"At the time I disciplined Larry Potts, he was the acting deputy director. Shortly thereafter, I sought to promote him to be deputy director of the FBI.

"In pressing for Mr. Potts' appointment as deputy director, I was not trying to minimize or downplay the significance of the punishment that I had imposed upon him. I did not appoint him deputy director simply because he is a friend . . . I considered his many years of public service to the Nation and to law enforcement . . . I considered his vast accomplishments in the FBI, including our work together during the VANPAC investigation for which President Bush personally awarded Mr. Potts an Exceptional Leadership Award . . . I consulted with numerous people inside and outside the FBI, including judges, a former attorney general. . . . It

The Branch Davidians believed in the imminent end of the world. Koresh taught that only the Davidians would survive, but first there would be a confrontation with the government, which he saw as evil. He quoted Revelation 11:7 as his proof: "And when they shall have finished their testimony, the beast that ascendeth out of the bottomless pit shall make war against them, and shall overcome them, and kill them." *FBI*

was their consensus that Larry Potts was an excellent and progressive leader, highly qualified to be deputy director. Like them, I placed great trust and confidence in Mr. Potts.

"Looking back, I recognize that I was not sufficiently sensitive to the appearance created by my decision to discipline and then promote Mr. Potts. Thus, I made a mistake in promoting Mr. Potts. I take full responsibility for that decision." Deputy Director Potts retired in 1997.

Waco, Texas

Thirty-three-year-old David Koresh, alias Vernon Howell, was the leader of the religious sect of the Branch Davidians, a splinter group of the Seventh Day Adventist Church. Koresh's group was located at Mount Carmel, near Waco, Texas.

According to FBI documents, there were allegations that some of the Davidians were being held against their will, which would be a violation of federal law. Some former members from Koresh's group alleged that he practiced polygamy with underage girls, physically abused children, and stockpiled illegal weapons. Koresh acknowledged he was the father to at least fourteen children. Some of his followers say he was a manifestation of God on earth. Outsiders say he was a child abuser and rapist.

Child Protective Services in Waco investigated the compound and made several unannounced visits but found no violations. The Bureau of Alcohol, Tobacco, and Firearms had been secretly investigating the group for alleged firearms violations.

The BATF suspected the Davidians were converting semi-automatic weapons to fully automatic weapons. The BATF was also advised that there was a rumor that Koresh was planning a mass murder/suicide in the spring of 1992 to coincide with Easter. Members of the group denied the allegation, saying that it was all just a rumor.

Koresh believed that his time to turn the other cheek was over, and it was time to fight. When not preaching or studying the Bible, many male members of the sect practiced firearms training on the firing range within the compound.

Taken from FBI records, surveillance footage, and audio recordings, the following is known: Koresh had a massive arsenal of weapons, including heavy automatic weapons. The constant noise of automatic weapons fire attracted the attention of the local sheriff. In Texas, it is illegal to own fully automatic weapons. An undercover BATF agent confirmed Koresh was converting semi-automatic weapons into fully automatic weapons, a violation of federal law.

In January 1993, the BATF began a surveillance of the compound from a property across the road. Robert Rodriguez, a BATF undercover agent, infiltrated the group, posing as a potential convert. He began to attend Bible study classes and, after a number of weeks, he was invited by Koresh to bring a gun to the firing range.

The BATF decided the illegal weapons gave them grounds for an arrest. The raid was set for 10 a.m. on February 28. However, twenty-four hours before the raid, the BATF discovered a local newspaper was about to expose Koresh's activities under the headline, "The Sinful Messiah." The BATF tried to stop the article. They were concerned that it would alert Koresh to the upcoming raid. The newspaper refused.

The three helicopters and seventy-five agents would have to move in before the element of surprise was lost. First, the undercover agent must get inside to make

For months, the Bureau of Alcohol, Tobacco, and Firearms (BATF) gathered evidence, through an undercover agent, of illegal arms possession against Koresh. The group had at least 150 automatic weapons, including AK 47s. There was at least one .50-caliber machine gun, eight thousand rounds of ammunition, and at least one explosive device. Here, the FBI SWAT members practice a forced entry. *FBI*

VOL.CXLII... No. 49,307   Copyright © 1993 The New York Times   NEW YORK, TUESDAY, APRIL 20, 1993   75 cents beyond 75 miles from New York City, except on Long Island.   50 CENTS

SCORES DIE AS CULT COMPOUND IS SET AFIRE AFTER F.B.I. SENDS IN TANKS WITH TEAR GAS

The wood-frame compound of David Koresh and his cult followers turned into an inferno of death yesterday as a standoff of 51 days was ended. — Agence France-Presse

Apparent Mass Suicide Ends A 51-Day Standoff in Texas

By SAM HOWE VERHOVEK
Special to The New York Times

WACO, Tex., April 19 — Hours after Federal agents began battering holes in the walls of the Branch Davidian compound and spraying tear gas inside, David Koresh and more than 80 followers — including at least 17 children — apparently perished today when flames engulfed the sprawling wooden complex on the Texas prairie.

Officials of the Federal Bureau of Investigation said they believed that Mr. Koresh, a self-described messiah who prophesied to his followers that they would meet their end in an apocalyptic confrontation with the law, gave the order to burn the compound down in the 51st day of a standoff with Federal agents.

F.B.I. officials said smashing the walls and filling the building with tear gas was intended to increase pressure on the cult members, who had resisted all previous demands for surrender. But the officials insisted that the tear gas was not flammable and that the fire was set by cult members who poured fuel around the perimeter of the compound and lit matches.

'They All Willingly Followed'

"David Koresh, we believe, gave the order to commit suicide and they all willingly followed," said Bob A. Ricks, a senior F.B.I. agent who has been here for most of the standoff, which began seven weeks ago with a deadly shootout between cult members and agents from the Federal Bureau of Alcohol, Tobacco and Firearms who wanted to search the compound.

Mr. Ricks said only nine people were rescued from the compound today, including one woman who had sought to return to the burning building and tried to fight off a Federal agent who came to her aid. Ammunition in the cult's storehouse of weapons exploded sporadically during the afternoon, hindering rescue workers.

Mr. Ricks said that so far "several bodies" had been found in a bus buried on the compound, and only "two or three" other bodies. The authorities believed that some of these were cult members who had been killed in the original confrontation on Feb. 28, he

said.

"We had hoped the women would grab their children and flee," Mr. Ricks said. "That did not occur and they bunkered down the children and allowed them to go up in flames with them." Mr. Ricks said it was only speculation at this point but that the authorities had received reports, apparently from some of the survivors, that the children had been injected with some kind of poison to ease their pain.

F.B.I. officials said they believed that 95 people were inside the compound when the fire began, including 17 children under the age of 10, and that it only knew of the 9 survivors, 4 of whom were at hospitals this evening and 5 of

Continued on Page A26, Column 3

RENO SEES ERROR IN MOVE ON CULT

Fatigue of Agents and Failure of Talks Brought Assault

By STEPHEN LABATON
Special to The New York Times

WASHINGTON, April 19 — Attorney General Janet Reno conceded tonight that in hindsight the Government's plan to assault the heavily armed cult near Waco, Tex., had been a mistake.

"It was based on what we know then," she said this evening on CNN. "Based on what we know now, it was obviously wrong."

Earlier in the day, a shaken and somber Ms. Reno said she had worried over the weekend that the plan could bring mass suicide, but she decided that it was "highly unlikely" and approved the operation.

Taking responsibility for the assault, she acknowledged that it had in fact led to a mass suicide, as members of the

Italians Support Political Reform By a Big Margin

By ALAN COWELL
Special to The New York Times

ROME, April 19 — After months of scandal, recession and Government paralysis, Italians voted overwhelmingly for political change in a referendum on Sunday and today that repudiated the country's leadership of the last 48 years, but that left the future uncertain.

Final computer projections late tonight, 10 hours after polls closed, showed 82 percent of voters endorsing a proposal to scrap the current system of pure proportional representation for most of the Senate and replace it with the majority voting used in other parts

Vietnam Report on Prisoners A Fake, Reputed Author Says

By PHILIP SHENON
Special to The New York Times

HANOI, Vietnam, April 19 — A Vietnamese general denied today that he had written in 1972 that Hanoi held more than twice as many American prisoners as it ultimately released. Any such report attributed to Hanoi is a forgery, he declared.

And a special envoy, sent by President Clinton to tell the Vietnamese that relations could not improve until the matter was cleared up, said he saw no reason to disbelieve the Vietnamese denial.

Nearly two weeks ago, Russian archivists turned over to the United States a Russian translation of what was said to be a secret report to Hanoi's Politburo given by Gen. Tran Van

Russian translation was supposedly based. If the Vietnamese report exists, General Quang said, it is a forgery that may have been prepared by someone interested "in undermining advances in relations between Vietnam and the United States."

At a news conference today after meeting with General Vessey, General Quang said of the 1972 report: "I did not write it. I tell you, never in my life have I made such a report, because it was not in my area of responsibility." He stressed that although he was

Continued on Page A6, Column 4

Law Firm for S. & L. Is Fined $51 Million

Jones, Day, Reavis & Pogue, one of the nation's biggest law firms, agreed to pay the Government $51 million to settle charges that it aided the financier Charles H. Keating Jr. in the fraud that brought on the costliest bankruptcy in the savings and loan debacle. The agreement came as a trial was about to begin.

The settlement, which is the largest against a law firm in the savings and loan rescue, also ends litigation against the Jones, Day partner in charge of work for Mr. Keating's Lincoln Savings and Loan Association, which collapsed in 1989 at a cost to taxpayers of $2.5 billion.

Business Day, page D1.

When the tanks rolled in to Waco, one FBI agent said, "How in the world did we get to this position, where we have tanks surrounding a church on the high plains of Texas? How could that happen in the United States of America? This tactic will not draw them out; it will only unite them, and drive them in (*New York Times* front page, April 20, 1993)."

sure the women and children were separated from the men. Rodriguez was inside, but with just an hour before the raid, he was told he must wait to see Koresh.

While the agent was waiting, a news cameraman, who was tipped to the raid, was on his way to the compound but got lost. He stopped a mailman for directions. The mailman happened to be David Koresh's brother-in-law, who called Koresh to warn him that the BATF was on its way.

Koresh had been suspicious of Agent Rodriguez. He confronted him less than an hour before the raid, and the element of surprise had slipped away. Rodriguez convinced Koresh he was true to the sect and slipped away to call the BATF to warn them that Koresh knows about the raid.

At that point, the BATF had another problem. One group wanted to delay the raid based on the loss of surprise. The other wanted to proceed anyway. The latter group won, and the agents prepared for the raid. The BATF plan was based on the element of surprise, and that plan had been compromised.

On February 28, 1993, the BATF raided the ranch. Inside the compound, the men directed the women and children to their rooms. The men would aggressively defend the compound. It is not known who fired the first shot. Nothing had prepared the BATF for the fusillade of gunfire the agents faced. The BATF agents did not have sufficient firepower to match the Davidians' automatic weapons. The gunfire was intense. Bullets were coming through the walls, and the BATF returned fire through the walls.

A local news crew captured the raid on film. The three BATF helicopters arrived late and landed under heavy fire from the compound. The BATF agents were pinned down and direct their fire toward the main building, where women and children fall victim to the gunfire.

Just one minute into the battle, one of the Davidians called 911. His call was routed to the sheriff's office in Waco. The Branch Davidians were calling for a cease-fire. The deputy who answered the call tried to contact the BATF, but the BATF communications officer had switched off his radio.

The BATF officers inside the compound were pinned down and also desperate for a cease-fire. Thirty minutes later, the deputy made contact with the BATF and attempted to broker a cease-fire between the 911 caller and the BATF. Koresh interrupted the dialogue and began a theological discussion with the 911 caller. After 90 minutes, a cease-fire is finally in place. The BATF withdrew with four of its agents dead and twenty-two seriously injured. Six Davidians had died, and Koresh was critically wounded. One hundred nineteen Davidians were inside the compound with Koresh, including forty-three children.

The day began with the goal of arresting one man but ended with a loss of ten lives. It would be the greatest number of casualties suffered by the BATF for a single mission in its history. Thus began a fifty-one-day siege—the longest federal siege in U.S. history at the time—watched by the world.

President Clinton adopted a wait-and-see attitude for the Waco standoff. However, since there were dead federal agents, the FBI stepped in to take control. Unfortunately, the FBI had arrived in the middle of the gunfight. It would negotiate with Koresh, who knew he was facing the death penalty and that he was still in control of the situation. Three hundred FBI agents were on the scene, including two dozen hostage negotiators. FBI snipers positioned themselves, and SWAT units were ready to breach the ramparts. The FBI set up a command headquarters eight miles away. The FBI agents were well versed in the Davidians' religion, cause, and allegiance to their leader. It would not be easy to bring anyone out unharmed.

The BATF reestablished telephone communications with Koresh, who was willing to talk despite his injuries. The FBI negotiators believed they could appeal to Koresh's ego and made him an offer they thought he would not refuse. The FBI offered Koresh the opportunity to record a message that would be broadcasted on national radio. In return, he and his followers would surrender peacefully. Koresh agreed to the terms and requested a tape recorder. The FBI appeared to have achieved a major breakthrough. On the third day of the siege, the Christian Broadcasting Network agreed to air Koresh's message to America. As Koresh ended his message, TV networks switched to Waco for live coverage of the Branch Davidian's surrender. Koresh, however, did not honor the agreement and told his devoted followers that God had told him to wait.

On the second anniversary of the Waco tragedy, a truck bomb exploded at the Alfred P. Murrah Federal Building in Oklahoma City, destroying the nine-story building. The explosion killed 168 people and injured 850 others. The FBI discovered that the bomb was wired incorrectly and the blast was half as powerful as planned. The bombing produced over seven thousand pounds of evidence for the FBI Laboratory to analyze. The FBI conducted over twenty-five thousand interviews in the case. Later, after a trial, convicted bomber Timothy McVeigh was executed. His accomplice, Terry Nichols, received life in prison. *FBI*

At that point, the FBI requested tanks and five combat vehicles, which Attorney General Janet Reno authorized. With the introduction of tanks, the FBI negotiators no longer control the situation. The Davidians saw no value in negotiating while they were facing an armed tank force. On day thirteen, the FBI cut electric power to the compound. It was cold at night, but Koresh's followers endured the hardships. Meanwhile, nineteen children were released during negotiations. By

On June 26, 1996, five thousand pounds of explosives packed into a truck exploded, drilling a crater thirty-five feet deep and ripping the front off an apartment building in the Khobar Towers. That act of terrorism killed nineteen Americans and injured scores of others. It was the deadliest bombing involving U.S. citizens in the Middle East since the October 23, 1983, truck bombing of a U.S. Marine Corps barracks in Beirut, Lebanon, which claimed 295 lives. The FBI deployed agents to investigate the Khobar Towers bombing. *FBI*

day forty-two, eighty-three people were living in the compound without electricity and running water.

With the negotiations stalled, the attorney general authorized appropriate deadly force if the FBI agents met with armed resistance. The FBI and BATF agents had been conducting around-the-clock operations, including psychological operations. Loud speakers broadcast auditory harassment, and at night, blinding searchlights lit up the compound. A few more Davidians surrendered and were held as material witnesses. Some would face charges and go on to trial. The FBI believed that the longer the siege continued the more likely Koresh would elect a murder/suicide pact similar to Jonestown, Guyana, where over nine hundred people committed suicide a decade before.

The FBI and BATF had destroyed everything outside the main building, but the Davidians had held their ground. The attorney general authorized the FBI to use CS tear gas. On April 19, the FBI launched a gas attack combined with pyrotechnic flash-bang grenades. The assault unexpectedly ignited the gasoline stockpiled inside the building. Fire consumed the complex, killing seventy-six Davidians, including twenty-seven children. David Koresh was found dead with a bullet in his head. The attorney general took responsibility for the debacle, and President Bill Clinton blamed the Davidians for the tragedy.

The government conducted an official investigation of itself. During a special inquiry before the Danforth Committee and during official testimony, the FBI denied the use of pyrotechnic devices. The committee issued a report concluding that the Davidians had started the fire. In 1999, however, the FBI admitted that the testimony it gave before the Danforth Committee was flawed. The FBI now admits to using pyrotechnic grenades on the day of the fire. The FBI's admission of incorrect testimony brought into question the validity of the committee's conclusions.

This devastating photo shows the wake of 2005's Hurricane Katrina. When Katrina hit the Louisiana coast, the FBI's disaster squad performed the grim task of helping to identify bodies. *Gerald Nino*

The government put some of the surviving Branch Davidians on trial. All were acquitted of conspiring to murder federal agents, but some were convicted of aiding and abetting voluntary manslaughter.

At first, Attorney General Reno explained in a *Washington Post* article dated April 20, 1993, that a paramount reason for approving the assault was that "babies were being beaten." FBI Director William Sessions said the next day there was no contemporary evidence of child abuse. Reno revised her statement several months later, agreeing there was no evidence of ongoing child abuse.

The images of the burning buildings at Waco and the killing of Randy Weaver's wife and son remain fresh in people's minds, even more than a decade after the episodes. To many people, it appears the FBI now labors under the presumption of guilt or noninnocence before the facts are known.

Critical Incident Response Group

In response to Ruby Ridge and Waco, the FBI formed the Critical Incident Response Group (CIRG) in 1994 to facilitate the FBI's rapid response to, and management of, future crisis incidents. CIRG deploys in response to terrorist activities, hostage situations, child abductions, and other high-risk repetitive violent crimes, including prison riots, bombings, air and train crashes, natural disasters, and armed standoffs.

In a new approach, the FBI learned to make proactive contacts with local militia leaders so that the two sides can voice their concerns and discuss issues in a nonconfrontational way, before a siege mentality sets in. The FBI can establish the initial contact simply by calling the local leadership and arranging an informal meeting at a mutually agreeable location. By talking, the FBI allows militia representatives to assess the character of the officers apart from the positions they hold. The episodes at Ruby Ridge and Waco taught the FBI many valuable lessons. It would not be long before those lessons were put to the test.

The Montana Freemen Standoff

On March 25, 1996, members of the Freemen barricaded themselves in on a 960-acre ranch in Brusett, Montana. The Freemen were a Christian Patriot group who believed in individual sovereignty and rejected the authority of the federal and state governments. In defiance, they set up a common-law court, banking, and credit system.

The standoff was precipitated when FBI agents arrested LeRoy Schweitzer, the group's self-taught legal strategist, and Daniel Peterson Jr., another Freeman, on charges of mail and bank fraud and passing millions of dollars worth of bogus checks. They and twenty-four of the Freemen were living on the ranch, which had been foreclosed on because the family who owned it had stopped making mortgage payments.

The Freemen reject the validity of the U.S., state, and county governments, refusing even to register their cars. Since they claimed the U.S. government had no jurisdiction over their

U.S. Senator Paul Wellstone and seven others died on October 25, 2002, when his plane crashed on Minnesota's Iron Range. The FBI sent an evidence recovery team to the crash site. When a government official is on board, the FBI takes all the precautions to make sure it was an accident and not a criminal act. The later investigation revealed pilot error caused the crash. *FBI*

If a biological threat is in the form of a letter, it is sent to a Centers for Disease Control–certified lab to ensure it is not contaminated. Then it is forwarded to the FBI Laboratory to test for fingerprints, DNA, and trace evidence. The FBI Behavioral Analysis Unit analyzes the letter's language and writing, which could provide important clues. The return addresses on the letters addressed to Senators Daschle and Leahy were phony: Franklin Park, New Jersey, exists, but the zip code, 08852, is for nearby Monmouth Junction. There is no Greendale School in New Jersey, although there is a Greenbrook Elementary School in South Brunswick Township, of which Monmouth Junction is a part. *FBI*

ranch, which they dubbed "Justus Township," they demanded a trial by other Freemen, using their own constitution. For months, they refused to leave the ranch, which they claimed as sovereign territory.

On day two, Schweitzer and Peterson appeared in federal court, refusing to allow the indictment to be read. U.S. Marshals and deputies, who set up camp outside the ranch's fence line, were joined by the FBI. The FBI wanted to arrest more than a dozen adults at the ranch on charges that included threatening to kill a federal judge.

The Freemen were known to be well armed. The FBI would attempt to negotiate a peaceful end to the standoff. Beyond the fence, FBI agents and other law enforcement agencies waited. The FBI had prepared for a long siege. Agents had everything they needed—long guns, body armor, and sidearms. Based on experience, they knew that their most valuable tool would be patience.

The FBI's new CIRG handled the Freemen siege, bringing in all FBI crisis units. The Hostage Rescue Team, additional SWAT personnel, hostage negotiators, behavioral scientists, and other specialists arrived on the scene.

With memories of the raids at Waco and Ruby Ridge still fresh in the minds of Americans, the FBI sought a peaceful solution to the standoff. The agents slowly increased the pressure on the Freemen, cutting phone lines and limiting family visits.

By day twenty-five, the FBI agents had become anxious. They brought in reinforcements in anticipation of violence sparked by the anniversary of the Waco, Texas, disaster and the 1995 Oklahoma City bombing. And yet, the day passed without incident. Organizers of a support rally had predicted some eight hundred people would arrive for the event. Instead, fewer than ten showed up.

Five weeks into the siege, Freemen leaders rejected an FBI proposal to meet face-to-face away from the ranch to discuss terms of surrender. By day sixty, the FBI prepared to end the siege, bringing in portable power generators near the ranch in advance of shutting off electric power. Later, the FBI evicted the media from the area surrounding the ranch after two television news reporters try to slip into the compound.

On day seventy, the FBI moved three armored trucks to within two miles of the compound. Two days later, they cut power to the ranch. Four more people gave up. There were sixteen Freemen left inside the compound. On day eighty, FBI agents met with the Freemen outside the ranch, and the last child was released.

On June 13, 1996, eighty-one days into the standoff, the last sixteen holdouts surrendered, ending the longest federal siege in modern U.S. history. Members of the group faced charges of threatening federal officials and defrauding banks and businesses of more than $1.8 million. For the peaceful resolution of the siege, officials credited the new crisis-management strategy that emphasized negotiations over violence.

Anthrax letters

Before September 11, 2001, a nuclear, chemical, or biological attack by terrorists was virtually unthinkable. Soon after the 9/11 terrorist attacks, however, the FBI was faced with a potentially disastrous biological attack. Two anthrax attacks became the worst biological attacks in U.S. history and the focus of the largest and most complex criminal investigations in FBI history.

One week after the World Trade Center and Pentagon terrorist attacks, the FBI believes someone mailed five letters containing anthrax spores. The letters

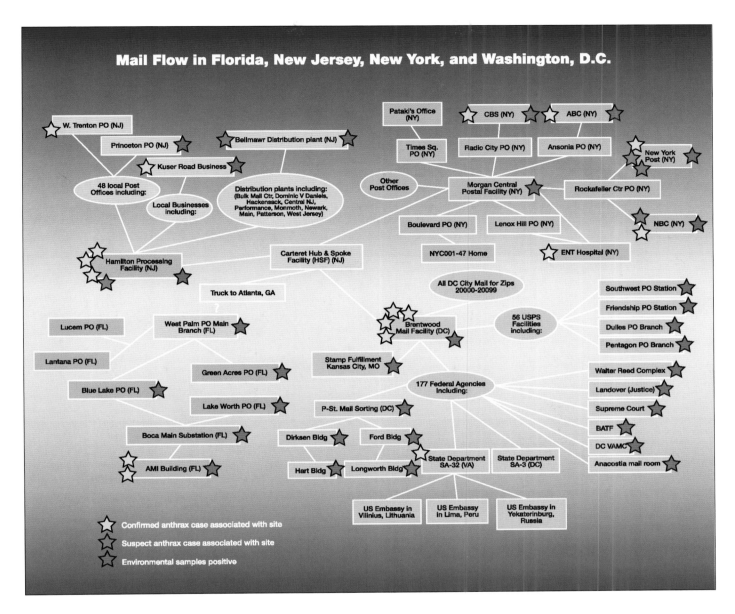

Mail Flow in Florida, New Jersey, New York, and Washington, D.C.

W. Trenton PO (NJ)

Princeton PO (NJ)

Kuser Road Business

Bellmawr Distribution plant (NJ)

48 local Post Offices including:

Local Businesses including:

Distribution plants including: (Bulk Mail Ctr, Dominic V Daniels, Hackensack, Central NJ, Performance, Monmoth, Newark, Main, Patterson, West Jersey)

Other Post Offices

Pataki's Office (NY)

CBS (NY)

ABC (NY)

Times Sq. PO (NY)

Radio City PO (NY)

Ansonia PO (NY)

New York Post (NY)

Morgan Central Postal Facility (NY)

Rockafeller Ctr PO (NY)

Boulevard PO (NY)

Lenox Hill PO (NY)

NBC (NY)

NYC001-47 Home

ENT Hospital (NY)

Hamilton Processing Facility (NJ)

Carteret Hub & Spoke Facility (HSF) (NJ)

All DC City Mail for Zips 20000-20099

Truck to Atlanta, GA

56 USPS Facilities including:

Southwest PO Station

Friendship PO Station

Dulles PO Branch

Pentagon PO Branch

Lucem PO (FL)

West Palm PO Main Branch (FL)

Brentwood Mail Facility (DC)

Lantana PO (FL)

Stamp Fulfillment Kansas City, MO

Walter Reed Complex

Green Acres PO (FL)

177 Federal Agencies Including:

Landover (Justice)

Blue Lake PO (FL)

Lake Worth PO (FL)

P-St. Mail Sorting (DC)

Supreme Court

Boca Main Substation (FL)

BATF

DC VAMC

AMI Building (FL)

Dirksen Bldg

Ford Bldg

Anacostia mail room

Hart Bldg

Longworth Bldg

State Department SA-32 (VA)

State Department SA-3 (DC)

US Embassy in Vilinius, Lithuania

US Embassy in Lima, Peru

US Embassy in Yekaterinburg, Russia

☆ Confirmed anthrax case associated with site

☆ Suspect anthrax case associated with site

☆ Environmental samples positive

The Centers for Disease Control analyzed the mail flow of the anthrax-contaminated letters. An FBI spokesman said, "We do know that the anthrax was mailed from 10 Nassau Street, Princeton, New Jersey, from a mailbox. We know the flow of the mail flow, and it would appear to many of us that have worked this investigation, that it's much more consistent with someone being an American-born and having some level of familiarity with the Princeton-Clinton, New Jersey, area." *CDC*

were postmarked Trenton, New Jersey, and dated September 18, 2001. Four of the letters were mailed to ABC News, CBS News, NBC News, and the *New York Post*, all in New York City. A fifth letter was mailed to the *National Enquirer* at American Media Inc. (AMI) in Boca Raton, Florida. Robert Stevens, a photojournalist, worked at a newspaper called the *Sun*, published by AMI, and was the first person to die from the mailings. Only the letters to the *New York Post* and NBC News arrived. The existence of the other two letters is suggested from the pattern of infections.

HMRT members use dive cameras to photograph a chemical crime scene. These cameras can be decontaminated and used again. An HMRT consists of special agents who have undergone a minimum of three hundred hours of training to obtain technician-level certification, and they recertify every year. *Henry M. Holden*

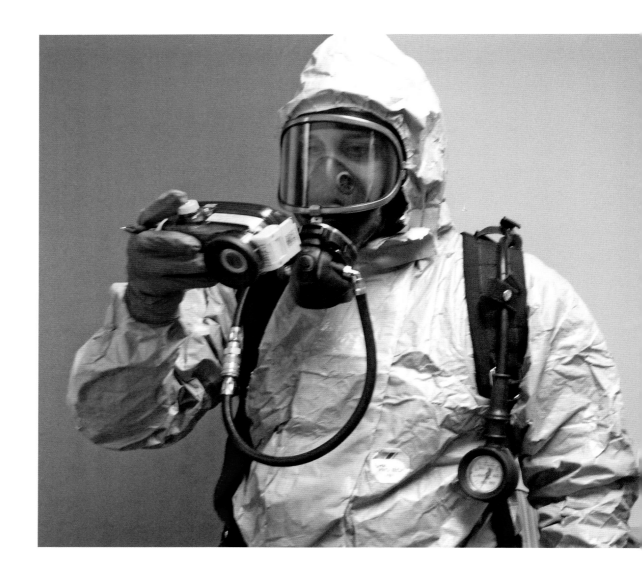

This is an FBI base of operations vehicle (BOV) used to respond to suspected or actual hazardous material incidents, serving as a science and technology platform. The forty-five-foot-long BOV can remain on scene twenty-four hours a day. It has a bunk room, shower, restroom, and a wide array of electronics. The two blisters above the cab are just two of the many antennae that can transmit both secure and nonsecure voice, data, and video. All FBI communications report to the BOV, where information is distributed via self-contained cell phone repeaters or to a satellite. *Henry M. Holden*

Inside the BOV, live video feeds can be sent to the FBI's Strategic Information and Operations Center (SIOC) in Washington. The BOV is equipped to safely package chemical, biological, and nuclear material for shipment to a laboratory. *Henry M. Holden*

Two more letters, postmarked October 9, 2001, also in Trenton, turned up three weeks after the first mailing. The letters were addressed to Senators Tom Daschle (D-South Dakota), and Patrick Leahy (D-Vermont). A Senate aide opened the Daschle letter on October 15, and the government shut down all mail service. The Leahy letter was discovered unopened in an impounded mailbag on November 16. It had been misdirected to the State Department mail annex in Sterling, Virginia, because a postal worker had misread the zip code. The postal worker contracted inhalation anthrax but survived.

The FBI believes all the anthrax letters were mailed from Princeton, New Jersey. All six hundred mailboxes that could have been used to mail the letters were tested for anthrax. Only one, the box at 10 Nassau Street, tested positive.

The material in the Senate letters was more potent than the first set of letters. It was a highly refined dry powder consisting of approximately one gram of almost pure spores. Earlier reports described the material in the Senate letters as "weaponized" or "weapons-grade" anthrax. However, in September 2006, the *Washington Post* reported that the FBI no longer believed this was true.

While the anthrax material had the potential to kill thousands of people, minimizing the public's exposure

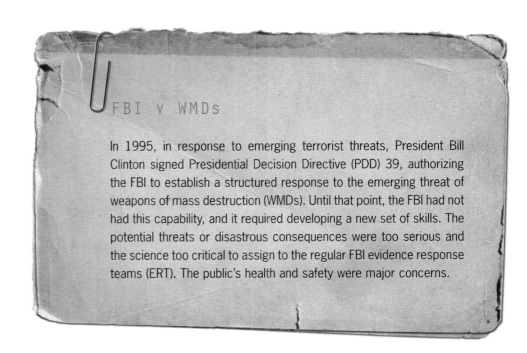

FBI v WMDs

In 1995, in response to emerging terrorist threats, President Bill Clinton signed Presidential Decision Directive (PDD) 39, authorizing the FBI to establish a structured response to the emerging threat of weapons of mass destruction (WMDs). Until that point, the FBI had not had this capability, and it required developing a new set of skills. The potential threats or disastrous consequences were too serious and the science too critical to assign to the regular FBI evidence response teams (ERT). The public's health and safety were major concerns.

In this simulated raid scene, the FBI agents use flash-bang grenades. HRT operators may sometimes use explosives to breach a door. In the Waco standoff, this tactic created the devastating fires inside the compound. *FBI*

was critical to controlling the spread. Quick deployment of the FBI's Hazardous Material Response Unit (HMRU) probably saved thousands of lives.

At least seventeen post offices and public office buildings were contaminated. Including cleanup costs, an FBI document put the damage in excess of $1 billion. Twenty-two people developed anthrax infections, eleven of the life-threatening inhalation variety, and five of those infected died.

In addition to the death of Robert Stevens in Florida, two people died from inhalation anthrax from unknown sources. The theory is that the two victims were probably infected through cross-contamination of the mail; Kathy Nguyen worked in New York City and Ottilie Lundgren, a ninety-four-year-old widow, was from Connecticut. The two other deaths from inhalation anthrax were employees of the Brentwood mail facility in Washington, D.C., who had likely handled one or more of the letters.

To date, one of the most exhaustive investigations in FBI history has yielded no arrests. However, the FBI has developed a linguistic and behavioral profile of the offender. The FBI believes the offender is a U.S. scientist who had access to the high-grade anthrax and knowledge of how to manipulate it physically for use as a weapon. Of the offender, the FBI has said, "It is highly probable, bordering on certainty, that all three letters (that were found) were authored by the same person. Letters one and two are identical copies. Letter three, however, contains a somewhat different message than the other letters. The anthrax utilized in letter three was much more refined, more potent, and more easily disbursed than letters one and two . . . While the text in these letters is limited, there are certain distinctive characteristics in the author's writing style. These same characteristics may be evident in other letters, greeting cards, or envelopes this person has written."

Among the behavioral characteristics, the FBI said the offender "is likely an adult male. If employed, is likely to be in a position requiring little contact with the public, or other employees. He may work in a laboratory . . . . He probably has a scientific background to some extent, or at least a strong interest in science, and likely has taken appropriate protective steps to ensure his own safety, which may include the use of an anthrax vaccination or antibiotics. He has access to a source of anthrax and possesses knowledge and expertise to refine it."

The FBI and postal inspectors have followed leads on four continents, conducted more than 9,100 interviews, issued more than six thousand subpoenas, and carried out sixty-seven authorized searches of houses, laboratories, and other locations. As of 2007, the case remains open. ∎

The United States Postal Inspection Service, Federal Bureau of Investigation and U.S. DOT Office of Inspector General

$120,000 REWARD

A reward is being offered of up to $120,000 for information leading to the arrest and conviction of the individual(s) responsible for the mailing of letters containing the poison ricin and ricin derivative.

Threatening communications inside each envelope made reference to pending hours-of-service regulations by the Department of Transportation; specifically, the number of hours truck drivers would be allowed to drive before a required rest period. The substance in the first letter was enclosed in a small metal vial.

"caution RICIN POISON"
"Enclosed in sealed container"
"Do not open without proper protection"

First letter discovered in Greenville, SC on 10/15/2003:

The following is a representation of the language contained in the threat letter:

"to the department of transportation: I'm a fleet owner of a tankard company.
I have easy access to castor pulp. If my demand is dismissed I'm capable of making Ricin.
My demand is simple, January 4 2004 starts the new hours of service for trucks which include a ridiculous ten hours in the sleeper berth. Keep at eight.
You have been warned this is the only letter that will be sent by me."

Second letter postmarked in Chattanooga, TN on 10/17/2003:

"Department of Transportation

If you change the hours of service on January 4, 2004 I will turn D.C. into a ghost town
The powder on the letter is RICIN
have a nice day"

Fallen Angel

The person(s) responsible for these threats infers a connection to the trucking/transportation industry, but any potential leads should be reported.

Anyone having information, contact the Tip Line 1-866-839-6241

All information will be held in strict confidence. Reward payment will be made in accordance with conditions of Postal Service Reward Poster 296, dated February 2000.

All Information will be Kept Confidential!

In October 2004, the FBI, U.S. Postal Inspection Service, and the U.S. Department of Transportation Office of Inspector General increased the reward money to $120,000 for information leading to the arrest and conviction of the individual(s) responsible for introducing threatening letters containing ricin into postal facilities in Greenville, South Carolina, and Chattanooga, Tennessee, in October 2003. _FBI_

In this training exercise, the Remotec ANDROS robot precedes a Hazardous Materials Response Team (HMRT) into a room suspected to be the site of homemade nerve gas. It is sampling the air from two detection devices onboard and feeding the contaminant levels in the air back to its operator. The robot is equipped with cameras, grippers, sensors, and tools that are useful during a chemical or bomb threat response. A robot can enter a dangerous area while the human operator is safely hundreds of feet away. *Henry M. Holden*

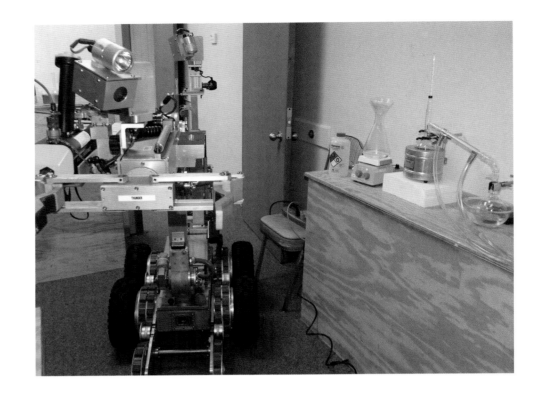

At a safe distance from the suspected site, the FBI technician reads the sensors from the Remotec ANDROS. *Henry M. Holden*

As the many small parts of TWA Flight 800 suggest, it was a long and tedious job to reassemble the airliner. The catastrophic explosion, just twelve minutes after takeoff, over the Atlantic Ocean on July 17, 1996, resulted in initial speculation that it was a terrorist attack using a missile or bomb. Just three weeks earlier, a bomb had killed nineteen Americans in the Khobar Towers in Saudi Arabia. The FBI's joint terrorism task force and the National Transportation Safety Board (NTSB) determined it was not a criminal or terrorist act. Yet, in 2007, the case is still open. *U.S. Coast Guard*

On May 7, 2000, a fire ripped through the headquarters of Holbrook Inc., an Olympia, Washington, timber company. Three weeks later, the Earth Liberation Front (ELF) issued a communiqué claiming credit on behalf of a group called "Revenge of the Trees." ELF is the collective name for anonymous and autonomous cells that use "direct action in the form of economic sabotage to stop the exploitation and destruction of the natural environment." The FBI classified ELF as a top domestic terror threat. *FBI*

Special Agent in Charge Gregory Jones, shown here, headed the investigation into a suspicious letter received by the clerk of the Eleventh Circuit Court of Appeals in Atlanta on December 22, 2004. The letter included specific threats against two circuit judges. FBI HazMat teams were deployed to the court to deal with the threat. The powder, letter, and envelope were collected and tested. The powder turned out to be detergent and tested negative for any biological or chemical agents. A similar letter containing a white powder went to the United States Supreme Court. The second letter, directed to the president, was sent in March 2005. The letter made specific threats toward President Bush and his family. This letter also contained a white powdery substance that proved to be detergent. The FBI traced the letters back to an inmate incarcerated in a Florida state prison. *FBI*

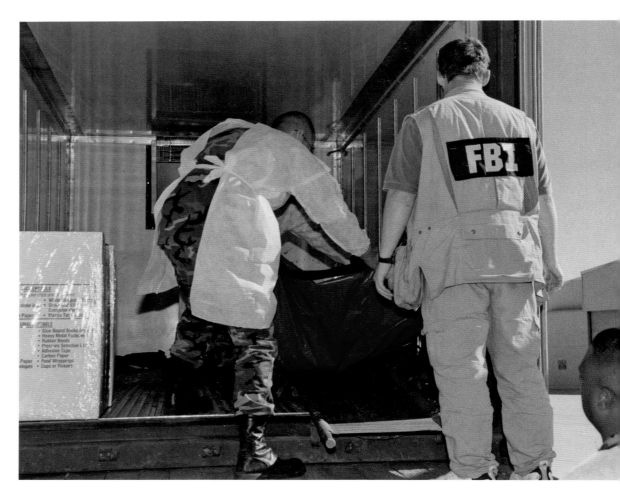

In the two months following Katrina, members of the disaster squad examined 816 victims. With help of personnel from other agencies, 155 bodies were positively identified through fingerprints. Efforts to identify the remaining victims continued at the FBI Laboratory. To date, not including 9/11 and the tsunami in 2004, the disaster squad has assisted in 230 disasters involving 10,687 victims. It has positively identified 6,809 victims by fingerprints, palm prints, or footprints. *FBI*

Special Agent in Charge of the Washington field office Van A. Harp directed two critical investigations. He was vacationing on September 11, 2001, in Hilton Head, South Carolina, with his wife, four children, and six grandchildren. His secretary paged him, and he flipped on the television to see the second plane slam into the World Trade Center. All planes were grounded, but an FBI plane received a waiver, and Harp was able to fly home to investigate the Pentagon attack. Within a month, he was confronted with the anthrax investigation. *FBI*

In January 2005, a freight train collided with a parked train in Graniteville, South Carolina, releasing a load of chlorine, killing nine people, and hospitalizing several hundred. Since the collision released poison gas and it was a possible criminal act, the NTSB investigation team requested FBI forensic assistance. The HMRT deployed to the accident site and documented the railroad switch involved in the derailment, retrieving the switch lock for forensic analysis. Investigators later determined a crew working on the parked train failed to reset the switch, causing the train to leave the main track, hit a parked train, and derail, spilling its hazardous load. *FBI*

On August 26, 1980, three men wheeled a piece of office equipment into the offices of the eleven-story Harvey's Resort Hotel in Lake Tahoe. On the case was stenciled "IBM." Once it was in place, the bomb was armed. The extortion note read: "This bomb is so sensitive that the slightest movement either inside or outside will cause it to explode." The only thing authorities could do to find out how to disarm it was to pay $3 million in unmarked $100 bills. The FBI X-rayed the device, found motion detectors, and confirmed what the note said. The FBI decided to disarm the bomb by taking out the detonator with a seven pound shaped charge of C4. Pressure waves move off an explosive at right angles, so by shaping the charge, it can aim the force of the explosion. It was a big gamble. In theory, the method should have worked. In reality, it toppled the bomb and a thousand pounds of dynamite blew a five story cavity into the building. No one was hurt. The FBI soon captured the bomber, John Birges Sr., who was sentenced to two twenty-year terms without parole. Harvey's rebuilt the casino bigger than it had been before the bombing. *FBI*

The International Criminal Tribunal for the Former Yugoslavia requested FBI forensic assistance to support a six-count indictment of mass murder by Yugoslavian President Slobodan Milosevic and four Serbian leaders. The FBI forensic team processed several sites in July 1999. The team exhumed the bodies of 124 victims and processed six "killing" areas. Field autopsies determined the cause of death to be multiple gunshots for the majority of the victims, although some died from blunt-force trauma. Victims ranged from a two-year-old boy to a ninety-four-year-old female. *FBI*

The HMRU maintains a twenty-four-hour-a-day ready status to deploy domestically or overseas in support of FBI criminal investigations and national security matters involving hazardous materials and other hazardous crime scenes. *Henry M. Holden*

In the recovery efforts of Egypt Air Flight 990, which crashed off the Massachusetts coast on October 31, 1999, the FBI Laboratory provided onsite forensic support. Examiners from the DNA, Chemistry, Explosives, and Latent Print Units and Evidence Response Team members assisted in the collection and separation of human remains, personal effects, and aircraft parts. *FBI*

Bomb Data Center specialists develop techniques, technology, and equipment that minimizes the hazards associated with bomb disposal, and they administer the training for the FBI's special agent bomb technician program. *Henry M. Holden*

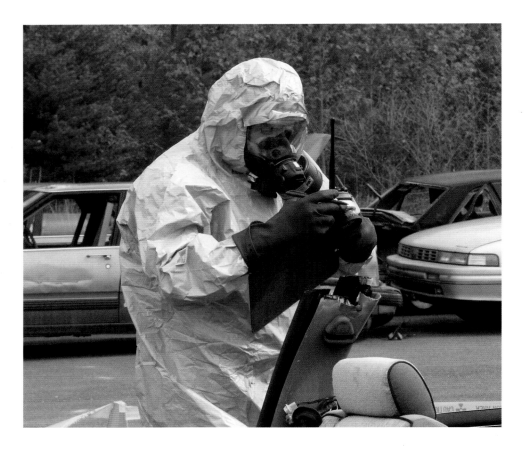

The FBI Hazardous Materials Response Unit responds to events involving the threatened, actual, illicit, or accidental use of chemical, biological, and radiological materials. It contains three collaborating entities: a scientific program, Hazmat ERT, and FBI Logistics. It provides rapid scientific and technical assessments of threats. *Henry M. Holden*

The anthrax investigation has parallels to another lengthy FBI investigation: the eighteen-year search for the Unabomber, who killed three people and injured twenty-three others in mail-bomb attacks. Agents pored over fifty-three thousand hotline tips and bomb parts, and searched massive computer databases, but the breakthrough did not come until the Unabomber issued a public manifesto. The document led to the 1996 arrest of Theodore Kaczynski, whose brother recognized his prose, and tipped the FBI. From the bomb parts, the FBI was able to reconstruct the bombs. *FBI*

FBI TEN MOST WANTED FUGITIVE

MURDER OF U.S. NATIONALS OUTSIDE THE UNITED STATES;
CONSPIRACY TO MURDER U.S. NATIONALS OUTSIDE THE UNITED STATES;
ATTACK ON A FEDERAL FACILITY RESULTING IN DEATH

USAMA BIN LADEN

Date of Photograph Unknown

Aliases: Usama Bin Muhammad Bin Ladin, Shaykh Usama Bin Ladin, the Prince, the Emir, Abu Abdallah, Mujahid Shaykh, Hajj, the Director

DESCRIPTION

Date of Birth:	1957	Hair:	Brown
Place of Birth:	Saudi Arabia	Eyes:	Brown
Height:	6' 4" to 6' 6"	Complexion:	Olive
Weight:	Approximately 160 pounds	Sex:	Male
Build:	Thin	Nationality:	Saudi Arabian
Occupation:	Unknown		
Remarks:	Bin Laden is the leader of a terrorist organization known as Al-Qaeda, "The Base." He is left-handed and walks with a cane.		

CAUTION

USAMA BIN LADEN IS WANTED IN CONNECTION WITH THE AUGUST 7, 1998, BOMBINGS OF
THE UNITED STATES EMBASSIES IN DAR ES SALAAM, TANZANIA, AND NAIROBI, KENYA.
THESE ATTACKS KILLED OVER 200 PEOPLE. IN ADDITION, BIN LADEN IS A SUSPECT IN
OTHER TERRORIST ATTACKS THROUGHOUT THE WORLD.

CONSIDERED ARMED AND EXTREMELY DANGEROUS

IF YOU HAVE ANY INFORMATION CONCERNING THIS PERSON, PLEASE CONTACT YOUR
LOCAL FBI OFFICE OR THE NEAREST U.S. EMBASSY OR CONSULATE.

REWARD

The Rewards For Justice Program, United States Department of State, is offering a reward of up to $25 million for information leading directly to the apprehension or conviction of Usama Bin Laden. An additional $2 million is being

On August 7, 1998, bombs exploded at the U.S. Embassy at Dar es Salaam, Tanzania, and in Nairobi, Kenya. The FBI investigated both bombings and, on June 7, 1999, the FBI placed Osama bin Laden on the Ten Most Wanted Fugitives list for his alleged involvement in the bombing of the two embassies in Africa. The FBI and other teams dedicated to tracking bin Laden and his network linked two dozen suspects to bin Laden. Four individuals were arrested and, on May 29, 2001, the U.S. Attorney's Office and the FBI announced their convictions in connection with the bombings. The four received life in federal prison without the possibility of release. The rewards are generally $100,000 but can range up to $5 million; in the case of bin Laden, the reward is $25 million. He remains at large in 2007. *FBI*

Members of the FBI, Federal Aviation Authority, and air force work together in the Crisis Action Center at McGuire Air Force Base during a simulated hijack exercise. *Department of Defense*

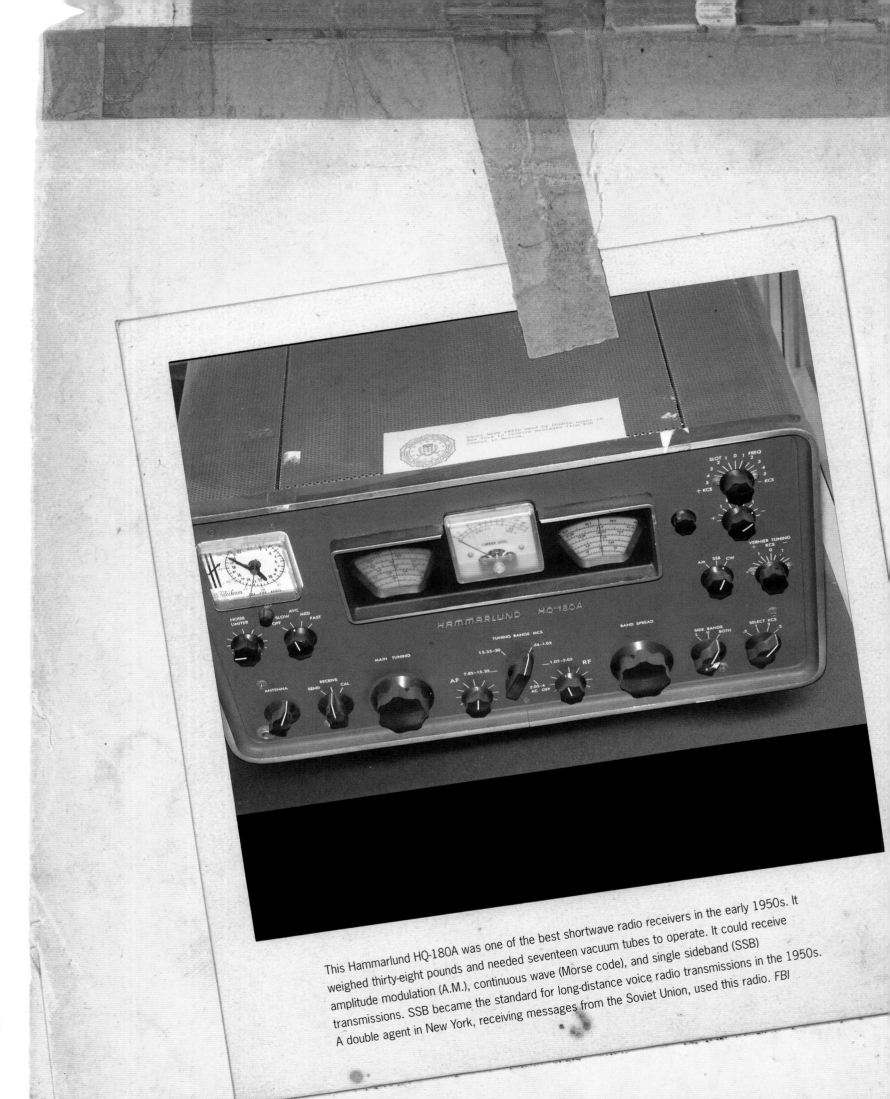

This Hammarlund HQ-180A was one of the best shortwave radio receivers in the early 1950s. It weighed thirty-eight pounds and needed seventeen vacuum tubes to operate. It could receive amplitude modulation (A.M.), continuous wave (Morse code), and single sideband (SSB) transmissions. SSB became the standard for long-distance voice radio transmissions in the 1950s. A double agent in New York, receiving messages from the Soviet Union, used this radio. FBI

212

Chapter 9

SNEAK AND PEEK
Domestic Surveillance and Wiretapping

Domestic surveillance has existed since the founding of the country; however, the equipment and techniques have become more sophisticated over the years. Since authorization in October 2001 of the Patriot Act (officially, the USA Patriot Act, or the Providing Appropriate Tools Required to Intercept and Obstruct Terrorism Act of 2001) there have been hours of debate on its encroachment into our private lives. Opponents of the legislations claim the president is not authorized to conduct warrantless surveillance. Others feel it is an effective weapon in the war on terrorism. Does the Patriot Act encroach on Americans' privacy through domestic surveillance, and is this anything new?

Federal Communications Act of 1934

On June 20, 1934, President Franklin Roosevelt signed the Federal Communications Act (FCA). The purpose of the act was to transfer jurisdiction over wire and radio communication to the newly formed Federal Communications Commission (FCC).

The party line was used for years by telephone companies. Up to six people shared the same telephone switching equipment. The equipment in the telephone central office was a safe place for wiretaps. Usually, trusted employees were used to wire the connections needed to extend a tap to a field location. *Library of Congress*

Section 605 of the act bans wiretapping. However, the law did not explicitly apply this ban against the "interception and divulgence" of communications "transmitted by wire" to federal agents. The loophole gave the FBI reason to continue employing wiretaps during criminal investigations.

In the provision of Section 605, it says: ". . . no person not being authorized by the sender shall intercept any communication and divulge or publish the existence, contents, substance, purport, effect or meaning of such intercepted communication to any person."

Historians note that Congress had intended this law to protect the integrity of the communications system, not the increased wiretapping that resulted. When the Supreme Court ruled in *Nardone v United States* (1937), it said that the Federal Communications Act forbade the use of evidence collected in wiretaps in federal courts. Since the court had found a statutory problem with wiretapping and not a constitutional prohibition, it was within the power of Congress to amend Section 605 to allow law enforcement to wiretap.

In 1938, both houses of Congress attempted to pass similar versions of such a bill, but each died in committee. Another attempt was made in 1939, but opposition from within the Executive Branch, and a Senate committee in 1940, killed the bill. Attorney General Cummings banned wiretapping, except when approved by the attorney general's office. This rule was not universally applied or consistently enforced, and the situation remained unresolved.

Warrantless Surveillance Goes to War

On May 21, 1940, President Roosevelt authorized the FBI to conduct warrantless electronic surveillance, with the prior approval of the Attorney General, ". . . of individuals suspected of subversion or espionage." The surveillance was to be . . . limited to German aliens. Nevertheless, the actions were still illegal. Roosevelt advised Hoover that he was to keep "no detailed record" of the cases where wiretaps were used.

Alexander Graham Bell demonstrates a telephone call between Salem, Massachusetts, and Boston. Almost immediately, the telephone became a means of eavesdropping. The wiretap received its name because historically a monitoring device was connected to the wires of the telephone line of the person who was being monitored. During the Civil War, the government eavesdropped on telegraph communications, and Southern Confederate General J.E.B. Stuart had an aide who tapped into the telegraph lines. According to Walter F. Murphy, author of *Wiretapping on Trial* (New York: Random House, 1965), New York City police in the years 1953 and 1954 tapped over 3,500 telephones; over half of them were public payphones. *Library of Congress*

SECRET

Memorandum to Mr. C. D. DeLoach
Re: "BLACK BAG" JOBS

have been operating this program for twelve years and
year the evaluation of the value of the information obtained
is included in our annual budget. In addition, the intelligence value of the information received has been beyond
calculation.

We have used this technique on a highly selective
basis, but with wide-range effectiveness, in our operations.
We have several cases in the espionage field, for example,
where through "black bag" jobs we determined that suspected
illegal agents actually had concealed on their premises the
equipment through which they carried out their clandestine
operations.

Also through the use of this technique we have on
numerous occasions been able to obtain material held highly
secret and closely guarded by subversive groups and organizations which consisted of membership lists and mailing lists
of these organizations.

This applies even to our investigation of the
Ku Klux Klan. You may recall that recently through a
"black bag" job we obtained the records in the possession of
three high-ranking officials of a klan organization in
Louisiana. These records gave us the complete membership
and financial information concerning the klan's operation
which we have been using most effectively to disrupt the
organization and, in fact, to bring about its near disintegration.

It was through information obtained through our
"black bag" operations that we obtained the basic information
used to compromise and to bring about the expulsion of
William Albertson, the former Executive Secretary of the
Communist Party New York District organization.

Through the same technique we have recently been
receiving extremely valuable information concerning political
developments in the Latin American field, and we also have
been able to use it most effectively in a number of instances

CONTINUED -- OVER

SECRET

SECRET

ROUTE IN ENVELOPE

OPTIONAL FORM NO. 10
MAY 1962 EDITION
GSA GEN. REG. NO. 27

UNITED STATES GOVERNMENT

Memorandum

TO : Mr. C. D. DeLoach   DATE: July 19, 1966

FROM : W. C. Sullivan   DO NOT FILE

SUBJECT: "BLACK BAG" JOBS

ALL INFORMATION CONTAINED
HEREIN IS UNCLASSIFIED EXC
WHERE SHOWN OTHERWISE.

The following is set forth in regard to your
request concerning what authority we have for "black bag"
jobs and for the background of our policy and procedures
in such matters.

We do not obtain authorization for "black bag"
jobs from outside the Bureau. Such a technique involves
trespass and is clearly illegal; therefore, it would be
impossible to obtain any legal sanction for it. Despite
this, "black bag" jobs have been used because they represent
an invaluable technique in combating subversive activities
of a clandestine nature aimed directly at undermining and
destroying our nation.

The present procedure followed in the use of this
technique calls for the Special Agent in Charge of a field
office to make his request for the use of the technique
to the appropriate Assistant Director. The Special Agent
in Charge must completely justify the need for the use of
the technique and at the same time assure that it can be
safely used without any danger or embarrassment to the
Bureau. The facts are incorporated in a memorandum which,
in accordance with the Director's instructions, is sent to
Mr. Tolson or to the Director for approval. Subsequently
this memorandum is filed in the Assistant Director's office
under a "Do Not File" procedure.

In the field the Special Agent in Charge prepares
an informal memorandum showing that he obtained Bureau
authority and this memorandum is filed in his safe until
the next inspection by Bureau Inspectors, at which time it
is destroyed.

Our most comprehensive use of this technique and
a measure of the outstanding success we have achieved with
it involves its use in

FJB/pcn

CONTINUED -- OVER

TOP SECRET

SECRET

TOP SECRET

Memorandum to Mr. C. D. DeLoach
re: "BLACK BAG" JOBS

recently through which we have obtained information concerning
growing   intelligence activities directed
at this country.

In short, it is a very valuable weapon which we have
used to combat the highly clandestine efforts of subversive
elements seeking to undermine our Nation.

RECOMMENDATION:

For your information.

no more such techniques must be used.

(Hoover)

The three-page FBI memorandum where
Hoover discontinued warrantless surveillance.
FBI

The U.S. Army's Signal Intelligence Service, the precursor to the National Security Agency, began a secret program in February 1943 later codenamed "Venona." The Venona Project was a long-running and highly secret collaboration between United States intelligence agencies and the United Kingdom's MI5, involving the cryptanalysis of messages sent by several Soviet intelligence agencies. *FBI*

On July 8, 1942, President Roosevelt barred all agencies except the FBI and the military from code breaking activities. In a turf-protecting move, the military interpreted this directive as authorization to deny signals intelligence to OSS.

In July 1946, Attorney General Thomas Clark (who rubber-stamped most of Hoover's biddings) wrote to President Truman asking him to renew Roosevelt's 1940 authorization of the warrantless wiretaps. Clark's letter quoted from FDR's original authorization but omitted one key sentence: "You are requested furthermore to limit these investigations so conducted to a minimum and to limit them insofar as possible to aliens." Truman approved the request unaware that there was an omission from the original authorization or that Hoover had written the letter sent by Clark. Clark, too, was apparently unaware of the omission. That omission gave Hoover unlimited authority to place an unlimited number of wiretaps on anyone at anytime.

Venona Project

The release of the Venona transcripts and material from Soviet intelligence archives after the collapse of the Soviet Union in 1991 added more information for the discussion of what had been going on in domestic intelligence gathering in postwar America. The Soviet records corroborated the general contention of Hoover and Senator Joseph McCarthy that communist spies had infiltrated the federal government. Other data (post–Cold War) has shown that Hoover and McCarthy overestimated the actual capacity of the Soviets to do military and economic damage to the United States.

The American Communist Party had senior members working for the Soviet Union. The communist spies included Julius Rosenberg, Theodore Alvin Holtzberg (a.k.a. Theodore Hall), Elizabeth Bentley, Alger Hiss, and others. Hall was an American physicist who provided nuclear secrets to the Soviets. He gave a detailed description of the Fat Man plutonium bomb, and the processes for purifying plutonium, to Soviet intelligence. Hall was never charged with a crime because the government felt it would compromise Venona. Hall suffered from Parkinson's disease and died of cancer at the age of seventy-four in England.

The Venona program ran from 1943 to 1980. Although it started with a fixed goal—to monitor Soviet diplomatic signals—National Security Agency (NSA) customers, the FBI, CIA, and Allied intelligence services asked that the program continue, as investigative leads developed further and there was hope that cover names would be revealed.

On September 1, 1947, Colonel Carter Clarke of the NSA briefed the FBI's liaison to the NSA, Special Agent S. Wesley Reynolds, on the breaks in Soviet diplomatic messages. Clarke was looking for Soviet cover names and wondered if the Bureau knew of any. Reynolds had a list of 200 cover names. Most of them were not found in the message traffic. Reynolds turned them over to the NSA, and the message fragments were placed in a safe and forgotten.

The FBI's investigations soon benefited from the NSA's work. On June 4, 1948, FBI Headquarters sent a top-secret letter to the Washington field office relaying information about Max Elitcher, a known communist. Elitcher maintained that Julius Rosenberg had attempted to recruit him as a spy. Although Elitcher shared many of Rosenberg and Morton Sobell's political beliefs, he claimed to have never passed secret information to either of them. Elitcher testified against Rosenberg, and said he accompanied Sobell to a location in New York, where Sobell passed film to Julius Rosenberg.

President Truman won the Democrat Party's nomination in July 1948, and the Republican-controlled Congress began hearings on the Soviet presence within the government. Elizabeth Bentley was called as a witness. The hearings produced dramatic charges, denials, and countercharges. To the credit of the FBI and NSA, Venona was not compromised during the investigation.

Wiretapping in the 1950s, 1960s, and 1970s

Every president since Franklin D. Roosevelt has asserted the authority to authorize warrantless electronic surveillance. President Eisenhower's attorney general, Herbert Brownell, gave Hoover authorization to conduct electronic surveillance, a practice Hoover had been ostensibly engaged in anyway, because the FBI was investigating espionage or an intelligence function in connection with internal security matters. Such bugging was often equivalent to criminal trespass and was illegal. Hoover was emboldened by the supposed sanctioning of these actions by the president.

Throughout the 1950s, wiretapping continued. By the early 1960s, however, the legal status of wiretapping had become clouded in a mass of conflicting laws, Supreme Court decisions, and policies. Civil libertarians had cause for concern— wiretapping evidence (illegal under FCA Section 605) could not be introduced into federal courts. A series of wiretapping hearings were held in Congress from 1961 to 1967 to search for some middle ground.

In August 1961, Robert Kennedy granted Hoover a blanket authorization for FBI request letters to telephone company officials to "secure lines for use in connection with microphone surveillances." Kennedy also wanted unrestricted use of wiretaps for the IRS and other unspecified serious charges. Hoover resisted. In 1963, Kennedy authorized Hoover to monitor the Reverend Dr. Martin Luther King Jr.'s SCLC and his residence on the condition that the FBI would seek Kennedy's reevaluation after thirty days. However, evidence seems to indicate that Hoover ignored the order. The taps remained in place until Attorney General Nicholas Katzenbach became aware of them and ordered them removed in 1968.

In 1965, President Johnson sought to bring some order to wiretapping policies by ordering all federal national security wiretaps to be conducted by the FBI (only) with approval of the attorney general. In 1967, the Supreme Court ruled in *Katz v United States* that wiretapping was equivalent to search and seizure, and required a warrant. The court also defined the specificity needed for the warrants (suspected crime, length of time, place, etc.). The Supreme Court did not rule out wiretaps in

On July 26, 1947, President Harry S. Truman signed the National Security Act, creating the precursor to the Central Intelligence Agency. Truman refused to agree with Hoover that the new Central Intelligence Group (later the CIA), which had replaced the wartime OSS, should become part of the FBI. Under this new law, domestic counterintelligence remained with the FBI. Other aspects of intelligence work also remained outside of the new CIA, specifically the army's cryptanalytic efforts. *Library of Congress*

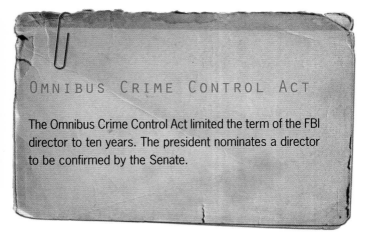

OMNIBUS CRIME CONTROL ACT

The Omnibus Crime Control Act limited the term of the FBI director to ten years. The president nominates a director to be confirmed by the Senate.

all circumstances and left open the possibility that warrantless national security wiretaps may be allowed.

Neither *Katz v United States* nor *United States v United States District Court* (1972) (known as the Keith case) challenged the president's unilateral authority in foreign intelligence cases. In *Katz*, the court explicitly declined to extend its holding that the Fourth Amendment required a warrant in electronic surveillance to cases "involving the national security" or "activities of foreign powers or their agents." The Supreme Court ruled the president does not have the constitutional power to authorize warrantless domestic security wiretaps. Its ruling, however, implied the president might have the authority to issue warrantless foreign intelligence wiretaps.

In 1968, in *Alderman v United States*, the Supreme Court said individuals are entitled to know if they are the subject of electronic surveillance, and data collected because of illegal electronic surveillance could not be introduced into evidence. This ruling more or less eliminated the usefulness of wiretaps for the FBI. In a short time, the pendulum had swung from wiretapping being given a wink and a nod by the courts, to wiretaps being virtually useless in federal law enforcement. And even if they were useful, the Fourth Amendment tightly controlled them.

Omnibus Crime Control Act of 1968

The Omnibus Crime Control Act was the nation's first comprehensive legislation describing the rules for obtaining wiretap authorizations and legalized electronic surveillance during criminal investigations. Surveillance was, however, subject to warrant requirements within the limits of the Constitution and as interpreted by Supreme Court rulings. The act also stipulated that it was not intended to "limit the constitutional powers of the president" in the national security arena. The act banned private wiretaps and allowed law enforcement wiretapping only if the investigators obtained a warrant meeting requirements defined by the law. It also allowed warrantless national security wiretaps only on the authority of the president.

In 1968, President Lyndon Johnson directed Hoover to tap the phone of Republican vice-presidential candidate Spiro Agnew on the suspicion that Agnew was telling the South Vietnamese that they would get a better peace arrangement from Nixon if he were elected president. The taps did not reveal that Agnew ever made such a deal.

On May 5, 1969, at the request of President Nixon and National Security Advisor Henry Kissinger, Hoover ordered the wiretapping of seventeen members of the White House, National Security Agency, and Secretary of Defense staffs, and four Washington reporters, to determine who disclosed the bombing of Cambodia, which was published in the *New York Times*. While the wiretaps never disclosed who leaked the information, they provided valuable political intelligence for the White House.

In the *United States v Truong* and *United States v Humphrey* espionage cases (1978), President Jimmy Carter had authorized warrantless physical searches by the FBI. In the only cases to date that directly address warrantless intelligence searches of foreign agents, the Supreme Court upheld the legality of the president's order if the primary purpose of the investigation was foreign intelligence gathering.

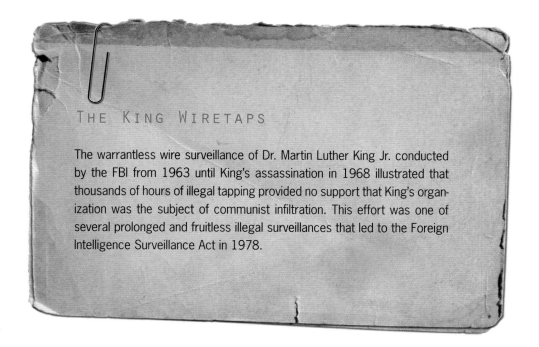

THE KING WIRETAPS

The warrantless wire surveillance of Dr. Martin Luther King Jr. conducted by the FBI from 1963 until King's assassination in 1968 illustrated that thousands of hours of illegal tapping provided no support that King's organization was the subject of communist infiltration. This effort was one of several prolonged and fruitless illegal surveillances that led to the Foreign Intelligence Surveillance Act in 1978.

This switchboard in the old telephone central office was an easy place to listen in on conversations. The operator could simply bridge both parties to an FBI agent listening in another room. Those telephone company employees were usually sworn to secrecy. President Roosevelt believed that the ruling in *Nardone v United States* applied only to criminal investigations and not to national defense investigations, whose purpose was not prosecutorial but to obtain intelligence. The Executive Branch thought itself free to wiretap anyone so long as the transcripts remained secret. *Library of Congress*

FISA

The FBI can apply to the Foreign Intelligence Surveillance Act (FISA) court for a special warrant to conduct searches or surveillance. The FISA court operates in secret, and FISA warrants are therefore not subject to public scrutiny.

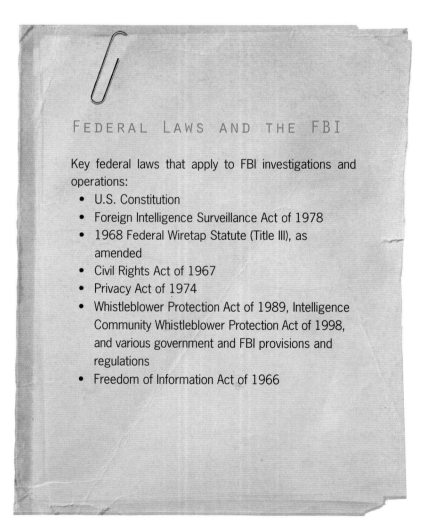

FEDERAL LAWS AND THE FBI

Key federal laws that apply to FBI investigations and operations:

- U.S. Constitution
- Foreign Intelligence Surveillance Act of 1978
- 1968 Federal Wiretap Statute (Title III), as amended
- Civil Rights Act of 1967
- Privacy Act of 1974
- Whistleblower Protection Act of 1989, Intelligence Community Whistleblower Protection Act of 1998, and various government and FBI provisions and regulations
- Freedom of Information Act of 1966

Foreign Intelligence Surveillance Act (FISA) of 1978

Because of the excesses of illegal wiretapping, Congress passed the Foreign Intelligence Surveillance Act (FISA). On October 25, 1978, President Jimmy Carter signed the FISA, which created a special court to review and approve, in secret, all government requests to install wiretaps and bugs relating to foreign intelligence investigations. FISA was initially limited to electronic eavesdropping and wiretapping, but in 1994, because of the Aldrich Ames espionage, the act was amended to permit covert physical entries in connection with security investigations.

Under the Fourth Amendment, a search warrant must be based on a probable cause to believe that a crime has been or is about to be committed. FISA, on the other hand, states that surveillance is permitted based on a finding of probable cause that the surveillance target is a foreign power or an agent of a foreign power, irrespective of whether the target is suspected of engaging in criminal activity. However, if the target is a "U.S. person," there must be probable cause to believe that the U.S. person's activities may involve espionage or other similar conduct in violation of the U.S. criminal statutes. A U.S. person may not be determined to be an agent of a foreign power "solely upon the basis of activities protected by the First Amendment to the Constitution of the United States," according to the act.

FISA Court

Throughout the twentieth century, the FBI used wiretaps and other surveillance methods without a warrant when it felt that national security was at risk. In some cases, the FBI and the CIA spied on domestic political groups, in clear violation of the Fourth Amendment. In 1972, the Supreme Court ruled that the president's authority over national security did not justify using domestic wiretaps without a warrant: "The freedoms of the Fourth Amendment," said the court, "cannot properly be guaranteed if domestic security surveillances are conducted solely within the discretion of the Executive Branch, without the detached judgment of a neutral magistrate." Six years later, Congress responded by passing FISA in an attempt to regulate the few cases (then) in which national security is at stake and in which law enforcement agents are either unable to procure a traditional warrant because they cannot show probable cause or are unwilling to do so because the information is classified or time is critical.

Wiretapping is a more accurate and benign technique to penetrate terrorist cells than the main alternative, which is recruiting informers, a dangerous and unreliable way tactic. The narrower the government's surveillance powers, the more it will rely on informants who provide information second-hand.

Observers point out that in spite of the government's vast power to comb through computerized records of banking and other transactions, the vast majority of the people who have seen their privacy invaded have not been aggrieved by rogue government officials. Some claim that media organizations do far greater damage to far more people with little or no accountability.

This type of passive surveillance is dangerous. While the agents concentrate on the suspects in front of them, someone has to watch their backs for any threats associated with the suspects. In 2005, the government made 2,176 secret surveillance requests under the Foreign Intelligence Surveillance Act. None of the requests were denied by the FISA Court. In contrast, the Department of Justice reported that law enforcement agencies across the country were authorized to conduct 1,773 wiretaps, which were issued under a more stringent standard. A report submitted in April 2006 to Democrat and Republican leaders in the House and Senate on secret wiretap warrants indicated that the government issued 3,501 National Security Letters during 2005. These letters can be used to obtain specific information about individuals without the government applying for a court-reviewed warrant. *FBI*

National Security Letters

In national security investigations, the FBI must follow up on every tip and every threat. The National Security Letters (NSLs) were created in the 1970s for espionage and terrorism investigations. NSLs predate FISA and enable the FBI to act quickly and unobtrusively. An NSL is a request for information. It does not authorize the FBI to conduct a search or make a seizure. These letters can be used to obtain information about individuals without the government applying for a court-reviewed warrant. If the recipient of an NSL declines to produce the requested information, the FBI cannot compel the individual to do so; only a federal court has that authority.

Long-range camera surveillance has long been a technique of the FBI. It is relatively safe but is only the first step in proving a criminal conspiracy. Physical and electronic surveillance have been carried out under most presidents since Woodrow Wilson, usually with a lawful warrant since the Supreme Court ruled it constitutional in 1928. However, it has also been carried out illegally, before and since that ruling. *Henry M. Holden*

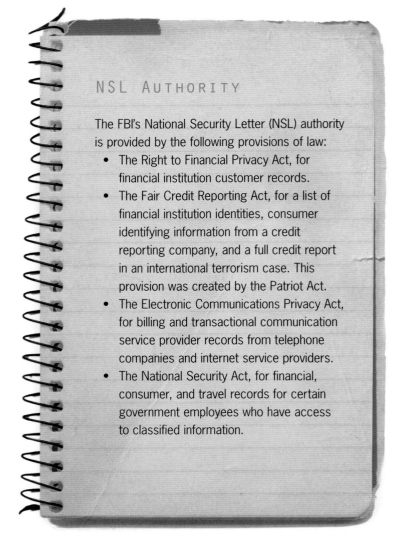

NSL AUTHORITY

The FBI's National Security Letter (NSL) authority is provided by the following provisions of law:

- The Right to Financial Privacy Act, for financial institution customer records.
- The Fair Credit Reporting Act, for a list of financial institution identities, consumer identifying information from a credit reporting company, and a full credit report in an international terrorism case. This provision was created by the Patriot Act.
- The Electronic Communications Privacy Act, for billing and transactional communication service provider records from telephone companies and internet service providers.
- The National Security Act, for financial, consumer, and travel records for certain government employees who have access to classified information.

The government cannot secure the nation against terrorist attacks unless investigators are equipped with tools that allow them to disrupt plots before they are carried out. These same tools must also protect civil liberties. National Security Letters, many argue, satisfy both requirements.

NSLs are subject to two important limitations. First, the FBI may issue them only to obtain information relevant to an international terrorism or espionage investigation. They are not allowed in criminal investigations or domestic terrorism investigations. Second, they may be used only to obtain narrow categories of information, such as credit card billing records, to attempt to learn the identity of a terrorist suspect. An NSL may not be used to obtain the contents of an e-mail or a telephone conversation. If the FBI goes beyond these legal constraints, the NSL implies the recipient could challenge it in court.

The NSL statutes prohibit a recipient from disclosing the fact that he received one. In international terrorism and espionage investigations, there are obvious reasons for this. If a terrorist were tipped off that the FBI was asking for his credit card billing records, he might flee, destroy evidence, or even accelerate plans for an attack.

On December 4, 1981, President Ronald Reagan signed Executive Order 12333, outlining new rules governing foreign intelligence and counterintelligence operations. Under this order, when requested by other intelligence agencies, the FBI can conduct, within the United States, investigations to "collect foreign intelligence, or to support foreign intelligence collection requirements."

COMPREHENSIVE CRIME CONTROL ACT
OF 1984

President Reagan signed PL 98-473, the Comprehensive Crime Control Act of 1984, extending federal jurisdiction to computer crimes and counterfeiting consumer goods. It also strengthened federal authority to seize and confiscate assets of drug trafficking, and it described the rules for obtaining wiretap orders. Title III of the act details how and in what circumstances warrants may be issued for monitoring phone lines and private, face-to-face conversations.

Electronic Communications Privacy Act of 1986

While some civil libertarians oppose wiretapping under any circumstances, by 1978, there was a national consensus that balanced a distrust of government (exacerbated by Vietnam and Watergate) against a fear of increasing crime and Cold War national security concerns. The consensus was that private wiretapping should be prohibited, and the executive branch of government should have the right to conduct electronic surveillance in support of legitimate law enforcement and national security objectives—but only when approved by the courts.

FORIEGN
COUNTERINTELLIGENCE

The FBI conducts foreign counterintelligence investigations under the authority of Executive Order 12333 and acts of Congress. The national strategies of the foreign counterintelligence (FCI) program are to:

- Prevent the penetration of the U.S. intelligence community, and U.S. government agencies or contractors;
- Prevent the compromise of U.S. critical national assets; and
- Conduct aggressive counterintelligence operations focusing on those countries that constitute the most significant threat to U.S. strategic interests.

Because of the first bombing of the World Trade Center in 1993 and the Oklahoma City attack in 1995, Congress passed the Antiterrorism and Effective Death Penalty Act in 1996. The law made almost sixty offenses, most of them terrorism-related, punishable by death and broadened the FBI's electronic surveillance and other search powers. *Henry M. Holden*

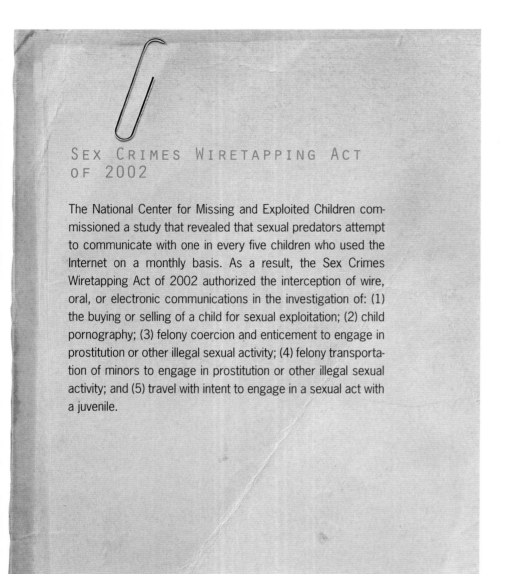

SEX CRIMES WIRETAPPING ACT OF 2002

The National Center for Missing and Exploited Children commissioned a study that revealed that sexual predators attempt to communicate with one in every five children who used the Internet on a monthly basis. As a result, the Sex Crimes Wiretapping Act of 2002 authorized the interception of wire, oral, or electronic communications in the investigation of: (1) the buying or selling of a child for sexual exploitation; (2) child pornography; (3) felony coercion and enticement to engage in prostitution or other illegal sexual activity; (4) felony transportation of minors to engage in prostitution or other illegal sexual activity; and (5) travel with intent to engage in a sexual act with a juvenile.

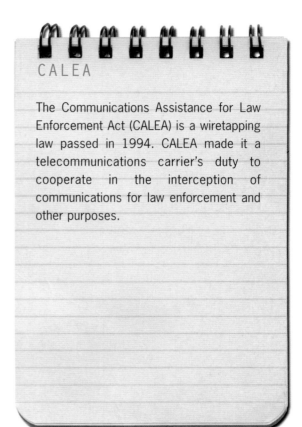

CALEA

The Communications Assistance for Law Enforcement Act (CALEA) is a wiretapping law passed in 1994. CALEA made it a telecommunications carrier's duty to cooperate in the interception of communications for law enforcement and other purposes.

This consensus brought about the Electronic Communications Privacy Act (ECPA) of 1986. This act extended the same privacy rights, and law enforcement and national security access, to digital and cellular telephone communications, as those applied previously to land-line telephones. The EPCA passed on a voice vote with little opposition.

One opponent to the bill argued on the floor of Congress, "I believe the bill represents an unnecessary expansion of federal wiretap authority, a procedure so evasive of the rights of citizens in a free society that it can only be made available for use under circumstances specifically approved by Congress."

Patriot Act

President George W. Bush signed the USA Patriot Act on October 26, 2001. This antiterrorism law provided the FBI with additional resources to hire critical support personnel, employ court-approved wiretaps against potential terrorists more quickly, seek additional information about potential terrorists more easily, and share criminal investigative information with counterterrorism investigators, other government officials, and more. Sections of the act amended the Foreign Intelligence Surveillance Act and the Electronic Communications Privacy Act of 1986. In 2006, Congress renewed the USA Patriot Act.

In 2005, a *Financial Times* article said cellular providers can ". . . remotely, without the owner's knowledge, activate the microphone even when its owner is not making a call." The U.S. Commerce Department's security office admits that "a cellular telephone can be turned into a microphone and transmitter for the purpose of listening to conversations in the vicinity of the phone." In November 2006, U.S. District Judge Lewis Kaplan ruled that the roving bug was legal because the federal wiretapping law is broad enough to permit eavesdropping, even of conversations that take place near a suspect's cell phone. The eavesdropping technique functions regardless of whether the power on the cell phone is on or off. Many cell phones cannot be fully powered down without removing the phone's battery. *Henry M. Holden*

This act has been hailed and condemned. The issues range from why the FBI has been slow in implementing terrorist watch lists and computer upgrades after 9/11 to questions about its investigations of peace groups.

"I'm very disappointed when I find that the FBI has been using new capabilities against Americans simply because they oppose the war in Iraq," said Senator Patrick Leahy, a ranking Democrat. He cited reports of FBI surveillance of a Seattle peace festival, a Catholic peace organization in Pittsburgh, and the Raging Grannies, another peace group.

FBI Director Robert Mueller III said that many of these assertions and rumors had already been put to bed by an investigation by the Justice Department's Office of the Inspector General (OIG), and that he welcomed another OIG investigation to deal with new rumors.

The warrant system serves as a restriction on law enforcement agents. Political science professor Christopher Banks writes, "Pre-Patriot Act law gave preference to safeguarding private telephone, face to face conversations, and electronic or computer messages . . . by prohibiting eavesdropping unless a warrant could be obtained in a set of narrowly defined circumstances."

September 11, 2001, illustrated, said the FBI and other government officials, that the current laws were too restrictive. As evidence, they pointed to Zacarias Moussaoui, an al Qaeda agent who aided and abetted the hijackers, and who was later convicted.

FBI agents working the same case could not talk to each other about the case if some agents were working it as a criminal case and others were working it as an intelligence case. Before the Patriot Act, some called this mandate "the wall."

For criminal matters, the FBI could apply for and use traditional criminal warrants. For intelligence matters, the rules were different. The attorney general could authorize surveillance of foreign powers and agents of foreign powers without any court review, but FISA regulated the intelligence collection directed at foreign powers and agents of foreign powers within the United States. Besides requiring court review of proposed surveillance, FISA required that a search be approved only if its

An aerial view of Building Six of the World Trade Center, the NYC Customhouse. Prior to September 11, some FBI agents were suspicious of Moussaoui because he had attended a flight school where he inquired about whether cockpit doors could be opened during flight, and he was not interested in learning how to land. He had also spent time in Pakistan, where al Qaeda had recruited many agents. Because the FBI could not demonstrate probable cause, it could not obtain a warrant to search Moussaoui's computer or tap his phone. "Consequently," writes Mark Reibling, in his book, *From Pearl Harbor to 9/11: How the Secret War between the FBI and the CIA Has Endangered National Security*, "the FBI lost its best chance to learn of Moussaoui's links to the other September 11 conspirators before they could strike." *James Tourtellotte CBP*

primary purpose was to obtain foreign intelligence information. It could not be used in place of criminal warrant requirements. The Justice Department interpreted this to mean that criminal prosecutors could be briefed on the information collected but could not direct or control its collection.

The prosecution of Aldrich Ames for espionage in 1994 re-energized issues about a prosecutor's role in intelligence investigations. The attorney general had authorized a warrantless entry to Ames' residence. The Department of Justice's Office of Intelligence Policy and Review (OIPR) is responsible for reviewing all applications to the FISA court. The OIPR thought the judge might rule misuse of the FISA because discussions had taken place between the FBI, on the criminal side of the house, and prosecutors. If the judge ruled FISA had been misused, the Ames case would be thrown out, and he would be free. This, however, did not happen.

Counterterrorism Evolves

In July 1995, the Justice Department's Executive Office for National Security issued formal procedures approved by Attorney General Janet Reno. These procedures regulated the way information was shared in the FBI between the intelligence and criminal squads and individual agents. In the opinion of many, the process was misunderstood and resulted in less coordination and sharing within the FBI. Although the attorney general's procedures did not include such a provision, the OIPR assumed a gatekeeper's role for passing information to criminal prosecutors. OIPR argued that this position reflected the issues of the chief judge of the FISA court. OIPR suggested that it would not present the FBI's warrant requests to the FISA court if it could not regulate the flow of information to the prosecutor's office. As a result, the information flow dried up.

The 1995 procedures dealt only with sharing information between agents and criminal prosecutors, not between FBI agents working the intelligence side and those working on the criminal side. Because of pressure from the OIPR, FBI management created artificial barriers between agents serving on the same squads. As a result, relevant information from the NSA and the CIA often failed to make its way to the criminal side of the house. Separate reviews in 1999, 2000, and 2001 concluded independently that information sharing was not occurring.

More misunderstandings followed. Investigators would not commingle domestic intelligence with foreign intelligence. Both prosecutors and FBI agents believed that they were not allowed to share grand jury information, although the prohibition applied only to a small number of cases presented to a grand jury, and some of those had exceptions. Finally, NSA began requiring its bin Laden–related reports to have prior approval before sharing them with criminal investigators of the FBI and prosecutors.

One assistant director said, "We had to report violations when criminal and intelligence agents talked to each other. My guys were always coming to me and complaining that they weren't allowed to share information between intelligence and the criminal side."

One U.S. attorney who was conducting a criminal investigation of Osama bin Laden in New York said, "We could talk to other law enforcement, ordinary citizens, and other U.S. government agencies, and to al Qaeda members. But, we couldn't talk to the FBI agents who were assigned to a parallel investigation of Osama bin Laden and al Qaeda. We could not learn information they had gathered. That was 'the wall.'"

The 9/11 commission report recounted how the distinction between criminal and intelligence matters prevented the FBI from taking any steps that might have led to unraveling the 9/11 plot before it took place. On August 29, 2001, an FBI agent in the New York field office asked FBI Headquarters to approve a criminal investigation to find Khalid al-Mihdhar, who turned out to be one of the 9/11 hijackers. Headquarters denied the request.

Roving Bugs

The Patriot Act was designed in part to tear down the wall that tied counterterrorism efforts in knots. It also gave the FBI the tools it needed to hunt down terrorists before an attack occurs. Before the Patriot Act, the FBI had to obtain a separate

THE FOURTH AMENDMENT

"The right of the people to be secure in their persons, houses, papers, and effects, against unreasonable searches and seizures, shall not be violated, and no warrants shall issue, but upon probable cause, supported by oath or affirmation, and particularly describing the place to be searched, and the persons or things to be seized."

Domestic surveillance, wiretapping, and the Patriot Act have provoked many Fourth Amendment challenges over the years.

authorization to wiretap each phone a suspected terrorist might use. By the time the FBI obtained nearly a dozen signatures on a wiretap application and the approval of a judge, the suspect would switch phones. In the time it took to obtain authorization, he could have committed any number of terrorist acts, potentially killing thousands of people.

Ironically, if the FBI were chasing drug traffickers or organized crime figures, it could obtain court authorization to wiretap a suspect regardless of what phone he was using. The media reported on the new powers contained in the Patriot Act without saying that the FBI already had such authority when pursuing drug dealers.

Under the Patriot Act, each roving wiretap has to be approved by a judge, so there is no question about infringing on civil liberties. Yet some have portrayed the act as a new invasion of civil rights. Those same critics claim that the FBI can use sneak-and-peek tactics in libraries to probe people's reading habits without informing the targets until after a search. But the FBI has always had authority, with a judge's approval, to conduct a search without telling the suspect until a later point in the investigation. The Patriot Act sped up the approval process.

Technology has to keep up with criminal creativeness and, in November 2006, Department of Justice officials approved a new surveillance technique called the "roving bug" (remote cell phone monitoring) for use against members of a New York organized crime family. The mob is highly suspicious of bugging activities, and the FBI had concluded that the mob was aware it was being bugged with conventional wiretapping.

A confidential informant reported that John Ardito, whom the FBI believed was a high-ranking individual in the Genovese crime family, conducted his business at certain restaurants. The FBI bugged the restaurants but had little luck with the conventional surveillance. Conversations recounted in FBI affidavits show the men were also suspicious of tails and avoided conversations on cell phones whenever possible. That led the FBI to implement the roving bugs. A U.S. district judge approved the actions in a series of orders in 2003 and 2004, and said she expected to "be advised of the locations" of the suspects when their conversations were recorded.

Earlier, a 2003 lawsuit revealed that the FBI had done this type of eavesdropping before. The suit revealed that the FBI was able to turn on, covertly, the built-in microphones in automotive systems such as General Motors' OnStar. When the OnStar system is remotely activated, the passengers in the vehicle cannot tell if someone is eavesdropping on their conversations.

A judge concluded that the roving bugs were legally permitted to capture conversations because the FBI had obtained a court order and undercover alternatives did not work. The FBI's "applications made a sufficient case for electronic surveillance," wrote the judge. "They indicated that alternative methods of investigation either had failed or were unlikely to produce results, in part because the subjects deliberately avoided government surveillance."

This prosecution was the first time a remote-eavesdropping mechanism had been used in a criminal case. Cellular service providers will not talk about this kind of surveillance. One provider said it "works closely with law enforcement and public safety officials. When presented with legally authorized orders, we assist law enforcement in every way possible." ■

A 1970 Herblock cartoon
The Herb Block Foundation

FBI ABROAD

In 1986, Congress authorized the FBI to investigate criminal acts against Americans that occur outside the United States. Three years later, it added authority for the FBI to make arrests abroad without the consent of the host country.

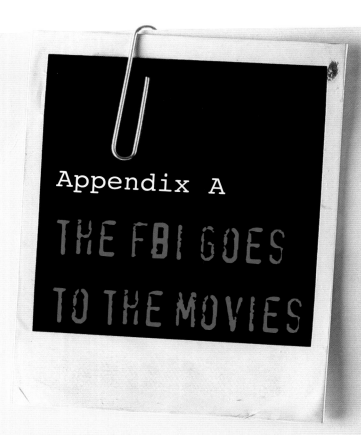

Appendix A

THE FBI GOES TO THE MOVIES

The story of the FBI as a law enforcement agency, ready to strike at any danger to the nation's welfare, is partly the result of J. Edgar Hoover's adroit manipulation of the media and the motion picture industry. Often, however, the actual work of its dedicated employees gave Hoover the raw materials for his icon building.

The FBI has long been a fixture in the nation's popular culture; over the years, it has been the focus of thousands of books, movies, and TV and radio shows, some rooted in fact, and others purely fictional. Comic books, "Junior G-Men" toys, and games helped build an iconic image.

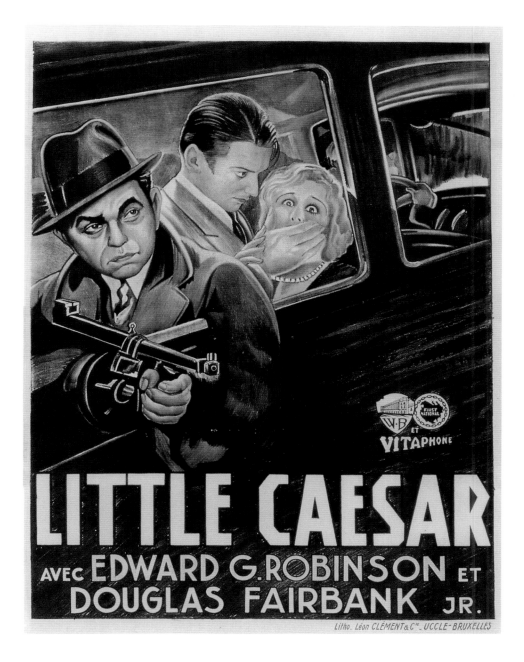

Little Caesar, a 1931 crime film, tells the story of a man who works his way up the ranks of the mob. Edward G. Robinson plays Al Capone. *Little Caesar* showed the world as seen through the eyes of a ruthless gangster. This was one of many films that infuriated Hoover as being disrespectful of the law. Jimmy Cagney's *G-Men* features none other than J. Edgar Hoover, making Hoover Public Hero Number One. *Henry M. Holden collection*

The FBI on film is a mirror of the American culture. The films reflect the turbulent times, prosperity, depression, international scheming, and espionage, and, as is often the case in other media, an inaccurate record. When "talkies" hit the silver screen, they brought a new level of fantasy for millions during the Great Depression. They enabled Hollywood to create more vivid pictures by enhancing a movie with dialogue and sound effects. It would also turn gangsters into violent yet charismatic counterculture heroes.

During the 1930s crime wave, Hollywood created movies about killers such as Al Capone. Hoover disapproved of the glorification of these murderers and thieves. He saw it as a challenge to law and order, and civilization itself, and he was determined to put a stop to this blatant disrespect for authority, especially his authority. Hoover

In *Federal Agent At Large* (1950), the federal agent is on the trail of gold smugglers in Mexico, when he crosses the path of hard-boiled lady criminal, Solitaire. Her criminal tendencies softened by romance, Solitaire decides to work with the agent instead of against him. The gang's *modus operandi* is ingenious; equally clever were the means by which they are brought to justice. The film is actually about Treasury agents, but in 1950, any "fed" was fodder for the silver screen. *Henry M. Holden collection*

began to open investigations and build files on those in Hollywood who were popularizing the gangster mystique.

Several classic gangster films (among the first of the talkies) spearheaded the wave of gangster glamorization and Hoover's disapproval. The lead role in each film, a gangster or a racketeer, achieved the status of a folk hero to be glorified. However, each in the end would meet his doom. Film censors at the time demanded that the gangsters pay back society for their evil ways, usually in a blazing gun battle. Gangster films rivaled the ever-popular Westerns, but they had a darker side. Usually, in the Western, the cowboy gives the villain a chance to draw. The single cowboy who battles for law and order was replaced by the gangster who operates in a dark violent world where no quarter is given.

In 1931, Hollywood released *Little Caesar* and *The Public Enemy*. Both glorified crime and illustrated the government's inability to deal effectively with criminals. In *Scarface* (1932), based on the story of Al Capone, there are forty-three murders, making it one of the most violent of the gangster films. It was the first film in which the gangsters use machine guns. Filmed in 1932, its release was delayed until it had been edited to the Hays Production Code standards.

Movie gangsters, played by such actors as James Cagney, Edward G. Robinson (who attended Capone's income tax evasion trial), and George Raft (well-known for his portrayal of a coin-flipping psychopath in *Scarface*), were portrayed as iconic heroes who possessed an aura of someone successfully defying society. In 1934, Will H. Hays, a former postmaster general, became the administrator of the Motion Picture Production Code Office (the Hays Office), Hollywood's official self-censorship group. Under pressure from FDR's attorney general, Homer Cummings, the Hays Office pressured Hollywood to stop producing films that glorified gangsters.

The Hays Production Code spelled the end of glorifying the criminal and the accompanying violence of the gangster lifestyle. The Hays Office forced studios after July 1, 1935, to obtain a certificate of approval before the film could be released. The amended code ended the depiction of the gangster as a folk hero and forced filmmakers to emphasize that crime did not pay (although the audience knew otherwise). It also demanded toning down the gore shown in brutal crimes. The production code forbade the use of a weapon by gangsters on camera because "it would corrupt the youth of America."

Hoover noticed how adroit the Hollywood tabloids were at garnering publicity for the industry's current stars. If a star were married but having an affair, the studio would focus on the star's family life, squashing rumors about illicit sexual encounters—that is, as long as the star was "box office." The ability of Hollywood's publicity machines to tell the public only as much as it felt the public should know, while keeping the dirty laundry in the closet, impressed Hoover.

Hoover would use the Hollywood model and become a skilled puppet master, manipulating the press, Hollywood moguls, and the public's perception of the Bureau for decades. However, it would often be a love-hate relationship. At Hoover's insistence, racketeers and gangsters, Nazis, kidnappers, and communists were hunted relentlessly by the on-screen G-men. Corporate crime and crooked politicians were almost nonexistent. There was a brief scene in *The FBI Story* that featured the Ku Klux Klan, but as long as Hoover held the puppet strings, there

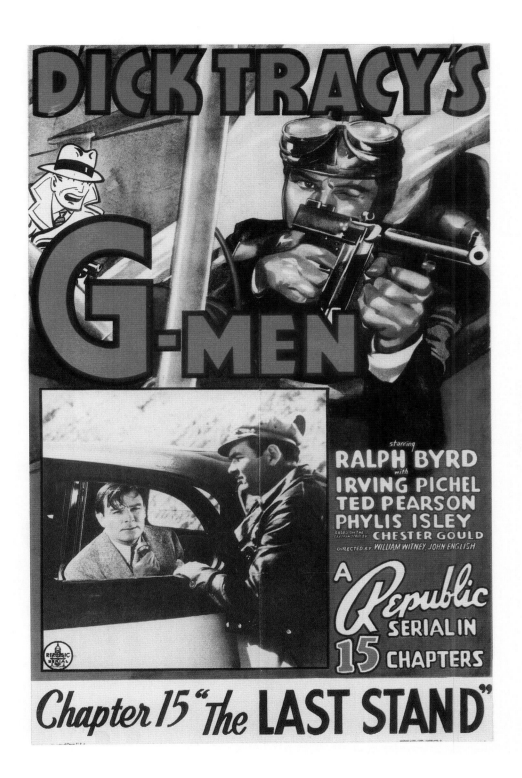

Dick Tracy's G-Men ran in movie theaters in 1939. The Serials were half-hour films designed to bring the viewer back, in this case, for fifteen weeks. The plot of the film was a bit bizarre: A mad doctor named Zanoff uses a drug to bring himself back from the dead after his execution in prison. Dick Tracy sets out to capture Zanoff before he can put his gang back together again. *Henry M. Holden collection*

Several movies put J. Edgar Hoover's G-men up against the toughest gangsters Hollywood could dig up. In the twelve-part cliffhanger, *G-men Never Forget* (1948), the future Lone Ranger, Clayton Moore, plays a starring role. *Henry M. Holden collection*

were no FBI films featuring the Klan, Al Capone, Murder Inc., or La Cosa Nostra. Those films would come after his death

Hoover first cultivated the friendships of the most influential reporters such as Walter Winchell, and Attorney General Cummings hired Harry Suydam, the Washington correspondent for the *Brooklyn Eagle*, to be the Bureau's public relations officer. Suydam introduced Hoover to the Hollywood elite—producers and directors, such as Jack Warner. He also hired Courtney Riley Cooper, a journalist and author. Cooper would ghostwrite Hoover's books in the 1930s, and more than two dozen articles about Hoover and the Bureau for *American Magazine*.

In 1935, the FBI took on a big box office role with the film *G-Men.* In it, James

In *Held for Ransom* (1938), a female FBI agent risks her own life by going after a group of people responsible for the kidnapping of a wealthy businessman. We can imagine Hoover's reaction to this film since he had purged the Bureau of female agents ten years earlier. *Henry M. Holden collection*

Cagney changed sides and dropped the violent criminal persona he plays in *The Public Enemy*. Instead, in *G-Men*, tough-guy Cagney plays a ruthless, revenge-seeking, impulsive FBI agent who infiltrates criminal gangs. The film showed the mean-spirited gangsters no mercy and watered down the violence to reflect a gentler FBI. It also introduced some romance—now FBI agents had wives and families. This film was the boilerplate for the films that followed: G-man gets the girl, loses the girl, wins

In *Down Three Dark Streets*, a 1954 film noir based on the novel *Case File FBI*, FBI agent John Ripley, played by hard-nose Broderick Crawford, investigates the three cases his murdered partner had been working on, hoping to find the killer. The film's climax takes place around the famous Hollywood sign. *Henry M. Holden collection*

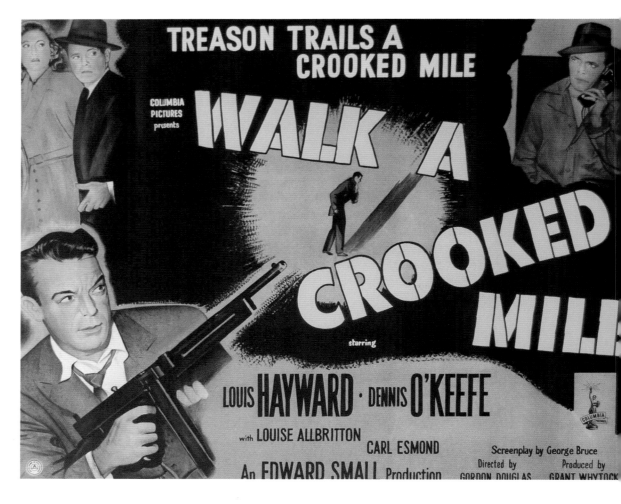

"Avenging FBI guns blast killers of G-men out of their holes," one promo for *Walk a Crooked Mile* (1948) proclaimed. The film involves a security leak at a Southern California atomic plant. The FBI fears that the information will leak to the Soviet Union. The investigation leads to San Francisco, where a communist spy ring flourishes, a portent of the Rosenbergs. *Henry M. Holden collection*

her back, and dispatches some no-good dirty rats in the process. It offered the public a new picture of FBI agents—college educated agents, who work as a team, aided by technology (and submachine guns in tight situations). It pulled together bits and pieces of almost every major crime the FBI had handled and condensed the history of the Bureau's first ten years into eighty-six minutes of a carefully scripted, dramatic crime fighting.

In the mid to late 1930s, the FBI bathed in glory, at least on film. In *Mary Burns, Fugitive* (1935), a young woman falls for a handsome young man, unaware that he is a gangster. The association results in her being tried and sentenced to a long prison term. However, the authorities allow her to escape, hoping that she will lead them to her boyfriend. Instead, she falls in love with an FBI agent. *Let 'em Have It* (1935) was another FBI gangbusters-in-action-type film, with pauses for romance. In *Whipsaw* (1935), Myrna Loy plays the glamorous member of a trio of jewel thieves. G-man Spencer Tracy goes undercover to join the gang. Loy falls in love

In *Federal Agents versus the Underworld Inc.* (1949), the female leader of an international crime ring steals a valuable artifact that can give her the power to control men's minds. FBI agents are dispatched to get it back and stop her evil plans. *Henry M. Holden collection*

with Tracy and quits the gang. However, Tracy arrests her after he recovers the jewels. The girl forgives Tracy when he is wounded in a wild gun battle with the rest of the thieves. *Show Them No Mercy!* (1935) was based on the real-life story of George Weyerhaeuser, whose kidnappers were caught by the FBI through tracing the serial numbers on the ransom money. This was another in a series of FBI melodramas blessed by J. Edgar Hoover. In *Public Enemy's Wife* (1936), a young woman is falsely imprisoned for a crime that she did not commit. The real culprit is her jailbird husband, a jewel thief with a jealous streak. She hopes to put her past behind her by taking up with a rich guy, keeping the affair secret lest her fugitive husband kill her lover. Of course, she ends up with the G-man.

The Street with No Name was another film noir made in 1948. Screen tough guy Richard Widmark is an up-and-coming crime boss trying to stake his claim in the criminal underworld. One FBI case baffles FBI Inspector Briggs (Lloyd Nolan). It involves the murders of a housewife and a bank guard. Both were killed by the same gun, yet there is no connection between the victims. Briggs sends his best agent undercover to penetrate the inner circle of the notorious gang. Everything goes according to plan, until an informant inside the police department tips off Stiles. *Henry M. Holden collection*

In 1936, the *Agent of Influence* was the first of twelve officially sanctioned, thirty-minute documentaries about the Bureau. It showed only what Hoover wanted the public to see—fingerprinting, chemical lab, firearms demos, and a few other peeks within the Bureau.

By 1939, the real public enemies were going the way of the flappers, breadlines, and bootleg booze, so Hollywood shifted gears. *Missing Evidence* opened that year, and it was about counterfeit sweepstakes tickets.

The anti-Nazi films made during World War II and the anti-communist films after the war would put Hoover and his FBI on the world stage. *Confessions of a Nazi Spy* is a 1939 spy thriller and the first blatantly anti-Nazi propaganda film produced by a major Hollywood studio prior to World War II. (There would be dozens of anti-Nazi and Japanese films after Pearl Harbor, which mirrored the tone in America, and continued through the 1950s). *Confessions* was based on articles written by a former FBI agent, who had been active in investigating Nazi spy rings in the United States. The Warner Brothers advertising copy read: "What do you know about the man next door?" Despite its controversial subject, the film was a major box office hit. The book, however, was banned in Germany, Japan, and some Latin American countries.

Persons in Hiding (1939) is about two low-level kidnappers who choose an unusually perceptive victim, one who is able to recall the flight paths of the airplanes that fly over the hideout. The crooks are soon captured. The movie was adapted from a book by the same name; Hoover claimed authorship, but it was a product of his ghostwriter, Courtney Riley Cooper. Cooper also wrote the introduction to the book and said, "The man is almost fanatical in the energy, the strength and time he gives to his job; it is nothing for him to work fourteen to sixteen hours a day." A perceptive reader might wonder how he had time to write the book.

Parole Fixer (1940) was another unofficial film in the J. Edgar Hoover series and was purportedly based on an actual FBI case. It revolves around the activities of a crooked attorney, who hatches a plot to kidnap a rich socialite. Another of the lawyer's stooges kills an FBI agent in the early scenes, thereby signing the lawyer's death warrant.

Pearl Harbor brought many changes to America. Soon after, two films of the attack came out: *Secret Agent of Japan* and *Little Tokyo*. Within three days of Pearl Harbor, Roosevelt put Hoover in charge of all censorship until a censorship czar could be appointed three days later. Hoover quickly persuaded Washington journalists, such as Drew Pearson and Walter Winchell, to sanitize their columns about the details of Pearl Harbor and other losses. Hoover would rule over Hollywood throughout the war. The restrictions Hollywood felt were always there, but the war added a sense of urgency and patriotism on the part of Hollywood to ignore its right to produce the real story.

The capture of the eight German saboteurs triggered *They Came to Blow Up America* (1943). The disclaimer said, "The picture you are about to see was not documented from the official records of the case of the eight Nazi saboteurs . . . this picture has been created to show Americans the dangerous warfare." The film stated it was an original story, and the FBI did not assist in the film, but the plot somehow seemed lifted from the real-life saboteurs' case. One of the film's stars, Ward Bond, was the second president of the Motion Picture Alliance for the Preservation of American Ideals, an anti-communist organization.

The House on 92nd Street (1945), based on double agent William Sebold, was the first of the "now it can be told" films released shortly after World War II. Twentieth Century Fox made it with the cooperation of the FBI. A *New York Times* review written by Thomas M. Prior says, *"The House on Ninety-Second Street* barely skims the surface of our counterespionage operations, but it reveals sufficient of the FBI's *modus operandi* to be intriguing on that score alone."

The second Red scare was at full throttle in postwar America, and *I Was a Communist for the FBI* (1951) blasts the communist menace. Employed by a Pittsburgh steel plant, Matt Cvetic poses as a communist to secure information for the FBI. Even his own family believes he is a Red and is hostile toward him. The American communists in this film are seen as cut from the same cloth of the 1930s gangsters, which they were not. A year later, a radio show would bear the same name.

Walk East on Beacon! (1952) features Republican California-senator-in-waiting George Murphy as a Jack Webb–style, just-the-facts-ma'am, G-man hot on the heels of a Red sleeper cell. It was based on a magazine article by Hoover (ghostwritten, of course).

My Son John (1952) is another Red scare propaganda film about two all-American parents who try to save their son from communism. Unfortunately, they are too late. Things get worse when an FBI agent shows up to tell the parents that their son is an enemy spy and his girlfriend is a commie. He eventually repents but is killed by his girlfriend's commie friends.

In *Pickup on South Street* (1953), a pickpocket (Richard Widmark) steals a wallet from Jean Peters that contains microfilm with top-secret government information. The theft sets off a frantic search for Widmark's character by the police and the FBI, who has a stake in securing the microfilm. In an obvious allusion to the Rosenbergs, FBI Agent Zara says in the film, "If you refuse to cooperate, you'll be as guilty as the traitors who gave Stalin the A-bomb."

Down Three Dark Streets (1954) is another documentary-style film about an FBI agent investigating three cases that his murdered partner had been working on, hoping to find the killer. Broderick Crawford plays an FBI agent (he had played FBI agents before, including none other than J. Edgar Hoover). When Hoover saw the dwindling box office returns on movies like this, he began to realize the public had its fill of anti-communist films and turned to a new approach with *The FBI Story*.

In *FBI Code 98* (1964), a bomb is found in the luggage of a businessperson on board

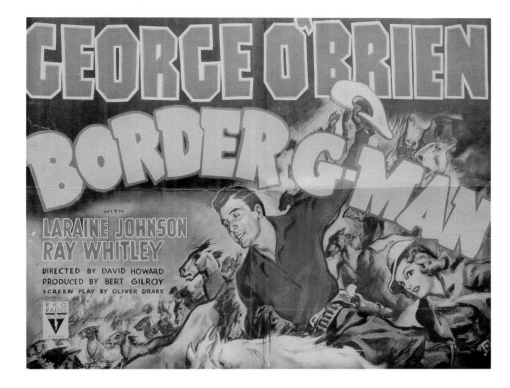

In *Border G-Man* (1938), a G-man is sent undercover to investigate a shifty businessman for violations of the Neutrality Act, one of the original federal laws that empowered the Bureau. This was based on reality. The FBI had been aware of ammunition and men being smuggled out of the United States and into Mexico in violation of the Neutrality Act for some time. The film straddled the Western and crime-flick genres. *Henry M. Holden collection*

In *FBI Girl* (1951), the girl is not an FBI special agent but an office clerk who steals some documents and is rewarded by getting murdered. The plot revolves around a governor planning to run for U.S. Senate who has a secret past that could prove damaging to his career: he is a convicted murderer, and that will become known if the FBI does a background check on him. He goes to a local crime boss for help. The racketeer arranges for the office clerk to take the incriminating file from FBI Headquarters, and then she is conveniently murdered. There is more than a wink and a nod to the Judith Coplon case there. *Henry M. Holden collection*

an airplane—a *Dragnet*-styled crime drama where a disgruntled mad bomber uses his heightened knowledge of electronics to stay one step ahead of the FBI. It is somewhat reminiscent of the mad bomber who terrorized New York City in the late 1950s.

Not long after Hoover's death, the pendulum of fortunes for the FBI began to swing off the chart in the opposite direction. By the time films like *Die Hard* came along in

1988, the formerly straight-laced Ivy-League FBI agents had morphed into foul talking, often reckless and vicious, maverick heroes. But one especially salacious film would add to an urban legend. *The Private Files of J. Edgar Hoover* (1977) takes a creative look at the public and private lives of the late J. Edgar Hoover. It is a no-holds-barred and nothing-too-sacred-to-expose film that includes strong hints of Hoover's alleged homosexuality and cross-dressing. Had Hoover been alive, one imagines he would have found a reason to incarcerate the individuals involved with the film.

Just as Hollywood had jumped on the gangster film bandwagon in the 1930s, it did not miss the drama and real-life activities of the modern mafia. Mario Puzo's 1969 book, *The Godfather*, spawned the movie of the same name in 1972 and several sequels. Rumors abounded that Puzo modeled Don Corleone after Carlo Gambino. The FBI was merely background scenery in this film. The words "mafia" and "Cosa Nostra" were not used in the film.

Dog Day Afternoon (1975) sympathizes with counterculture robbers and heaps scorn on law enforcement. Actor James Broderick, as a cold-blooded FBI agent, takes charge and precipitates a bloodbath.

Manhunter (1986) is one of the early films about the Bureau's hunt for serial killers. William Peterson plays a profiler who attempts to get into the mind of a charismatic Hannibal Lecter. *The Silence of the Lambs* (1991) stars Jodie Foster and Anthony Hopkins (the FBI was consulted on this film, and it was filmed partly in Quantico). It was followed by *Hannibal* (2001) and *Red Dragon* (2002), a remake of *Manhunter*.

In 1988, Hollywood peaked with more FBI films than any year since 1935. In *Shoot to Kill*, an FBI agent and his mountain guide track a killer trying to cross from Washington State into Canada. In *Little Nikita* (1988), Jeff Grant (River Phoenix), without telling his parents, applies to the Air Force Academy. Running the necessary background checks, FBI Agent Parmenter (Sidney Poitier) discovers that Jeff's parents are Russian deep-cover sleeper spies. In *Married to the Mob* (1988), Michelle Pfeiffer plays Angela de Marco, a woman given a new lease on life when her hit man husband (Alec Baldwin) is killed. Angela finds a soul mate in Matthew Modine's character, a straight-arrow FBI agent who draws her into a scheme to seize the mob's boss. *Mississippi Burning* (1988) was based on the investigation into the real-life murders of three civil rights workers in Mississippi in 1964. The movie focuses on two fictional FBI agents (portrayed by Gene Hackman and Willem Dafoe) who investigate the murders.

In *Point Break* (1991), Keanu Reeves plays a young hotshot FBI agent up against bank robbers who use the masks of ex-presidents during their heists. This was one of a long line of films that have depicted FBI agents as bureaucratic morons.

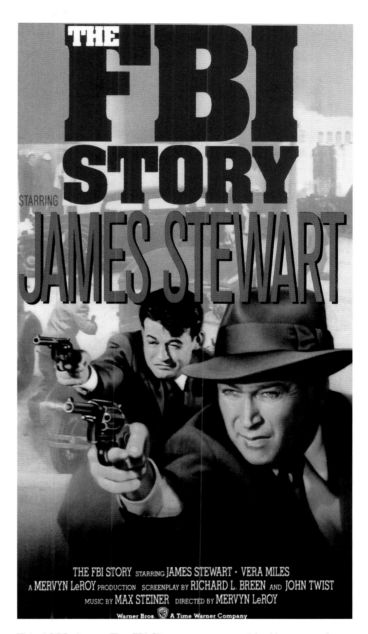

This 1959 drama *The FBI Story* was approved by Hoover and based on files released by Hoover to the movie makers. The most common criticism was that the film played more like propaganda than a stand-alone film. Although the film has largely been forgotten, it is based on Pulitzer Prize–winner Don Whitehead's history. It stars Jimmy Stewart as an FBI agent. Hoover had tight control over the film, approving the script and the actors and actresses. *Henry M. Holden collection*

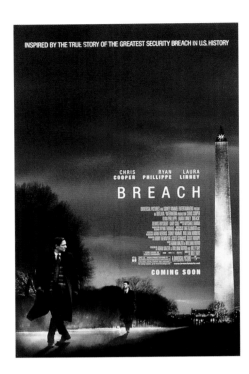

Breach (2007) was based on the real-life spy story of disgraced former FBI agent Robert Hanssen. Hanssen was charged with selling American secrets to Moscow for $1.4 million in cash and diamonds over a fifteen-year period. On July 6, 2001, he pled guilty to fifteen counts of espionage. He was subsequently sentenced to life in prison. The film producers consulted with the FBI on the technical details of the script. *Henry M. Holden collection*

JFK (1991) examines the events leading to the assassination of President Kennedy (and an alleged subsequent cover-up). Members of the CIA, mafia, military-industrial complex, Secret Service, FBI, and Kennedy's vice president, Lyndon Johnson, are implicated in the film as co-conspirators with motives for Kennedy's assassination and/or the cover-up afterward.

In *Donnie Brasco* (1997), Special Agent Joseph Pistone, alias Donnie Brasco, works undercover for five years to infiltrate the Bonanno crime family in New York City. Pistone is selected to be an undercover agent because of his Sicilian heritage, ability to speak Sicilian dialect, and acquaintance with the mob from growing up in Paterson, New Jersey.

In *Johnnie Mae Gibson: FBI* (1997), Lynn Whitfield stars as Johnnie Mae Gibson, the first African-American female FBI agent to work undercover.

Miss Congeniality (2000) stars Sandra Bullock as an undercover FBI agent. A sequel followed in 2005.

The Watcher (2000) was set in Chicago. A retired FBI agent who has been chasing the same serial killer for most of his career eventually burns out, retires, and moves to the Midwest. The serial killer follows him and continues his killing spree.

Catch Me if You Can (2002) is based on a true story and concerns a young con man, played by Leonardo DiCaprio, who steals more than four million dollars in the 1960s through forgery and other frauds by assuming different disguises. Tom Hanks plays the FBI agent hot on his trail. The FBI agent gets his man in the end. The DiCaprio character is eventually let out of prison to work with the FBI in the check fraud division.

In *Blood Work* (2002), an ailing veteran FBI agent gets a second chance when he receives the heart of a murder victim. The murder victim's sister visits the agent (Clint Eastwood) to remind him that he is alive only because he received her sister's heart. She asks him to pay her back by investigating the unsolved murder.

The tagline for *National Treasure* (2004) is "The greatest adventure history has ever revealed." In the movie, Nicholas Cage is the descendant of an early American patriot. He discovers the legendary Knights Templar treasure, rumored to be the most awesome bounty in human history, is hidden somewhere in America. The founding fathers and clues from a hundred-dollar bill and the reverse side of the Declaration of Independence lead to the location of the treasure. But in order to find the treasure, the Declaration of Independence has to be stolen from the National Archives. Harvey Keitel plays a grim FBI agent.

In *The Kingdom* (2007), a terrorist bomb detonates inside a Western housing compound in Riyadh, Saudi Arabia, igniting an international incident. FBI Special Agent Ronald Fleury, played by Jamie Foxx, quickly assembles an elite team and negotiates a secret five-day trip into Saudi Arabia to locate the persons behind the bombing. Saudi authorities are unwelcoming of Americans and consider them interlopers into what they consider a local matter. The film is a fiction based in part on the Khobar Towers bombing in 1996 and reflects to some degree the difficulty the FBI had in collecting crime scene evidence. It is unrealistic in its portrayal of a mere four FBI personnel taking down an entire terrorist cell. ∎

The Dick Tracy cartoon, created by artist Chester Gould in 1931, became an icon of American pop culture. Tracy made his silver screen debut in *Dick Tracy* (1937), *Dick Tracy Returns* (1938), and *Dick Tracy's G-Men* in 1939. In the serial, Dick Tracy portrays an FBI agent, or "G-man," based in Los Angeles. After Gould's death, artists Dick Locher and Mile Kilian continued the cartoon, adding the crime-stoppers' textbook and one of the FBI's Ten Most Wanted posters. *FBI*

Chester Gould's early cartoons mirrored the violence of Chicago during the 1930s. When America entered World War II, Gould created the Nazi spy, Pruneface, who was not only a machine design engineer but also dabbled with nerve gas. Tracy, like the FBI, used the latest crime fighting techniques and technology. After the war, Tracy started using the two-way wrist radio. In 1964, he upgraded it to a two-way wrist radio/TV. *FBI*

Appendix B

SPECIAL AGENTS— DIED IN SERVICE

Edwin C. Shanahan	1925	Johnnie L. Oliver	1979
Paul E. Reynolds	1929	Charles W. Elmore	1979
Albert L. Ingle	°1931	Jared Robert Porter	1979
Raymond J. Caffrey	1933	Terry Burnett Hereford	°1982
W. Carter Baum	1934	Robert W. Conners	°1982
Samuel P. Crowley	1934	Charles L. Ellington	°1982
Herman E. Hollis	1934	Michael James Lynch	°1982
Nelson B. Klein	1935	Robin L. Ahrens	1985
Wimberly W. Baker	1937	Jerry L. Dove	1986
Truett E. Rowe	1937	Benjamin P. Grogan	1986
William R. Ramsey	1938	James K. McAllister	°1986
Hubert J. Treacy Jr.	1942	Scott K. Carey	°1988
Percy E. Foxworth	°1943	L. Douglas Abram	1990
Harold Dennis Haberfeld	°1943	John L. Bailey	1990
Richard Blackstone Brown	°1943	Stanley Ronquest Jr.	°1992
Joseph J. Brock	1952	Martha Dixon Martinez	1994
John Brady Murphy	1953	Michael John Miller	1994
Richard Purcell Horan	1957	William H. Christian Jr.	1995
Terry R. Anderson	1966	Charles Leo Reed	1996
Douglas M. Price	1968	Paul A. LeVeille	°1999
Anthony Palmisano	1969	Leonard W. Hatton	2001
Edwin R. Woodriffe	1969	Robert Russell Hardesty	°2005
Gregory W. Spinelli	1973	Gregory J. Rahoi	°2006
Jack R. Coler	1975	Barry Lee Bush	°2007
Ronald A. Williams	1975		
Trenwith S. Basford	°1977	*°Cause of death: accident in the line of duty (aircraft,*	
Mark A. Kirkland	°1977	*automobile, gunfire, or training)*	

Appendix C

TIMELINE

1908
An investigative branch of the Department of Justice is created; this branch would evolve to become the Federal Bureau of Investigation

1910
The Mann Act is passed, making the transport of women across state lines for immoral purposes illegal.

June 1917
J. Edgar Hoover begins working with the Department of Justice legal staff.

January 1920
Prohibition begins. Organized crime begins its rise in the United States.

August 1921
William J. Burns is appointed director of the Bureau of Investigation; J. Edgar Hoover is named assistant director.

May 1924
J. Edgar Hoover is named acting director of the Bureau of Investigation.

October 1925
Edwin C. Shanahan becomes the first FBI Agent killed in the line of duty.

June 4, 1928
Supreme Court upholds that the use of wiretap evidence in a federal court did not by itself violate constitutional guarantees in the Fourth and Fifth Amendments against unreasonable searches and seizures and self-incrimination.

March 1929
Al Capone is arrested by Bureau agents.

November 1932
The FBI Laboratory is created.

June 1933
The Bureau of Investigation becomes the Division of Investigation. The Kansas City Massacre occurs.

June 7, 1933
Congress authorizes use of subpoena power in sabotage cases.

June 1934
Federal agents in Chicago kill John Dillinger.

July 1934
The Division of Investigation becomes the Federal Bureau of Investigation.

August 19, 1938
President Franklin Roosevelt declares he favors larger appropriations for military intelligence services to expand counterespionage activities in the United States.

June 26, 1939
Soviet communication is intercepted between New York and Moscow that will be the subject of the Venona Project.

September 1, 1939
World War II begins as Germany invades Poland.

September 2, 1939
Whittaker Chambers reveals espionage activities of Alger and Donald Hiss to Assistant Secretary of State Adolph Berle.

September 4, 1939
French intelligence informs American Ambassador William C. Bullitt in Paris that Alger and Donald Hiss are Soviet agents.

September 6, 1939
A presidential directive gives the FBI the sole responsibility for investigating espionage, counterespionage, and sabotage.

August 1940
The disaster squad is created when the FBI is called upon to identify its agents involved in an airplane crash in Virginia.

December 7, 1941
United States enters World War II.

June 1942
Four German saboteurs land on Long Island. Four others land in Florida. All eight are arrested by the FBI.

March 1950
The FBI's "Ten Most Wanted Fugitives" program begins.

June 1957
The FBI arrests Colonel Rudolf Ivanovich Abel, a Soviet espionage agent. He is sentenced to thirty years in prison but is later exchanged for U-2 pilot Francis Gary Powers.

November 1963
President John F. Kennedy is assassinated. President Lyndon B. Johnson orders the FBI to investigate.

June 1964
Three civil rights workers are murdered near Philadelphia, Mississippi.

July 4, 1966
President Johnson signs the Freedom of Information Act (FOIA).

January 1967
The National Crime Information Center (NCIC) becomes operational.

June 1968
James Earl Ray is arrested in London. He is later convicted of the assassination of Dr. Martin Luther King Jr.

May 2, 1972
J. Edgar Hoover dies after 48 years as director.

May 1972
The new FBI Academy opens on the United States Marine Corps base at Quantico, Virginia.

April 1978
The use of laser technology to detect latent fingerprints begins.

1983
The Hostage Rescue Team became operational.

1984
The National Center for the Analysis of Violent Crime (NCAVC) is established at the FBI Academy. A Computer Analysis and Response Team (CART) is established to help field offices retrieve computer evidence.

1988
The FBI employs 9,663 special agents and 13,651 support personnel.

April 1994
The Critical Incident Response Group (CIRG) is created to more effectively deal with hostage-taking and barricade situations.

September 1995
The FBI announces an undercover investigation, "Innocent Images," which targets child pornography over the Internet.

June 1997
Timothy McVeigh is convicted of the bombing of the Murrah Building in Oklahoma City, one of the worst acts of domestic terrorism in American history.

May 1998
Eric Robert Rudolph is placed on the FBI's Ten Most Wanted List after being charged with the Centennial Olympic Park bombing in Atlanta and the bombing of a Birmingham abortion clinic.

August 1998
Bombs are detonated near United States embassies in Nairobi, Kenya, and Dar es Salaam, Tanzania, killing 223 people. Among the dead are twelve Americans and thirty-eight Foreign Service Nationals.

June 1999
Osama bin Laden is placed on the FBI's Ten Most Wanted List for his alleged involvement in the 1998 bombing of the U.S. embassies in Kenya and Tanzania.

September 1999
The FBI announces the ground breaking for its new Laboratory facility in Quantico, Virginia.

February 2001
Special Agent Robert Hanssen is arrested and charged with committing espionage.

September 2001
Terrorists attack the World Trade Center in New York City and the Pentagon in Washington, D.C.

October 2001
The FBI responds to anthrax-laden letters.

December 2001
Director Mueller announces a reorganization of FBI Headquarters to meet evolving challenges.

Appendix D

ACRONYMS AND ABBREVIATIONS

APL—American Protective League

ASAC—assistant special agent in charge

BOI—Bureau of Investigation

CDC—Centers for Disease Control

CI—confidential informant

CIRG—Critical Incident Response Group

COINTELPRO—Counter Intelligence Programs

CALEA—Communications Assistance for Law
Enforcement Act

COMINFIL—communist infiltration in the United States

COMPIC—communist infiltration, motion picture industry

CORE—Congress of Racial Equality

CPUSA—Communist Party USA

CT—counterterrorism

DNC—Democratic National Convention

DOJ—Department of Justice

ELF—Earth Liberation Front

ERT—evidence response team

FBIHQ—FBI Headquarters

FOIA—Freedom of Information Act

G-man—"government man"

HMRU—hazard materials response unit

HRT—hostage rescue team

IG—inspector general

JTTF—joint terrorism task force

LEO—law enforcement officer

Legat—legal attaché

NAACP—National Association for the Advancement of
Colored People

NCIC—National Crime Information Center

NJTTF—national joint terrorism task force

NOI—Nation of Islam

NTSB—National Transportation Safety Board

OIPR—Office of Intelligence Policy and Review

OSS—Office of Strategic Services

RICO—Racketeer Influenced and Corrupt Organization Act

SAC—special agent in charge

SIOC—Strategic Information and Operations Center

SCLC – Southern Christian Leadership Conference

SLA—Symbionese Liberation Army

SWAT—special weapons and tactics

UC—undercover

Appendix E

BIBLIOGRAPHY

Ansley, Norman. "The United States Secret Service: An Administrative History," *Journal of Criminal Law, Criminology and Police Science*, XLVII (May–June 1956).

Batvinis, Raymond J. *The Origins of FBI Counterintelligence.* Lawrence: University Press of Kansas, 2007.

Bock, Alan W. *Ambush at Ruby Ridge.* New York: Berkley Publishing Group, 1996.

Crowdy, Terry. *The Enemy Within: A History of Espionage.* New York: Osprey Publishing, Limited, 2006.

Donner, Frank J. *The Age of Surveillance: The Aims and Methods of America's Political Intelligence System.* New York: Knopf, 1980.

Felt, Mark, and John O'Conner. *A G-Man's Life: The FBI, Being "Deep Throat," and the Struggle for Honor in Washington.* New York: PublicAffairs, 2006.

Freeh, Louis J., with Howard Means. *My FBI.* New York: St. Martin's Press, 2005.

Gentry, Curt. *J. Edgar Hoover The Man and the Secrets.* New York: W. W. Norton & Company, 1991.

Goode, James. *Wiretap: Listening in on America's Mafia.* New York: Simon & Schuster, 1988.

Hack, Richard. *Puppetmaster: The Secret Life of J. Edgar Hoover.* California: New Millennium Press, 2004.

Hoover, J. Edgar. *Masters of Deceit.* New York: Pocket Books, 1959.

Jeffreys-Jones, Rhodri. *American Espionage: From Secret Service to CIA.* New York: Free Press, 1977.

Jensen, Joan. *The Price of Vigilance.* New York: Rand McNally & Company, 1968.

Karpis, Alvin. *The Alvin Karpis Story.* Berkeley: University of California Press, 1972.

Kessler, Ronald. *The Bureau: The Secret History of the FBI.* New York: St. Martin's Press, 2002.

———. *The FBI.* New York: Pocket Books, 1993.

Lewis, James R. (ed.). *From the Ashes: Making Sense of Waco.* Lanham, Maryland: Rowman & Littlefield, 1994.

Lindberg, Richard. *Return to the Scene of the Crime: A Guide to Infamous Places in Chicago.* Chicago: Cumberland House Publishing, 1999.

Mason, Alpheus Thomas. *Harlan Fiske Stone: Pillar of the Law.* New York: Viking, 1956.

Moynihan, Daniel Patrick. *Secrecy: The American Experience.* New Haven: Yale University Press, 1998.

Nixon, R.N. *The Memoirs of Richard Nixon.* New York: Warner Books, 1979.

Powers, Richard Gid. *Secrecy and Power: The Life of J. Edgar Hoover.* New York: The Free Press, 1987.

Reavis, Dick J. *The Ashes of Waco: An Investigation.* New York: Simon & Schuster, 1995.

Spannaus, Edward. "The Mysterious Origins of J. Edgar Hoover," *American Almanac*, August, 2000.

Sullivan, William C. *The Bureau: My Thirty Years in Hoover's FBI.* New York: W. W. Norton & Company, 1979.

Summers, Anthony. *Official and Confidential: The Secret Life of J. Edgar Hoover.* New York: Penguin Group, 1993.

Tabor, James D. and Eugene V. Gallagher. *Why Waco? Cults and the Battle for Religious Freedom in America.* Berkeley: University of California Press, 1995.

Theoharis, Athan G. (ed.) et al. *The FBI: A Comprehensive Research Guide*. New York: Checkmark Books, 2000.

———. *From the Secret Files of J. Edgar Hoover*. Ivan R. Dee, 1991.

Thibodeau, David and Leon Whiteson. *A Place Called Waco: A Survivor's Story*. New York: Public Affairs, 1999.

Whitehead, Don. *The FBI Story: A Report to the American People*. New York: Random House, 1956.

Wright, Stuart A. (ed.). *Armageddon in Waco: Critical Perspectives on the Branch Davidian Conflict*. Chicago: University of Chicago Press, 1995.

Websites

citypages.com/databank/25/1244/article12543.asp

nativeson.wordpress.com/2006/08/01/secrets-uncovered-j-edgar-hoover-passing-for-white/

fas.org/irp/ops/ci/hanssen_affidavit.html

FBI website (www.fbi.gov)

spartacus.schoolnet.co.uk/USAhooverE.htm

usdoj.gov/usao/eousa/foia_reading_room/usam/title9/131mcrm.htm

Other

G. Bonaparte testimony, before hearings before the House Committee on Appropriations, January 17, 1908.

Charges of Illegal Practices of the Justice Department, Hearings Before the Senate Committee on the Judiciary, Congressional Record 66th Congress, 3rd Session, 1921.

Department of Justice. *Report on the Relationship between U.S. Recording Co. and the FBI and Certain Other Matters Pertaining to the FBI*. January 1978.

———. *Report to the Deputy Attorney General on the Events at Waco, Texas*, February 28 to April 19, 1993.

———. *Report of the Staff of the Senate Select Committee on Intelligence: An Assessment of the Aldrich H. Ames Espionage Case and Its Implications for U.S. Intelligence*. 103rd Congress, Session 51, 1994.

U.S. Congress. Senate. Committee on Government Operations. Permanent Subcommittee on Investigations. *Hearings on Riots, Civil and Criminal Disorders*. 90th Congress, 1st Session/91st Congress, 2nd Session, 1967–1970.

U.S. Congress. House. Committee on Internal Security. *Hearings on Domestic Intelligence Operations for Internal Security Purposes*. 93rd Congress, 2nd Session, 1974.

U.S. Congress. Senate. Select Committee to Study Governmental Operations with Respect to Intelligence Activities. *Hearings on the National Security Agency and Fourth Amendment Rights*. Vol. 6. 94th Congress, 1st Session, 1975.

U.S. Congress. Senate. Select Committee to Study Governmental Operations with Respect to Intelligence Activities. *Hearings on the Federal Bureau of Investigation*. Vol. 6. 94th Congress, 1st Session, 1975.

———. *Book II, Intelligence Activities and the Rights of Americans* (and *Book III, Supplementary*). 94th Congress, 2nd Session, 1976.

"Loan of Detectives." *Washington Evening Star*, April 21, 1908.

"Espionage Exists." *Washington Evening Star*, April 22, 1908.

"Reno Says, 'I Made the Decision,' " *Washington Post*, Apr. 20, 1993.

Index